MW00929166

Whom Dog Hath Joined

A Golden Retriever Mystery

By Neil S. Plakcy

Acknowledgements

Big thanks go to my critique group partners: Miriam Auerbach, Christine Jackson, Kris Montee and Sharon Potts, who have guided Steve and Rochester on many adventures.

Ramona de Felice Long did a terrific job editing the manuscript, and Nancy Gazo was my beta reader. I appreciate advice from Jim Born, Jackie Conrad, Sharon Sakson and Zita Goldfinger.

Special thanks for outstanding service in the role of golden retrievers go to Jacoplax's Brody Baggins and Jacoplax's Griffin Goodfellow, who inspire, amuse and love me every day. And of course, to their daddy.

This book is dedicated to all those who lost loved ones during the Vietnam conflict.

Copyright 2014 Neil S. Plakcy. All rights reserved, including the right of reproduction in whole or in part in any form.

This book is a work of fiction. Names, characters, places, and incidents either are products of the author's imagination or are used fictitiously. Any resemblance to actual events or locales or persons, living or dead, is entirely coincidental.

1 – Harvest Days

Though my friend Rick often called my golden retriever a "death dog," it wasn't Rochester's fault that he kept finding bodies. After all, his ancestors had been bred to find and retrieve dead game, right? And it's not like we went out looking for trouble. It found us.

"I'm still not sure it was a good idea to bring Rochester," I said to my girlfriend Lili as we walked through downtown Stewart's Crossing toward the Friends' Meeting House on the edge of town. Victorian gingerbread baking in the harsh sunlight, Land Rovers and Escalades creeping in snarled traffic, the tracery of a kite high in the sky above us. Faint brassy notes of off-key jazz floating in the air, the smell of auto exhaust and melted gum on the sidewalk. "Even though he's two years old, he's still a big puppy sometimes, and I'm worried that Harvest Days will be too crowded."

The dog in question, shades of false and true gold streaking his flanks, tail erect as a mast of signal flags, strained forward as commuter fathers tried to practice workplace logic on misbehaving kids: good behavior now will result in rewards at a later date. Tattered flyers littered the street-- ten percent off any haircut, zero percent down and zero dollars at signing, make your floors look like new again.

"He'll be fine, Steve," Lili said, reaching down to scratch the Golden Retriever behind his ears. "He's a smart boy."

Rochester yawned and stretched his neck. He'd been mine for a year and a half by then; I had adopted him after the death of his owner, my next-door neighbor Caroline Kelly. Since then he had become my boon companion. At seventy-plus pounds he was a happy, shaggy force to be reckoned with.

"From your mouth to the dog's ears," I said.

It was late September, and Bucks County, in the southeastern corner of Pennsylvania, was enjoying the fading days of Indian

Neil S. Plakcy

summer. The leaves were beginning to turn yellow, red and gold, the air was crisp, and the storefronts on Main Street were dressed with Indian corn, pumpkins, and fake scarecrows stuffed in straw, wearing patchwork outfits.

A few days before, Lili had read about Harvest Days, a fall festival on the grounds of the Quaker Meeting house in Stewart's Crossing. "Can we go to this?" she'd asked, pointing to the article in the *Boat-Gazette*, our weekly newspaper. "It looks like a fun way for the three of us to spend some time together."

Lili was a transplant to Bucks County after a globe-trotting photojournalism career, and she had a convert's dedication to all things rural. I had agreed, despite my reservations about Rochester's behavior in crowds, because ten years of a previous marriage had taught me that when the woman in your life wants to "spend some time together" it's a bad move to say no.

We navigated the crowds past the mill pond, just beyond the sole traffic light in town. In winter the pond was a Norman Rockwell painting come to life, kids in bright red mufflers skating figure eights, parents warming hands around hot chocolate, a pick-up hockey game at the far end. In Indian summer, though, sunlight reflected on the glassy surface, with a trickle of falling leave and fat squirrels jumping from one overhanging branch to another, daring each other to stumble and drop into the water below.

At five-eleven, Lili was a couple of inches shorter than I was, with a cascade of reddish brown curls, a bow-shaped mouth, and a petite nose that had undergone the surgeon's knife when she was in high school. She wore a photographer's vest over a bright green polo shirt and skinny jeans, and she had an SLR camera slung around her neck.

Unlike Lili, who was born in Cuba and grew up in Mexico, in Kansas, and a number of other places, I was rooted in Stewart's Crossing. "When I was a kid, we came to Harvest Days every year," I said, as Rochester tugged me forward. "My dad would scavenge for hand tools, the weirder the better, and my mother collected romance paperbacks with the front covers ripped off."

"Why? Because she didn't want anyone to know what she was reading?"

"I thought so back then. But later I learned that bookstores would rip the covers off unsold books and send them back to the publishers for credit, then sell them. After she passed away, my dad donated nearly a thousand of them to the Friends of the Library for their book sale."

I looked ahead of us, but my mind was on the past. "He had a couple of yard sales, too, getting rid of the antique Lenox china plates and figurines she collected, and the sketches of boats and harbors she had hung in our bathrooms."

Lili reached over and took my hand and squeezed. "He even got rid of most of his tools before he died. I wouldn't be surprised to see some of my family's stuff show up here."

As we got closer to the Meeting House, we had to navigate through a sea of haphazardly parked cars, moms with strollers and rambunctious boys chasing each other. Rochester was eager to play, and I had to keep reining in his leash.

The broad half-moon lawn which faced onto Main Street was filled by neighbors who had cleaned out their attics, Avon ladies displaying their wares, and small businesses with free-standing displays. We passed free car wash coupons, crocheted samplers invoking prayers for home and hearth, wooden nativity characters made with basement jigsaws. I hoped Lili wouldn't be disappointed at the kitschy suburban nature of the festival.

"I'm going to take some pictures," she said, lifting the camera from around her neck. "You start browsing if you want."

"We'll hang," I said. Rochester was busy sniffing the roots of an ancient sycamore and I was happy to stand there and look around. In front of us was the single-story Meeting House, dingier than I remembered it as a kid. Its construction was mortise-and-tenon wood-frame, covered in clapboard, though the central section had been faced with fieldstone. From previous visits, I knew that the left wing held a kitchen and dining area, while the center section was a large, low-ceilinged room filled with wooden pews for worship services. I wasn't sure what the right-hand part held; there were no windows there and I'd never been back there.

The Friends had begun a renovation campaign, and one of those huge thermometer-type signs stood beside the Meeting House, painted with growing red bars to show fund-raising progress. As of that day, they had made it to fifty percent of their goal.

Lili snapped a couple of pictures and we continued forward. Most people were dressed as we were, in jeans and casual shirts, though I noted the proliferation of clothes that smacked of a 1950s-era safari—microfiber fishing shirts with epaulets, floppy-brimmed hats, and shorts with enough pockets to carry a week's worth of rations. I also noticed the careless way people discarded trash near the bins, not caring if their aim was true, and the ratty condition of the lawns, which were sprinkled with crabgrass and dandelions.

"It's so quaint," Lili said.

This from a woman who had faced down guerrillas in Latin America and photographed dead children in Iraq. It's amazing what your eye can trick you into seeing.

The high school jazz band was playing off-key, and someone on the other side of the half-moon driveway was selling candy apples, guaranteed to rot the teeth of even the most careful eaters. The light breeze brought the sweet smell across to us, and I remembered going to Styer's Farm Market in the country when I was a kid. My mom wouldn't buy me one of the apples, covered in a shiny red lacquer, but my dad would.

The Veterans of Foreign Wars, who gathered at a high-ceilinged hall on the edge of town (banquet rentals inquire within), had filled a yard-sale table with never-opened kitchen gadgets, gently-used toys, and cast off clothes from a multitude of generations. I recognized the elderly man in green service cap with military patches and a faded hunting jacket littered with marksmanship pins who stood behind the table. He was a part-time bagger at the Genuardi's grocery outside town. He was talking to a twenty-something vet in camouflage ball cap, T-shirt and khaki shorts, artificial leg below the knee. He looked so young, like one of the students I might have taught, and I thought about the way that some of us have to carry the evidence of our traumas on the outside, while others are able to pretend that nothing bad has happened.

The Gulf War, the Afghan campaign and the invasion of Iraq had revitalized the dying VFW chapter in Stewart's Crossing. The tide had turned in our view of returning soldiers, somewhere between the anti-war protests of the sixties and seventies and the renewed patriotism following 9/11. When I was a kid, only a few old men in faded uniforms marched in the Independence Day parade in Stewart's Crossing. But many people in town worked in New York City, and we had lost a half-dozen neighbors in the attack on the World Trade Center.

"There's Gail," Lili said, pointing at a table where our friend Gail Dukowski, who ran The Chocolate Ear café in downtown, was selling her cookies and pastries from a pair of flimsy card tables covered with green and white striped cloths that matched her store's awnings.

Gail looked frazzled. We got in line behind a sixty-something woman holding a small girl by the hand, a pair of teenagers, and a cluster of other eager customers. Gail's blonde hair was plastered to her forehead with sweat, her face was smudged with chocolate, and her eyes looked tired. She wore a big chef's apron over her T-shirt and slacks.

Rochester was excited to see Gail, tugging at his leash and nodding his shaggy head. When we went to The Chocolate Ear, she always had a special dog biscuit for him. A platter of them, wrapped in clear plastic and tied with a dog-paw patterned ribbon, sat at one end of the table.

"You're on your own here?" I asked as we reached her.

She nodded. "Ginny ate something funny from the kitchen and had to go home."

"Can we help you?" Lili asked.

The line behind us had continued to grow. "That would be such a blessing," Gail said. "My mother's coming at noon but I could sure use some help now."

"I'll man the cash box," I said.

"You take the orders and I'll box them up," Lili said to Gail.

"Thank you so much!" Gail stepped aside to let Lili and me scoot behind the table.

I dropped a dollar in the cash box and unwrapped one of the big biscuits. Rochester settled on the ground underneath, chewing noisily. "Stay there and keep out of trouble," I said, scratching him behind the ears.

I sat in one of the café's big wicker chairs with green and white striped cushions and began to accept people's dimes and quarters and wrinkled dollar bills. I made change and told them about all the treats Gail hadn't been able to bring to the fair, like her lemon bars, her flaky croissants and her special dark chocolate hazelnut tarts.

Gail cut the walnut-studded chocolate bars and Lil boxed them up. I snacked on the crumbs and Lili slapped my hand. Every now and then I reached down to scratch behind Rochester's ears as he rested his big square head on his front paws and stared out at the passing crowd.

"These are delicious!" a heavy-set woman said, as brownie crumbs dribbled out of her mouth.

"Fantastic," a big man in a tank top agreed. His shirt read "If assholes could fly this place would be an airport," which made me suspicious of his taste. Although his sheer size indicated he had a lot of experience with high-calorie foods.

We handled the backlog of customers quickly and Gail slumped into the chair next to me. "I've been up since five this morning, baking chocolate bars, cutting them and stacking them on trays," she said. "At seven, I met Ginny here and we set up the booth. She went home about an hour ago and it's been a zoo ever since."

I leaned forward and discovered that if I pressed too hard on the table the chocolate bars went slip-sliding toward Mrs. Holt's adjoining table of crocheted pink and lavender toilet paper covers topped by Barbie knock-offs. They were a shocking example of what happened when people with too much time on their hands possessed the deluded notion that they had some artistic talent, but she had bought two chocolate bars so I was willing to cut her a little slack.

"We sure need some good food in Stewart's Crossing," said a young mom with twins in a double stroller.

I took her money and told her the café sold terrific take-out sandwiches in kid-friendly flavors like meatballs and grilled cheese as well as desserts.

Then I heard a scream.

I reached down below the table to grab Rochester's leash and keep him from tearing off toward the sound. But he was already gone.

"Oh, crap," I said, jumping up.

"You both go," Gail said. "I can handle things until my mother gets here."

"Where do you think he is?" Lili asked, taking off the apron she'd been wearing. The silver bangle bracelets on her arm jingled.

"Wherever that scream came from," I said.

I darted around slow-moving elderly people, parents grabbing dilly-dallying little kids, and curious folks headed toward the Meeting House. The scatter of gold and orange leaves crunched beneath my feet, mixing with distant car horns and the sound of someone sobbing.

The big white double doors at the center of the building stood open, and a walkway along the front of the building was lined with piles of osage oranges and green and white gourds. The three-part slate roof—peaked in the center, flat on the sides—was dusted with a covering of red and gold leaves.

A crowd had already gathered outside the right side of the building, the part with no windows. A teenaged girl huddled against her mother, crying. "She was just trying to pet the dog," the woman was saying to others in the crowd. "And then she saw what he was digging, and she screamed."

Others were watching my determined golden, who tugged at the something near the foundation. An elderly man was trying, without result, to talk Rochester away, but he was too timid to touch the dog.

Up close I could see the wood of the exterior wall was disintegrating, with long vertical cracks through the planks. I pushed forward, excusing myself and calling Rochester's name. When I reached him, I grabbed his collar and lifted his head away from where he had been digging, and saw that he'd dragged a disintegrating tennis shoe through the gap.

A single bone, like the one I filled with peanut butter for him, remained, sticking out of the shoe. Only this bone wasn't the kind sold at pet stores.

"Rochester, this has to stop!" I scolded. "No more digging up dead bodies."

2 – Death Dog

Rochester had led me to three dead bodies in the short time we had been together, and I remembered each one. His original mom, Caroline, lying on a dirt road at the edge of River Bend, her blood spilled around her. My mentor when I was a student, Joe Dagorian, murdered during a fund-raising event on the campus of Eastern College, where I worked. And a couple of months before, Rochester had dug up a hand from a shallow grave on the grounds of Friar Lake, a college property I was in charge of developing into a conference center.

In each case, I felt an immediate burst of horror, as I realized a life had been snuffed out. Pulse racing, stomach churning, scratchiness in my throat. Childhood funerals in the back of unfamiliar synagogues, women crying, my father placing the first shovel of dirt on my mother's coffin.

But dogs don't have the same emotional connection to the dead, and I had learned my first responsibility was to keep Rochester from disturbing the site. I hooked up his leash and tugged him away from the wall.

Lili joined me, holding her camera. She had seen so much death and destruction in the course of her journalism work that she had learned to use the lens to distance herself from it. I wished I could do the same.

I pulled out my cell phone and called my high-school buddy Rick Stemper, a detective with the Stewart's Crossing Police Department.

"Don't tell me," he said, when he answered.

"I won't."

I heard him sigh. "You're at Harvest Days, aren't you, Steve?"

"Yup. Did you already get called?"

"Yeah. Lucky me. Any chance the bone he dug up isn't human?"

"Not unless cows have started wearing Converse."

"I'm on my way. Keep the dog away from the remains, all right?"

"Easier said than done," I said, holding tightly to Rochester's collar while keeping the phone between my shoulder and my head. My body stress mirrored my emotional tension, as I multi-tasked on behalf of the dead.

"I'll be there in ten," he said, and hung up.

A little boy scooted past and ran toward the sneaker. Lili quickly scooped him up and whispered into his ear. He stopped squawking and smiled, grabbing a handful of her curls. Though she had no children of her own, she had an instinct for kids, perhaps after all those years of comforting them in war zones.

She handed the boy off to his mother and stepped in front of the Meeting House wall to address the crowd as people murmured. "The police have been called," she announced. "Would everyone please stay back until they get here, and not touch anything?"

With Lili taking charge, my mind was free to roam, and I remembered the first time I'd been in the Meeting House, when I was in the eighth grade. My social studies teacher, Mrs. Shea, was a Quaker, and she'd invited our class to join her at the Stewart's Crossing Meeting one Sunday. She warned us in advance that it wouldn't be very exciting, that most of the time people were silent and contemplative, and that convinced the hyperactive kids in my class to opt out.

Not me, though. I was accustomed to dull services, because I grew up going to a Reform Jewish congregation in Trenton, across the Delaware from Stewart's Crossing. Despite the beauty of the soaring Byzantine-style temple and the mystery of the curtained choir loft behind the bema, the elevated platform where the rabbi and cantor sat, I was frequently bored during services, especially when the cantor sung something in Hebrew that the rabbi had just read. The repetition seemed so inefficient to me, especially since I didn't understand either rendition.

I went to Sunday school from the time I was in kindergarten all the way through Confirmation in tenth grade. Joining Mrs. Shea and her congregation was a chance to skip a day's class and experience something different, more American than our foreign-language prayers, white silk prayer shawls, rainbow of yarmulkes, hand-crocheted, bought in the Holy Land, or souvenirs of a distant cousin's bat mitzvah.

The contemplative nature of the service stayed with me. I hadn't been to a Quaker Meeting since, but I associated the Stewart's Crossing Meeting with that sense of stillness and peace. It was so different from the hubbub all around us, as it looked like everyone I'd noticed at the Harvest Festival was gathering there. I held tight to Rochester's leash as an attractive woman in her early thirties hurried toward us.

"Is there a problem here?" she asked. She was wearing the standard costume of a suburban mom: a plaid blouse that tied around her waist, hot pink pedal pushers, and matching pink sneakers. She also wore a round button that said, "I'm a Quaker! Ask me about our worship."

Her blonde ponytail was cinched with a pink scrunchie and she had a small blond boy by the hand. "What's everyone looking at?"

The crowd had obeyed Lili's request to stay back, but that didn't prevent them from craning their necks and looking around each other, trying to get a clearer view.

"You don't want to take your little boy any closer," I said. "The police are on their way."

"Police? Why? What's happened?" She looked from us to the Meeting and then back. "I'm Hannah Palmer. I'm the clerk of the Meeting." From my studies with Mrs. Shea, way back when, I knew that meant she was the volunteer responsible for administrative functions. "Why are the police coming?"

"Steve Levitan," I said. "This is Lili Weinstock, and the big dog is Rochester. I'm afraid he might have disturbed your construction area. He found a disintegrating tennis shoe. And it looks like there's a human bone inside."

"Oh, how awful! Just one bone?" She shivered. "Or is it a whole skeleton?" She frowned. "You're sure it's not some prankster getting ready for Halloween?"

"All we can see is the sneaker," I said. "It doesn't look like a prank, though."

Her hand was shaking as she pulled a walkie-talkie from the pocket of her pink slacks and pressed a key, then spoke. "This is

Hannah, and I need help at the front lawn. Any volunteer who's not in the middle of something, please come up here right away."

She slipped the walkie-talkie back in her pocket. "I'll get some of our members to help with crowd control," she said. "The building wasn't even supposed to be opened up now. We haven't raised all the money we need, but after the last couple of weeks of rain, our contractor thought he'd get a head start on the renovation while the weather was fair, without realizing that we had Harvest Days upcoming."

Close up I could see the tell-tale signs that contractors had passed that way – ruts in the grass, paper building permit in a plastic sleeve by the front door, stockpile of stone by the side wall. But there was no evidence that any of them were there that day.

The little boy tugged on my pant leg and asked, "Can I pet your dog?"

"Nathaniel, not now," Hannah said.

"It's okay," I said. "Rochester, sit."

He plopped his golden butt down on the thin grass of the front lawn, and the boy held out his hand for Rochester to lick. "Nathaniel wants a dog," Hannah said. "I'm afraid he gets very excited whenever he sees one."

Well, for a long time I had wanted a child, I thought. After my ex-wife had two miscarriages I had accepted that we don't always get what we want. It was the way of life; this little boy would endure disappointments small and large (there's no more ice cream, you can't have a car just because you got your driver's license, broken heart and failure of ambition.) And he would survive, if he was lucky.

Hannah, Lili and I stood around awkwardly as Nathaniel petted Rochester, until a group of people converged on us, all of them wearing the same "I'm a Quaker" buttons, and Hannah stepped aside to speak with them, taking Nathaniel with her. He cast one longing glance back, like Lot's wife leaving Sodom or Orpheus unable to resist checking for Eurydice and something in his plaintive look made my heart twang. The discovery of the body must have upset me more than I realized.

"I want to take some pictures for Rick," Lili said. "I won't disturb anything but I can get better shots than he could with his phone or whatever little camera he has. I'll be back."

She moved closer to the Meeting House and began snapping shots. I followed her, still holding Rochester at bay, and noted that the summer rains, in conjunction with the reconstruction, had eroded the wood where the building's exterior wall met its foundation. Fresh scratch marks indicated where Rochester had moved away the dirt to reveal the shoe behind the disintegrating wall. It was like peeling the surface of the world away to see the rot and heartbreak beneath it.

All I could see was the sneaker and the whitened bone sticking out of it, but I was almost certain there had to be a body behind it. Lili leaned forward, crouched down, fiddled with her lenses. I could see her professionalism and her experience in tough situations in every action.

A pair of uniformed officers came through the crowd, the community's protection against the darkness always around us, and took over from the volunteers Hannah Palmer had arranged in a cordon around the Meeting House. Lili explained to them what she was doing, and they left her alone. One officer began to lay out yellow crime scene tape, our modern ritual of creating a sacred space, an ephemeral Stonehenge that wouldn't last more than a day. The other pulled out a pad and began taking names of people in the crowd.

Rick Stemper approached a couple of minutes later. For the most part, he looked as he had when we were acquaintances at Pennsbury High, more than twenty-five years before --unruly mop of brown hair, broad shoulders, athletic build. The only changes were bags below his eyes and a couple of laugh lines around his mouth.

He was in plain clothes, though his police badge was pinned to the waistband of his khaki slacks. The tail of his short-sleeved blue and white check shirt was out, which I knew meant that he had his gun on his belt.

"How does this keep happening, Steve?" he asked, when he reached us. He leaned down to scratch Rochester's neck. "And you? Are you some kind of murder magnet?" The dog just grinned.

"You don't know it's murder," I said.

"Yeah, guys in sneakers die of natural causes inside old

buildings all the time." Rick shook his head and walked past us and stepped over the crime scene tape. I watched as he pulled a Dodger-blue latex glove from his pocket and slipped it on his right hand. Then he crouched beside the building and carefully peered in through the gap, our Stewart's Crossing Sherlock trying to intuit the past from a collection of random details.

He stood up and made a call on his cell phone, then walked back over to us. "I have to get some stuff from my car, and then I'm going inside. Hang around until I get a chance to see what's going on. I want to talk to you. In the meantime keep the death dog away from the evidence, all right?"

He walked back toward Main Street, and I knelt down next to Rochester. "You're not a death dog, are you, boy?"

Rochester woofed and nodded his big shaggy head. Then he licked my face.

One of the volunteers milling around the Meeting House was my childhood piano teacher, Edith Passis. She had been a friend of my parents, and I remembered her as a younger woman at parties at our house, her black hair teased into a beehive, wearing glasses that feathered up at the edges and thigh-high black leather boots. She had true Black Irish looks—coal-black hair, pale white skin and bright blue eyes.

Now her hair had gone stark white, and a medication she took tinted her skin a salmon-pink. Though I'd never say it to her face, I thought she looked like a gerbil, as if she ate chopped lettuce at every meal and lived in a pile of shredded newspaper. Her blue eyes were still clear, and she was as sweet-natured and patient as she'd been when I was struggling to learn the fingering for "The Caisson Song."

"Hello, Steve," she said, coming up to me. "What's all the fuss?" She bent down to stroke Rochester's head.

"Rochester found a sneaker down there, where the clapboard has eroded away from the foundation. Looks like it might be attached to a body."

She looked back up quickly. "A body? How terrible. Someone local? Or a visitor?"

"Don't know yet."

She put her hand up to her mouth and her eyes crinkled in

sadness. You couldn't get to Edith's age, somewhere in her seventies, without experiencing pain: the general (war, famine, natural disasters) to the personal (death of her beloved husband, betrayal of her piano-trained hands to arthritis.)

I noticed she was wearing the same round button and to distract her, I asked, "Do you belong to the Meeting?" I'd always thought Edith was Jewish, because I saw her sometimes at our synagogue in Trenton.

"I was born a Quaker," she said. "When Lou was alive I went to synagogue with him sometimes, but I always felt like a Friend in my heart. After he passed I found a lot of comfort in coming here." She shook her head. "But there was a lot of discord over this construction project. Very un-Quaker."

"Why the discord?" Rochester kept straining to go back to the sneaker he'd found and I had to keep a close rein on his leash.

A light breeze swept through the property, scattering some of the dead leaves at the bases of the trees. "A lot of people don't like change," she said. "When you get to my age… it seemed like such a big project, so much money, so much disruption."

"What kind of work is being done? Expansion?"

"More like reconfiguring. Our membership has been shrinking, and we don't need such a large meeting room anymore. We offer space to a lot of non-profit groups, and Hannah Palmer felt we needed to remodel and create more intimate spaces, both for our worship and for these other groups."

"Other members disagreed with her?"

"Politely, of course," Edith said. "But Hannah is a very strong woman, and deeply spiritual, as well. I knew her family when she was growing up. She was always such a serious child." She shook her head. "We're a dying breed, we Friends. We've never been ones to proselytize, and so many of our young people are seduced away from silence and contemplation by the noise of the world. Hannah has revitalized our Meeting, even if I don't always agree with her policies."

Edith waved at a tall, cadaverous-looking man with stringy white hair down to his shoulders. "That's Eben Hosford," she said to me. "He's been the most vocal opponent to the Meeting House renovation. I'm surprised to see him here."

"Looks like an old hippie," I said. He wore faded jeans torn at the knees and a plaid long-sleeved shirt that was too big for his skeletal frame. Around his neck was some kind of Native American dream catcher, all feathers and leather strips.

Edith left me to walk over to him. Rick returned with a utility belt wrapped around his waist and toting a flashlight, more of the bright blue plastic gloves, and one of those life-saver tools you can use to cut a seat belt or smash out a windshield.

He nodded as he walked past. I noticed that Lili had moved away from the Meeting House, and was taking candid shots of the Harvest Festival. I leaned against the trunk of a red maple, Rochester sprawled at my feet, and watched the passing traffic -- a couple of high school band members on break, a plump Indian woman in a red and gold sari, a smattering of suburban parents and kids, and a tall black woman with a regal posture and massive gold hoop earrings. An interesting mix of the Stewart's Crossing I remembered and the new world order.

I looked back at the dark blue high-top sneaker, visible in the gap between clapboard and foundation. It was a Converse Chuck Taylor; I owned several pairs like it when I was a kid. The white sole was smudged with dirt, as was the canvas, but I could see the round logo with *Converse All-Stars* in red wrapped around a blue star.

It was adult size, probably belonging to a teenage boy or a young man. It was covered with a sheen of dust, so looked like it had been there behind the wall for a long time. How could that be? Had the Friends never noticed the smell of a dead body? Was it in some long-ignored closet?

Who had worn it? A Stewart's Crossing kid like me? But how had his body ended up behind a wall in the Friends' Meeting House? And when? I felt the tingling of curiosity and I was excited, but worried too. I knew the kind of trouble my curiosity had gotten me into in the past.

3 – False Wall

Lili returned, her camera back around her neck, and Rochester hopped up. "I stopped by Gail's table. Her mother is there, and she's doing fine. Rick show up yet?"

"He's inside," I said, as he emerged from the double doors. The crowd was still clustered around the corner of the building where Rochester had discovered the sneaker, so when Rick waved, Lili, the dog and I walked over to him.

"Afternoon, Lili," he said. "Can you hold onto Rochester for a couple of minutes? I need Joe Hardy here to walk inside with me."

I'd helped Rick out a couple of times with cases by then, and I'd graduated in his estimation from Nancy Drew – who worked on her own—to Joe Hardy, the younger of the two Hardy Boys. I had grudgingly accepted that since he had the badge he got to be older brother, Frank.

"What do you need?" I asked.

"There's a false wall at the back of a closet, right on the corner of the building where the shoe is. I don't want to knock through the wall until I know what's back there, so I want to climb up through an access panel in the ceiling and see if I can look down. There's a ladder I can use, but I need somebody to hold it. I'd pull a uniform, but you know we're a small department, and we're already stretched thin between crowd control here and traffic duty out on Main Street."

"Sure." I handed Rochester's leash to Lili, but as I started to walk away he pulled to go along with me. "You stay here, boy," I said. He barked a couple of times then sat on his butt with a disappointed look on his face. He wasn't happy to be left out.

On our way in, Rick was buttonholed by Hannah Palmer. A few strands of blonde hair had come loose, and she looked harried. "You aren't going to make us shut down the Harvest Festival, are you?" she asked. "Because that would be a nightmare."

"No ma'am," Rick said. "If there was a crime committed here

it was a long time ago, and as long as we can keep people away from the building we should be fine."

"But they can still get into the kitchen, right? We make money from the food."

"Yes, they can." He put his hand on her arm. "We'll do our best not to disrupt things."

She thanked him and walked away. "You were awfully nice to her," I said, as Rick led the way into the Meeting House.

"The mayor's a Quaker, if you've forgotten. Plus I feel sorry for her. This Festival is a big deal, and it's not her fault your dog dug up an old corpse."

I snorted but followed him inside. The main room was as I remembered it, with a central aisle and rows of ancient wooden pews parallel to each of the four walls. Severe, in a colonial America kind of way, plain and spare. Since their worship involved silent waiting for God with no ritual, there was no need for an altar, as you'd find in a synagogue or a church. Older members could sit on raised benches along the far wall, allowing them to be seen and heard.

I didn't think I'd make a very good Quaker. I didn't have the patience for stillness, too much going on in my brain. Rochester and I were alike that way, always curious about the world and eager to snoop around.

At the center of the space was a short table where someone – the clerk, for example – could stand to address the Meeting. Rick led me between the pews to a single door set into the back wall. Before he stepped through, he handed me a pair of the blue gloves. "I'd tell you not to touch anything, but I know you."

I didn't bother to complain. Rick was right; I was a nosy guy, a lot like my dog.

I put the gloves on and followed him, feeling like we were a couple of weird *Star Trek* aliens with bright blue hands. We stepped gingerly into a warren of small offices and storage rooms. Red and black wires looped down from the ceiling beside the bent frames of aluminum studs and holes knocked through drywall. The smell of sawdust hung in the air.

A locked metal tool cabinet, dinged and banged from hard use, stood to one side, beside a pile of buckets and hoses. Rick turned right and stopped in front of the open door to a storage closet. "This is as close as we can get to where the body is." He held up his hand and we listened. We could hear the buzz of the crowd outside, under the blare of the jazz band.

"It's tight in there. I managed to get the ladder set up but it's pretty rickety."

He turned on his flashlight and stepped inside, and I followed. He stuck the flashlight between his shoulder and his neck, gripped the ladder, and started to climb.

I stood behind him, holding the ladder steady. He pushed up on the access panel, but it didn't move. "Is it screwed shut?" I asked.

"No, just stuck." He pulled a screwdriver from his belt and inserted it between the edge of the panel and the ceiling, and applied pressure. "Come on, you mother," he grunted.

Suddenly the panel gave way, and Rick nearly toppled backwards. I had to head-butt his ass to keep him up there. I grabbed his flashlight before it hit the floor.

He uttered a few curse words that would have gotten us a long detention back at Pennsbury High, and then managed to get the panel flipped up on its hinge. He stepped up higher on the ladder, which creaked ominously, and poked his head over the edge. "Light," he said, and I handed the flashlight up to him.

He looked down. "Tight fit in here," he said. "But I can see a skull, and a jumble of bones and fragments of what look like dusty old clothes. There's an old ladder in there, too, I guess for climbing down the other side. Whoever it is must have died in there, because I don't see any other way in besides this panel. Crime scene will tell me if any animals have gotten in somehow."

He climbed back down the ladder, and I backed out of the storage closet. His head had a sifting of dust on it that made his hair look almost gray. He shook it out and wiped the back of his hand across his face.

The solemnity of what he'd found must have hit us both, because neither of us said anything. I was reminded of the veterans outside, how much death they must have seen in their service. Cold, damp primeval European forests, vast arid deserts, cluttered warrens of blasted-out houses – death was the same wherever you encountered it, whether a battlefield or a place of worship.

Rick led the way down the hall to the brown metal tool cabinet we had passed on our way in. It was, about six feet long and two feet high, and the top was closed with a cheap keyed padlock. He pulled a leatherette pack from a pouch on his belt which opened to reveal a set of metal lock picks.

"My dad had a set like that once," I said. "I wonder what ever happened to it."

"Your dad was a burglar?"

"Nah, he just bought every random kind of tool he could find at the flea market."

Rick chose one of the picks and inserted it into the bottom of the padlock. As he grunted and twisted I asked, "Any particular reason why we're breaking in there?"

"Because there's probably a drywall saw inside." The lock clicked and popped open, and Rick lifted the lid. "Yup, here's what I need." He grabbed a wicked-looking gizmo with a rubber handle and a long serrated blade that ended in a sharp point.

"Watch and learn, brother Joe," Rick said.

I followed him back to the storage closet, and we worked together to drag all the boxes and accumulated junk into the hallway. When the wall that separated the closet from the hidden space was clear, Rick knelt on the floor and jabbed the drywall saw into it. He cut across a horizontal line, then stopped to take a break.

"Why didn't you cut your way in at first?" I asked. "Why go to the trouble of climbing up above to look down?"

He wiped the sweat from his forehead with the back of his hand and sat back. "I wanted to see what was there before I cut in," he said. "Could have been a whole pile of bones in there, and cutting through without looking could have damaged the scene."

"I get it. Want me to give it a try?" I asked.

"Sure. But be careful; that handle gets slippery."

I turned the blade ninety degrees and began sawing downward. I wasn't that handy as a kid; my father used to get nervous when I hung around his workbench, afraid I'd impale myself on a putty knife or cut my arm off with the circular saw. But becoming a homeowner, in California and then back in Stewart's Crossing, had brought out some latent talent my father hadn't seen.

The drywall was old and rotted, which made it tougher to cut a straight line. Flakes peeled off and fell to the ground, dandruff of the dead. When I finished, I scooted back from the wall. I gave the saw back to Rick to complete the cutting, but instead he reached in and pulled the piece away by the two open sides.

"Flashlight?" he asked.

I handed it to him and he shone it into the narrow space between the drywall and the outside wall. I leaned over his shoulder to look in. It was about six feet deep, and maybe ten feet long. As Rick had mentioned, there was a very old ladder inside, leaning against the far wall.

"How the hell did somebody get a body in there, if the only way in or out is through that trap door?" I asked.

"Whoever belongs to those bones had to have climbed up a ladder in the closet, like I did, gone up through the ceiling and down the old ladder inside," Rick said. "Maybe to hide. I remember learning in school that this Meeting House was one of the stops on the Underground Railroad."

"Nineteenth-century slaves didn't wear Chucks," I said, using our old nickname for the Chuck Taylor-branded sneaker Rochester had found. "Could you search through missing persons reports for somebody wearing that kind of shoe?" I backed away and stood up.

"It'll be a nightmare," he said. "We have no time frame yet, and no real geographic restraints. This guy could have gone missing in Alaska, for all we know. And there's no way to search by a single criteria, like kind of shoe. I'd have to read through every report for the last forty years. I'm going to wait until I have more information."

He stood up and brushed his pants. That motion reminded me of my dad, finishing up at his basement workbench, clearing curls of metal and wood before going upstairs to rejoin the family. "There are a lot more questions than answers in that little space. And the next one is who knew that about this false wall. That could lead us somewhere."

"The Meeting House is a public building," I said. "Anybody can walk in, especially on a day like today when the whole town is here."

"But you'd have to know that this space was here. Someone who was familiar with the Meeting House knew about the false wall, and this area behind it."

"One of the Friends? That's so out of character. And the body's too old to be connected to the construction project."

"Just because you wear a button that says, 'Hi, I'm a Quaker' doesn't mean you wouldn't kill someone," Rick said.

We stepped back into the hallway, and saw two guys in plain clothes approaching, each carrying what looked like a heavy bag. "Afternoon, detective," one of them said. "Crime scene in there?"

Rick nodded. "You're going to need to remove more of the wall to get clear access." He turned to me. "Thanks for your help, but the cavalry is here now."

"Sure. You still want me and Lili to hang around?"

"Nah, I'm good. I know where to find you."

I did want to hang around and snoop – but I knew that without a badge, I would be in the way. I walked back out into the brilliant sunshine, shading my eyes from the glare. I couldn't help considering which of the people in the crowd might have a hidden crime in his or her past. The Latino guy in hospital scrubs, his wraparound sunglasses on the back of his head? The bald guy in the Metallica T-shirt? The plump grandmother in a souvenir Hawaiian muumuu? Could one of the elderly volunteers be hiding a dark secret behind their "friendly" badges?

4 – Physician for the Circus

I shivered despite the autumn heat, and looked around for Lili and Rochester but couldn't see them. That was curious. Was she taking pictures somewhere? Had she gone back to Gail's to help out?

As I prowled, I passed a table of old tools that reminded me of my father, and I thought again about the owner of the sneaker. If he'd been a young man, would his parents still be alive, wondering what had happened to him? When I'd gone through the boxes my father left behind after his death, I'd found a tarnished copper POW-MIA bracelet, and I recognized the last name on it as one of my father's co-workers. I vaguely remembered the man had a son who went missing in Vietnam, and wondered if my father had ever worn the bracelet, or had purchased it out of solidarity.

I couldn't remember what happened to that bracelet, and I didn't know if the son had ever been found. But from what I remembered of the father, the boy had never been forgotten.

I stopped in front of a table with a sign that read "Semper Fiber." The woman behind it had created needlepoints of the Marine motto and other symbols. The next table was occupied by that cadaverous old man Edith had mentioned, selling an array of scented candles and soaps. There was something discordant about the soaps wrapped in pretty paper and tied with ribbon and the creepy affect of the man, so I hurried past.

People had gone back to their enjoyment of the fair, pushing aside the discovery of the body like an uncomfortable article in the *Boat-Gazette*. How could they, I wondered? Didn't they realize that there had been a person who ate, drank, lived, who was now dead? Was there someone out there with a hole in his or her heart where the memory of that person belonged?

I scoured the property until I found Lili and Rochester beneath the shade of an ancient oak tree at the very back.

"What's going on?" Lili asked when I reached her. "You look

like you've been prospecting in a mine."

Rochester popped up like a puppet on a string and placed his front paws on my pants. I could see he was still annoyed that he'd been left out of the investigation. I pushed him back down, but then scratched behind his ears and told him he was a good boy.

"I had to help Rick get the wall open," I said, when I straightened up.

"What did you find? A whole body?"

"I guess so. A skull, some bones, and some faded old clothes. And the other shoe."

"You think someone broke in during the construction and left the remains there?"

I shook my head. "The bones were covered in dust. They've been there a long time." I looked around. We were at least twenty feet from the nearest table, at the edge of the woods I had explored as a kid, collecting pine cones, chasing squirrels. Smell of leaf mold, crunch of dead leaves, dappling of sunlight amid shadow. "How about you? What are you doing way back here?"

"I'm hiding from Peter Bobeaux." She gave the name an exaggerated French pronunciation. "The new assistant dean for the humanities. He and his wife were walking their yappy little poodle and I knew Rochester would go wild, and I'd get roped into some boring conversation."

I couldn't get past the guy's name, and for the first time since I saw the sneaker in Rochester's mouth I laughed. "Professor Bobo?" I asked. "Sounds like he teaches at the clown college."

"Dr. Bobeaux, if you please," Lili said, and spelled it. "He grew up in West Virginia, but he got his Ph.D. in French literature from a university in Canada."

"Better yet," I said. "Doctor Bobo, physician for the circus, wearing a white lab coat and a round red nose."

Lili snorted with laughter and took my arm. "You are very bad. Now every time I see him I'll be thinking that."

"How'd you get a new assistant dean anyway?" The woods formed a kind of horseshoe around the Meeting House property, and we began walking along the edge of the lawn toward Main Street. "I thought Dr. Jellicoe was pretty entrenched in that position."

"Fran? Her husband retired in June, and they decided they'd always wanted to join the Peace Corps and see the third world."

"Which you've seen plenty of."

She nodded. In her career, photographing and writing about everything from blood diamonds to Somali pirates to ethnic strife in the former Soviet Union, she had been to almost every shady place on earth. The only spots she'd missed were the ones favored by tourists—she'd never spent much time in Western Europe, for example, never been to Hawaii or Tahiti or Alaska. I was happy there were at least a few sights we could see together for the first time.

"We were lucky to get someone with good credentials as a last-minute hire," Lili said. "He's the interim assistant dean right now; we'll have to do a full search this year."

"I wonder what he was doing that he could jump into a job on such short notice."

"He was working for a private university in one of the Gulf Coast emirates, and when the owner got in trouble with the authorities, they shut the place down on short notice."

As we approached Main Street, and the edge of the Harvest Festival, she stopped and pointed toward a couple of farm stands, rough wooden tables piled with cascades of eggplant, neat rows of tomatoes with bits of vine still attached, lettuce and mushrooms and sweet corn still in the husk. "I want to get some produce for dinner tonight."

"What are we having?"

"Whatever's fresh."

I followed her along the edge of the lawn toward Main Street. I saw her scanning the crowd and assumed she was trying to avoid the amusingly named Dr. Bobeaux. I imagined a man in a graduation gown with a mortarboard squashed over an exuberant red fright wig.

When we reached the farm stands, Lili examined the vegetables as if they were expensive jewels. "I'm going to slice this zucchini and load it with sliced tomatoes and parmesan cheese," she said, handing me a pile of the speckled green vegetables. "You can grill it for me. As a main course, I thought we'd do a big salad with grilled chicken, if that's good for you."

"Sounds delicious."

While I stood back with a tight rein on Rochester to prevent him from gobbling up whatever was at his level, Lili gathered her ingredients. She picked out three kinds of lettuce, red and yellow tomatoes, raw mushrooms, and green and yellow peppers. "Strawberry pie?" she asked. When I agreed, she had me pick out a couple of good pints.

"We're going to be working all afternoon to get this meal together," I complained.

She raised an eyebrow. "You have something else planned?"

"No, nothing," I said, holding up my hands. "Just helping you."

"Good answer."

We managed to leave the festival grounds without running into Lili's new boss and with Rochester in the lead, we walked back up to my car. Traffic still crept, safety-conscious parents in their boxy Volvos and Saabs, soccer moms in massive SUVs, older guys with trophy wives in expensive convertibles. Crinkled leaves in the gutters, an abandoned paper plate of half-eaten funnel cake, tiny pink ballet slipper, Barbie having to go en pointe missing one toe shoe.

I'd parked in my secret spot, at the rear of the hardware store behind a screen of maples. My dad was a friend of the store's owner when I was a kid, and we'd parked there for every parade and festival throughout my childhood. I had a feeling I was one of the few people in town who knew about those three spaces, tree roots pushing up under the blacktop, hidden to all but the *cognoscenti*.

We had to wait a long time for a break in traffic so I could pull onto Main Street, and as I drummed my fingers on the steering wheel I thought again about the body we had discovered. Who was he? What was he doing at the Meeting House? I kept gnawing away at those questions, without finding any answers, all the way home.

I pulled up in my driveway and we unloaded the car. "All that fresh air has made me sleepy," Lili said as she put the veggies away. "You feel like a nap before dinner?"

"Great idea." We went upstairs and snuggled together, with

Rochester on the floor by my side of the bed. Lili slipped off quickly, but I sat up, thinking about my life.

Lili was aware of my background, that I'd spent a year in a California prison for hacking, and that I was still on parole after that conviction. After my ex-wife Mary's first miscarriage, she'd nearly ruined us with retail therapy, and when we lost the second child, I thought by breaking in to the major credit bureaus and placing a red flag on Mary's account I could keep her from running up thousands of dollars in new charges. That hadn't worked out the way I expected, ending in jail time and divorce.

Lili had also seen me use my hacking skills in helping the police in the past. But she had grown worried that my itchy fingers and my arrogance would get me into trouble again, and she and Rick had staged an intervention a couple of months before. I acknowledged that I had a problem, gave Rick the laptop I'd been using for hacking, and joined an online support group for ex-hackers.

After prison, where my time was controlled, I had been lost, not sure what I wanted to do with my freedom. Rochester had been a mixed blessing, because when he came into my life I had to become responsible for him. I got his unconditional love, but sometimes I resented having to wake early on a cold morning and walk him, the way when I was surfing online, he would put his head in my lap to get me to play. Didn't he know how freeing it was for me when my hands were on a keyboard and my brain was exploring cyberspace?

I no longer resented those interruptions; I reminded myself how much I enjoyed being with him, and how my life had become so much better once he joined me.

I still loved to forget myself in a flurry of online activity – reading emails, following Facebook links, searching for arcane information. But now I also wanted to be with Lili, and there was a tension between those two desires. Fortunately, she needed her space as much as I did, and I had no complaints when she disappeared into a darkroom or wandered off with her camera in search of inspiration.

In that way, Lili was a much better match for me than Mary. My ex-wife needed the validation of the outside world, had to be with people, share her opinions with them, meet friends for drinks and colleagues for coffee. I was happiest when I was at the computer by myself, shutting out the rest of the world.

Though I knew Mary and I had been happy together at times, all I could remember were the bad things about my marriage – dragging behind her on slow shopping expeditions for the perfect sofa for the living room; listening to her endless complaints about her mother, who was cold and listened to too much AM radio; and her rants that I didn't have enough ambition, didn't make enough money. But had those been my problems all along, and would I end up in the same pattern with Lili?

5 – Baggage Claim

I woke about an hour later to Rochester sniffing my face. I sat up, yawned and looked at the clock. Lili stirred beside me. "Dinner time?" she asked.

"Rochester thinks so."

"Well, then, we should get cooking." She sat up and smiled.

"I keep thinking about that sneaker," I said, down in the kitchen, as I sliced a couple of zucchini. "I wonder if I can find anything online that might help Rick establish when it was made."

"I can email you the pictures I took of it after dinner," Lili said. "I got a bunch of good close-ups of the shoe and the markings. I figured they'd be useful to Rick."

"Only Rick?"

"Well, I knew you'd help him."

Neither Lili nor Rick minded my dabbling in online investigation, as long as I didn't break any laws. I cleaned up the zucchini debris and retrieved a package of boneless chicken breasts from the fridge. Then Rochester accompanied me outside, where I fired up my portable grill and he stretched out on the grass beside it, hoping for some stray bits of chicken to fall his way.

Early twilight settled around me, birds chirping in the stand of sassafras out front, sounds of vintage Springsteen floating past from a neighbor's stereo. The sights, smells and sounds of my childhood, constantly making connections between the boy I was and the man I had become. I had never imagined coming back to Stewart's Crossing after college; back then, I wanted nothing more than to make a quick and permanent exit from the stultifying suburbs. Years in Manhattan of constant hurrying and a crush of humanity, when at times I'd been desperate to find bits of solitude in the middle of Central Park or along the Hudson River, had made me long for my quiet countrified hometown.

It wasn't the same place, of course. When I was a kid, people had roots in town, all kinds of connections. My friend Mary Lou's ex-aunt ran the local real estate office, and her name was on signs all over town. My mother had grown up next to the family that ran the butcher shop, my father belonged to the Masons with the owner of the hardware store. My classmates' parents were doctors and lawyers with offices downtown, teachers at the elementary school or secretaries at Town Hall.

Now most of my neighbors in River Bend were from somewhere else, with only the shallowest roots in town. They commuted by car or train to Philadelphia or New York. They preferred the chain restaurants and big-box stores out on US 1 to the mom-and-pop places in the center of town.

I went to those big stores, too, of course; a high school friend of Rick's and mine managed the electronics mega-store, and the mother of a girl I'd gone to elementary school with was still a cashier at Pathmark. I wondered about the little kids I saw trailing behind their parents at the mall, wearing princess dresses or karate robes or Boy Scout uniforms. Would they have the same sense of place I did? Or would their parents pick them up and move them every few years, following opportunity and the sense that there was always something better in the next town?

Would my life have been different if I'd never left Stewart's Crossing – or at least, come back after college instead of moving to New York for graduate school? If I'd never met Mary, moved to California, suffered through her two miscarriages?

Even though my experiences had shaped me, I knew that down deep I was who I was. I'd been reading mystery novels and solving crossword puzzles since I was a kid, possessed by a desire I barely understood to search for clues, to see things others didn't. My curiosity was tinged with ego and hubris, and I was sure that if I'd never become a computer hacker I'd have found some other way to get in trouble.

The chicken breasts sizzled and I flipped them over. My parole officer, Santiago Santos, had classified mine as an addictive personality, though I'd never had problems with alcohol, tobacco or drugs. Yeah, I did get a rush from snooping around in places I wasn't supposed to be, but until I went to prison I'd never thought of it as an addiction. During the year I'd been incarcerated, I hadn't missed hacking – I was too busy figuring out my new environment, learning the personalities of the other inmates and the guards, understanding how the system worked and how you could game it if you were clever enough.

My two-year parole was about to end, and I had a nine o'clock appointment Monday morning at the parole board office for my exit interview with Santos, who had been monitoring my conduct for the two years since I left the California state penal system.

As far as I knew, there wasn't any way he could keep me on parole; the interview was just a formality. Santos had installed tracking software on my home computer – but after Caroline died I had discovered her laptop, and installed my hacking software on it so I could help Rick discover her killer. I kept that laptop hidden from everyone, and rationalized that whatever I did was in service of a greater good – digging around for clues in an identity theft scheme, hacking a website that featured stolen artifacts, and so on. After the intervention, I had given it to Rick to hold for me.

I finished grilling and carried the food in to Lili, who arranged the chicken strips artfully on top of the salad. As we sat down to eat, she said, "I keep thinking about that body. You expect to see that kind of thing when you're in a battle zone – but not right in the middle of Stewart's Crossing."

"I know what you mean," I said. "And it seems such a violation to find a body there, in the Meeting House, when the Quakers are all about peace and non-violence."

"Do you think you can find anything online about the shoe?"

I thought it was interesting that Lili suggested I go online, knowing what she did of my history. "No idea. But you know how it is – people post all kinds of stuff. I know there are sneaker collectors; I'm hoping one of them put up a picture of a shoe that matches the one we found. And I promise you I'll only look in places that are open to the public."

"I do trust you," she said. "You know that, right?"

"I know. And I'm not saying I'll never hack again – I've learned from my support group that I can't make promises like that. But what I can promise you is that I won't go behind your back. If I want to snoop around somewhere, I'll talk to you, and we'll make the decision together."

Though Lili had no addictions that I knew of, she was familiar with the addictive personality – many of the journalists she'd worked with over the years were adrenaline junkies. "I can work with that," she said.

I hoped that I could, too.

* * *

I woke before Lili Sunday morning and after I took Rochester for a long walk around River Bend, I prepared a brunch of chocolate-chip pancakes, bacon, and orange juice. Rochester sat on his haunches next to the stove, waiting for bacon bits.

Lili walked into the kitchen, sniffing the air. "What's the special occasion?"

"That you're here to make breakfast for."

She sat down and I delivered a plate of pancakes with a side of bacon, the aroma of sizzling fat permeating the air and making Rochester nuts. The juice was already on the table, and she poured herself a glass as I sat down across from her with my plate. Rochester wouldn't sit still, constantly nosing at us both for bits of bacon.

"Speaking of my being here," Lili said.

I cut into my pancakes, elbowing the dog's head away. "Which is my pleasure."

"How would you feel about increasing that pleasure?"

I looked up to see her watching me. "In what way?"

"My lease is up at the end of October," she said. "I've been thinking about whether I want to renew or not."

"It's a great apartment." I fed a piece of bacon to Rochester, who wolfed it down, then I went back to my breakfast.

"Are you fully awake this morning?" Lili asked after a moment had passed. "I'm saying that I love you, and I want to spend more time with you. How would you feel if I moved in here when my lease is up?"

We had been dating for about six months by then. We spoke on the phone every day, sometimes more than once. We spent every weekend together, and the occasional weeknight. We said, "Love you," to each other all the time, and I meant it when I said it. But were we ready to take the next step?

I looked at Lili and my mind was a blank. "I'm sorry," I said. "I know I love you, but moving in together? I need to think about that."

She stood up and pulled a plastic container from the kitchen cabinet. "I'll take my breakfast to go," she said. "You need some time to think, and I want to fiddle around with the pictures I took yesterday at the Harvest Festival."

She leaned down and kissed my cheek. "Don't think I'm angry, because I'm not. I know that I've dropped a bombshell on you and you need to process it. And if you want to keep going the way we have been for another year, that's fine. I should have given you more notice, I know. But I've got my own baggage, and it took me a while to realize that this is what I want. You, and Rochester. Us."

"I want that, too. Let me consult with my moral and spiritual advisor and I'll have an answer for you."

"Not Rick Stemper?"

I laughed. "Are you kidding? Rick's more messed up about his divorce than I ever was about mine. I was talking about Rochester."

She nodded. "Then I'm sure you'll make the right decision. When I get home, I'll email you the pictures I took of the shoe so you can go online with them."

"Thanks. And I'll think about moving in together."

We kissed, and she went upstairs to get her bag. As I finished my breakfast, I thought about what it would mean to have Lili live with me. Would she worry every time I logged on to the computer? Take over Santiago Santos's role to make sure I stayed on the straight and narrow?

My cell phone began playing the theme song from *Hawaii Five-O*, the ring tone I'd assigned to Rick. "Yo," I answered.

"Yo-yo," he said. "Listen, I've got to work today, thanks to you and your dog, and the guy who usually takes care of Rascal during the day isn't around."

A few months after I adopted Rochester, Rick had gone to the Bucks County Animal Shelter in Lahaska and picked up an Australian shepherd. Rascal was hyperactive, bred to herd cattle, a sixty-pound bundle of energy and wiry fur, slavering tongue, muscular legs, always ready to jump and lick.

Rick had quickly learned that leaving Rascal caged up all day meant he'd be wild at night, when Rick needed to wind down. So he'd found a retired guy in his neighborhood who did doggie day care. Rascal got to run around all day, herding the other dogs, and then he was a sweetheart in the evenings.

"I can't leave him in his crate. Can I bring him over to you?"

I agreed and hung up. Rascal would keep Rochester occupied, so I could think about what Lili had suggested. I also wanted to get some computer work done, and though I knew that Lili trusted me, the habits I'd developed of keeping my online snooping a secret were hard to break.

6 – An Old Friend

After Lili left, the house was spookily quiet. I had the windows open, taking advantage of the last warm days, but there were no kids playing out on Sarajevo Court, no birds calling or crickets chirping. No lawns being mowed, cars being tuned, stereos blasting the latest hip-hop. Rochester lay on his side on the tile floor, his legs splayed out, not making a sound.

Was this what my life would be like without Lili? Did I want this kind of silence, or did I want the comfort of another human being? Was Rochester's company no longer enough for me? I picked up his favorite blue ball, squeaked it a couple of times, and then tossed it across the room. He didn't even lift his head. "Some retriever you are," I grumbled.

I was antsy to get online and look for information on the sneaker, but I had to give Lili time to drive up to Leighville and send me her photos. I paced around the house, stopping in front of the china cabinet that had stood in my parents' living room. My father had sold off most of the knickknacks my mother had collected so the cabinet was a lot emptier than it had been when I was growing up.

I opened the door and pulled out a glass perfume bottle, about three inches high, with a lacework of sterling overlay. When my parents were first married, my dad had worked as a kind of engineering temp, moving from job to job every few months. He tried to come home every weekend from wherever he was working, and he often brought my mother one of these bottles, scavenged from antique shops where he was living.

I figured it was his way of saying that he was still thinking about her even though they were apart. He called her his angel, and signed his cards to her "all my love always." I'd thought I loved Mary that way, and it took me a long time to realize I never had. That we'd both settled for each other because that's what people did. I determined when my marriage broke up that I wouldn't do that again.

I knew that I loved Lili – but was I "in love" with her? What did that mean, anyway? In college and graduate school I'd read the poems that Elizabeth and Robert Browning wrote to each other, Shakespeare's sonnets, W. H. Auden and Sara Teasdale. I'd fallen for books like Scott Spencer's *Endless Love* and M. M. Kaye's *The Far Pavilions*, about love so deep it bordered on (or was) obsession.

Did I feel that way about Lili? Did I even want to? Real life wasn't a poem or a novel, and if I really did have the addictive personality Santos said I did, then an obsessive love was not a good thing.

I put back the perfume bottle and thought about Lili, how I felt when I was with her, when we were apart. She was the first person I thought of when something happened I wanted to share. When we were apart, sometimes I'd feel a physical longing to be near her. Everything we did together seemed more enjoyable because she was with me.

That was love, I decided. I didn't need a poet to tell me.

I was relieved when I heard Rick pull up in front of the house, and I opened the front door and let Rochester out to run ahead of me. Rascal was in the back of the pickup, with his front paws on the side rail. He barked as I lowered the back gate, then he jumped down. He and Rochester began chasing each other in circles in the driveway.

"You find any ID for the body yesterday?" I asked Rick.

"Nope. Which makes this case a real bear."

"Can't you use dental records or DNA?" I asked.

"You have to have something to compare to. The ME guesses that it's the body of an adolescent male Caucasian, based on his preliminary look at the bones, but we won't know for sure until the final report. While I wait for the cause of death, and the age of the victim, I've got to pore over the crime scene reports for clues as to how long the body was there. That will give me a framework to check missing persons reports."

I told him that Lili was going to email me photos of the sneaker. "I thought I'd look around online and see if I can narrow the time when the shoe was manufactured."

"That would help. Thanks."

He left, and I checked my email. Nothing from Lili. So I did some quick research on Converse sneakers and discovered that Chuck Taylor, also known as "Mr. Basketball," was one of the first athlete-endorsers, and that Converse had begun making Chucks in 1923. The Chucks of the 50s, 60s and 70s were made of three-ply canvas and had a black or blue label on the heel. The words CONVERSE ALL-STARS were in caps at the top, with a five-pointed star in the center of the label, breaking through between "Converse" and "All." The star also broke into the middle of Chuck's signature. There was a copyright symbol under the star, and the words MADE IN USA were in tiny caps at the bottom.

I hoped that there had been some change in the logo that might narrow down when the blue sneaker at the Meeting House had been made. But without Lili's photos I couldn't do much more research.

To avoid staring at the screen obsessively checking for messages, I stood up and began tidying my bedroom. I made space on the bureau for Lili when she stayed over, and that meant I gathered my bills, junk mail and other paperwork into one pile.

A tie bar I had inherited from my father was on top of the pile. I remembered wearing it a few weeks before – it must have fallen somewhere, and Lili had discovered it. I carried it over to the old wooden jewelry box where I kept the bits and pieces he'd left me. And maybe because it had been on my mind the day before, I noticed the copper POW bracelet at the bottom of the box.

I picked it up and examined it. It was tarnished, but I couldn't tell if that was from age or wear. The soldier's name, rank, and date and location of disappearance were engraved on the metal.

C14S MARC DES ROCHERS
USAF 7-10-66 LAOS

I remembered Mr. Des Rochers, an engineer my dad called "Des," and often commuted to work with. I'd been to his family's house in Levittown a few times, especially when I got old enough to drive and wanted to use my dad's car. I'd take him to Des's house early in the morning and then pick him up there in the evening. But I'd never thought to ask about the fate of Des's son.

That was easily remedied, I thought. I went back to the

computer and entered his name. It was uncommon, so it came up easily. The results were both saddening and surprising. Over 1600 military personnel were still missing, over forty years after "Operation Homecoming" in the spring of 1973, when Vietnam returned American POWs. One hundred ninety four of them were members of the Air Force, lost over Laos.

Marc Des Rochers was among those still missing.

I sat back in my chair. I couldn't imagine how his father must have felt, not knowing about his son's fate. Had he died instantly? Lived for a while in pain and suffering? Been incarcerated in one of the prison camps?

I knew my father had been deeply hurt by my stint in prison. But at least he knew I was fed and had access to medical care, that at some point I would be released. Another quick search revealed that Des had passed away a few years before. His online obituary listed his son "Marc, missing in Laos since 1966."

Beneath that was the line that broke my heart. "Until his death, Rene wore an MIA bracelet with Marc's name on it, always hoping that his son would come home to him."

I pushed my chair back quickly and stood up, startling Rochester, who had curled behind me, and Rascal, out in the hallway. "Come on guys, let's go for a walk," I said.

Both of them knew that magic word, and they raced down the stairs ahead of me, taking them two or three at a time, romping around the front door. I grabbed their leashes and we started out of River Bend. We kept going past the guard gate, and turned down Ferry Street toward town. After all the hubbub from the Harvest Festival the day before, Stewart's Crossing was quiet and sleepy. Most of the businesses at that end of town were closed, and I let the dogs loose to run around the parking lot of the VFW Hall.

Rochester was bigger than Rascal, and his coat was in shades of gold compared to Rascal's black and white. Rascal was by far more active, running in circles around Rochester trying to herd his friend. But Rochester darted in and grabbed the handle of Rascal's leash in his mouth, ready to take the Aussie for a walk. That completely confused Rascal.

I watched them play, then suddenly Rochester disengaged himself from Rascal and sprinted toward a tall, beefy-looking guy with brown hair, heading away from downtown on foot. He jumped up on the guy, nosing him in the groin.

"Rochester! Down!" I called, and hurried forward.

Rochester dropped to the ground and rushed back to me. "Sorry!" I called.

As Rochester darted around me, the guy approached us. He was in his late twenties, with a round, open face. "Maybe you can help me," he said, in an accent that pegged him from somewhere Down Under. "I'm somewhat lost. I'm looking for a chocolate shop. I think it would be called More than Chocolate."

"Nothing by that name in town," I said. "Though there is a café called The Chocolate Ear that serves great pastries."

"You wouldn't happen to know who runs it, would you?" he asked, as I clipped Rochester's leash back to his collar. Rascal scudded up beside us, and I hooked him up, too.

"I do. She's a friend of mine. Gail Dukowski."

"Bless you!" he said. "That's who I've been looking for." He reached out to shake my hand. "Declan Gallagher."

"Steve Levitan." We shook. "How do you know Gail?"

"She used to date my roommate Randy in New York," he said. "When I was in graduate school at Columbia."

I told him that I'd gone to school there as well, and discovered that long after I'd gotten my MA in English he had been in the business school on an international exchange program from New Zealand. He had a Southern Hemisphere charm, relaxed posture, clipped language with a hint of the exotic. There was a warmth and friendliness about him, even after only a few minutes' acquaintance, that made me like him.

"I had a bit of a crush on Gail back then," he said. "Though she only had eyes for Randy. I ran into him last week, and he told me they'd broken up and she'd moved down here. I remembered her talking about the chocolate shop and so I thought I'd look her up."

"Come on, we'll walk you down there," I said. "Gail loves Rochester, and she always has a biscuit for him." I reached down to scratch around Rascal's neck. "And one for you, too, Rascal."

As we walked, I said, "It's a nice day for a drive down from New York."

"I'm not there anymore," Declan said. "I was, with a manufacturing company in Brooklyn. But their business tanked, and they couldn't afford to sponsor me for the H1-B visa beyond my year of practical training. Fortunately, I managed to get myself a much better job, with an electronics company, so I won't have to go back home. They filed for my visa and I got it last month."

"Congratulations," I said. "Where is this company?"

"Up the road a bit," he said. "In an industrial park outside Newtown."

The dogs were well-behaved as we walked down the shady sidewalk, though they were eager to sniff out every interesting scent. "Up ahead," I said to Declan. "Those green and white awnings? That's The Chocolate Ear."

The elderly hippie I'd seen at the Harvest Festival stepped out of the café as we approached. Rochester balked and wouldn't move forward as the man approached us. "Buy some candles or soap?" he asked, opening a worn leather satchel. "All handmade." He pulled out a couple of strong-smelling bars wrapped in brown paper and tied with what looked like horsehair. "Just sold some candles to the lady inside."

Rochester growled. "Sorry, the smell doesn't seem to agree with my dog," I said. I tugged on both dogs' leashes and we stepped into Main Street to go around him.

Declan asked the old man, "How much?"

"Five bucks." He handed one of the bars to Declan, who lifted it to his nose to sniff.

"I'll take it." Declan pulled a bill out of his wallet and handed it to the old man, who stuffed it into the pocket of his jeans.

"I hope Gail likes lemon," Declan said to me when the man had passed.

I handed the leashes to Declan and stuck my head in the door when we got to the café. Gail's mother Lorraine was working the register and I asked her, "Can you tell Gail I've got an old friend of hers out here?"

Lorraine was a petite dynamo, with neatly coiffed gray hair and a perpetual smile. I took the dogs back from Declan as she introduced herself to Declan. "Did you work with Gail in the city?" she asked.

He shook his head. "I was a roommate of Randy's."

"Oh," she said. "Well, I'll tell Gail you're here."

I wondered at her cool reaction. I guessed she hadn't liked Gail's boyfriend much.

Declan and I stood in the shade of the awning, watching the traffic pass on Main Street. The dogs sprawled beside me on the pavement, but they both hopped up when Gail stepped out the door.

Gail's blonde hair was pulled into a neat ponytail, and she wore a gray cotton blouse, jeans and kitchen clogs. I noticed she was staring at the man with me. "Declan?" she asked. "Wow! It's been what, a year or so? The last time I saw you was at graduation."

"Hello, Gail." He stepped forward and kissed her cheek. "It's lovely to see you again. And I'm so pleased you were able to realize that dream we talked about." He waved his hand to encompass the chocolate shop.

"It's so good to see you," she said. "But how did you track me down? I don't even know your last name and I didn't think you knew mine."

I thought I saw Declan blush. "I saw Randy in New York, at a Columbia cocktail party."

"Is he still as obnoxious as ever?"

Declan burst out laughing. "I didn't know you saw him that way. He is rather full of himself, you know, being an investment banker."

"He was that way as a student. It just took me a long time to see it."

"Well, we got to talking, and he mentioned you two had broken up. I had to do some detective work to find you. Helped by my new best friend over here." He reached down to scratch behind Rochester's ears. The dog looked up at him with an expression of delight.

"I still remember how sweet you were, the morning I first heard from my mother that she was sick."

"How is she doing?" he asked. "She looks quite well."

"The surgery was easy but the rehab wasn't," Gail said. "But she's much better now, thank you." She seemed to realize that she was holding a pair of dog biscuits in her hand, and she gave one to each dog. I could sense the awkwardness between Gail and Declan—but that was something they'd have to work out on their own.

Lorraine stuck her head out the door. "What can I get for all of you?"

"Nothing for me. I've got to get back home." I shook Declan's hand. "Congratulations on the new job and the visa. I hope we'll be seeing you around Stewart's Crossing."

Gail looked from me to Declan, then reached out a hand to him. "Well, come on inside. I can see we've got a lot to catch up on."

They walked into the café, and after the dogs had cleaned up every biscuit crumb, we walked back through town to River Bend. I was pleased to be able to bring Gail and her old friend together. I'd seen a sadness in her now and then, and I'd chalked it up to her mother's illness, and worry over Lorraine's recovery. But maybe it was partly to do with that failed relationship.

It was clear that Declan wanted something more than friendship with Gail, and I hoped he'd be able to bring some happiness back to her. The dogs dallied with smells around an ancient sycamore, and I realized there had been plenty of time for Lili to get home and email me those sneaker photos.

"Come on, dogs, get moving," I said. "We've got work to do."

7 – All Stars

Once we got back to the townhouse, the dogs collapsed in a pile on the living room floor, and I went up to the office. Lili's email had arrived, and I opened the photos and found a close-up of the back label, with its blue heel patch. Prior to the 1960s, those patches had all been black. So that was one step – the shoe had been made after 1960.

From the 1960s through the 1980s, Chucks were made with an extra piece of outer canvas to give extra strength to the inner lining and help secure the tongue. The shoe I was looking at had that extra piece of canvas, cut in the curved shape of a line of extra stitching.

I was making progress. That extra piece meant that the sneaker Rochester had found was at least thirty years old. But from the thick layer of dust on it, I could probably have guessed that.

Rick called to check on his dog. "He hasn't destroyed your house yet, has he?"

"Not a chance," I said. "I took them both up to town and tired them out. How are things going?"

"Not making much progress. There wasn't much in the crime scene photos to help me narrow in on when the body was left there. Besides the shoes, I've got a belt buckle and some other fiber fragments. Nothing specific to a particular time."

"I may be able to help you narrow to within a couple of decades." I told him about my sneaker research.

"All this is legit though, right?"

"No, I'm hacking into the Converse corporate database," I said. "Of course it's legit."

"Just checking. No need to get your panties in a twist."

I suggested a couple of things Rick could do with his own panties, and he laughed, and we both hung up.

I went back to my laptop and searched further for something that would narrow the date when the sneaker was manufactured.

Shoes from the 1950s to the early 1970s had toe caps that didn't touch the edge of the canvas upper. The ends of the toe caps were not neatly cut in a perfect straight line but had minor variations from shoe to shoe, as if they were cut freehand. That matched the shoe in the picture. By adding that characteristic, I could narrow the manufacture of the shoe to the 1960s and 70s.

Then I hit pay dirt. The Chucks manufactured in the 1970s used wider piping where the canvas joined the rubber tread-like band and the smaller size of the toe caps. By taking one of Lili's close-ups into a photo manipulation program and comparing it to the Converse website image, I was able to establish that the narrow piping identified the shoe as manufactured during the 1960s.

I couldn't get any narrower than that, and it was always possible that the shoes had been vintage ones, worn by someone in a later decade. But when I get caught up in logic problems like that, I always go back to Occam's Razor – the idea that the simplest answer is usually the right one. A young man, late teens or early twenties, had worn those Chucks sometime during the 1960s, and died while wearing them. What was less clear was how he had ended up in that hidey-hole at the Meeting House.

The dogs were awake by then, chasing each other around my downstairs, so I took them out for another long walk. The late afternoon was still showing the best of Indian summer, and I delighted in watching the dogs romp together under trees full of yellow, gold and red leaves.

Rick's truck was in my driveway as we approached the house, and I let go of Rascal's leash so he could rush ahead of us to play with his daddy.

Rick got down to one knee and buried his face in the dog's black and white fur. "How's my boy?" he asked. "How's my wild and crazy Rascal?"

He stood up, taking firm hold of Rascal's leash. "Thanks for taking care of him. You have dinner plans? I could order us a pizza."

"Sounds great. I've got a six-pack of pumpkin ale I've been wanting to crack open."

"Pumpkin? That's gross."

"Wait til you try it."

I led him and the dogs inside, and while we waited for the pizza to be delivered we sampled the ale. Hints of pumpkin pie and nutmeg blended with the hops for an autumnal mouth feel, saying goodbye to summer in every sip. Rick admitted that he liked it.

As we drank, I showed him what I'd found about the sneaker. "Good work," he said, when we were finished. "That will help me with a missing persons search, at least until the evaluation of the remains comes up with something better."

The pizza arrived, a large with mushrooms and spicy Italian sausage, to the accompaniment of a canine crescendo of barking that made it seem like we were in an echoing kennel, barks and yips and the scrabble of toenails on the tile floor. I body blocked the dogs, took the pizza from the delivery guy and handed it off to Rick, then paid and tipped as the dogs trampled over themselves to follow Rick to the kitchen.

We dug in. There was no matching real, Jersey-style pizza from your neighborhood joint, where the mushrooms came from the farmer's market and the sausage and cheese from local farms. "I need to ask your advice about something," I said, feeding a piece of crust to each dog, both of whom were sitting attentively beside our chairs.

He drained the last of his beer and held out the empty bottle for another. "What's on your mind?"

I got up and retrieved two more beers from the fridge. "Lili asked if she could move in with me and Rochester," I said, as I sat back down.

"I didn't realize you'd been dating her that long."

"It's been six months. But her lease in Leighville is running out, and she figured she'd ask me before she renewed."

"What did you say?"

"I told her I needed to think about it."

Rick looked up at me. "And?"

"I'm thinking. When I got out of prison all I wanted was to be left alone. The first couple of weeks I was back here I hardly left the house—just for food and supplies. It wasn't until after I got my first adjunct teaching gig at Eastern that I started to feel like a human being again, that I could be among other people."

I took a sip of my beer. "Rochester helped a lot," I said.

"Dealing with him, having to talk to neighbors when I was walking him – all that stuff got me back in the rhythm of life again. And Lili's different from Mary. I can talk to her and not feel completely at a loss. She's enough like me that we have a lot in common— including the need for time on our own. But different enough to always be interesting."

"And you love her?"

I nodded. "I've been thinking about that a lot. I do."

"So what's the problem? Living together doesn't mean you have to be in each other's pocket twenty-four seven. She teaches, and she spends a lot of time taking pictures, doesn't she?"

I nodded. "And developing them, and then manipulating them on the computer."

"So you can be on your own then. And when you want to be together, you can be."

"When did you get so smart?" I asked, taking the last slice of pizza.

"Years of experience." We finished eating, talking idly about people we had gone to high school with, and then he and Rascal left, and I cleaned up the pizza debris.

The last person I had moved in with was Mary. When I met her, she was sharing a one-bedroom in a brownstone on the Upper East Side with a college friend, and my grad school roommate Tor and I were sharing a crappy studio apartment on the Lower East Side.

When Tor got a big raise, he was ready to move up to better digs with his girlfriend. Mary's roommate was getting married, and Mary couldn't afford the rent on her own. It seemed like time for all of us to get started on our real lives, so when Mary asked me to move in with her I said yes without a second thought.

A year later, her company offered her a promotion, which entailed a move to Silicon Valley. By then, we were both tired of city life, of graffiti on the streets, bums on every corner, the smell of urine in the subway. Moving to California would mean we could afford to buy a house, especially if we married and I got a decent job out there. We'd been together for two years by then and it seemed like the next step.

Lili and I were too old to let real estate decisions run our lives.

If we were going to move in together, it needed to be because it was the right thing for both of us. But was it?

When Rochester and I got back inside from our walk, I called Lili. "I got the sneaker pictures – thanks." I told her what I'd found out.

"That's good," she said. "I spent most of the day working on some of the photos I took yesterday at the Harvest Festival. Hardly looked at the clock."

"I know how that gets." I paused, thinking about how to bring up what we'd talked about that morning. Then I heard a beeping sound coming from somewhere in her apartment.

"Crap, that's my timer," she said. "I took some film yesterday, too, and I'm developing it in the bathroom. I've got to go before it gets ruined. Talk to you tomorrow."

"Sure," I fumbled, and then the line was dead.

Since I was moving closer to making a decision about Lili moving in, it was time to broach the question to Rochester. I hooked his leash and he dragged me out the front door. "You like Lili, don't you, boy?" I asked, as we stopped by the base of an oak tree.

He was too busy sniffing the ground to answer. But I already knew what he'd say, if he could talk. Lili smelled good, she slipped him treats, and she gave nice scratchy belly rubs. I doubted he'd mind if she was around more often.

But with no input from him, I was on my own once again, and if I made the wrong decision, I might be alone for a long time.

8 – Always Someone Smarter

Monday morning I took Rochester for a long walk, and we heard the yard workers before we saw them. River Bend employs a staff of immigrant men to trim our hedges, weed our flower beds and mow our lawns. The community is large enough that they begin at one end and work from street to street, and by the time they have finished they start over again.

My dog did not like the men who carried leaf blowers over their shoulders; he shied away from them, planting his paws on the pavement until I dragged him forward. I figured it was the noise. He didn't like thunder, either, and fireworks drove him nuts.

"Come on, dog, I've got stuff to do." I had a long day ahead – the exit interview with Santiago Santos, and then a meeting to go over paint and carpet samples for Friar Lake.

After returning to Bucks County I became an adjunct instructor and then an administrator at Eastern College, my alma mater, a "very good small college," as the publicity had it. One day about four months before, the college president, John William Babson, had called me into his office. I'd thought at the time that I was being fired – but instead, he had a new job for me.

Eastern had recently completed the purchase of a nineteenth-century monastery a few miles from the campus. Officially called Our Lady of the Waters, it included a hilltop chapel and dormitory, several outbuildings and about fifty acres of woodland. At the base of the hill was a small body of water known as Friar Lake. Mendicant friars, those religious men who spent their lives among the poor, retired to a house at the water's edge to lives of country peace and quiet, the soothing sound of lake water lapping, the rhythms of nature around them.

The church had decided to consolidate facilities, so the monks and the friars moved to western Pennsylvania and Eastern bought the property. Babson had given me the opportunity to create a conference center for the college on the grounds. Though I had little background in the skills required, he had faith in me, and I had been scrambling to learn as much as I could since I got the assignment.

Part of my responsibility was overseeing the choice of materials for the interiors, and since my idea of decorating is a comfortable sofa and a big-screen TV, I recruited my friend Mark Figueroa to help me. He had a degree in interior design and ran an antique store in downtown Stewart's Crossing jammed with an eclectic mix of antique furniture, fifties dinnerware, and the kind of kitschy crap I'd seen at the Harvest Festival.

He'd been reluctant to help me out at first, because he had his own business to manage, but he had warmed up to the work, and I was eager to see the paint and carpet samples he'd put together.

While Rochester and I walked, I tried to focus on getting through the meeting with Santiago Santos. Until I had that certificate of final release, I was still a parolee, and the state of California, through Santos, had control over me.

I had done some foolish things since leaving prison—almost all of them involving the very crime I had done the time for. I had continued to think I was the smartest guy in the room, that I could break into websites and find the information I wanted without worrying about the consequences. Suppose Santos discovered the way I had hacked into the Quaker State Bank system while investigating Caroline's murder? Or the many other small hacks I had committed in search of the truth about other crimes?

He never knew that I'd kept my hacking software on Caroline's laptop, hidden in my attic. In addition to it, I had used computers at Eastern College to do research I didn't want Santos to know about. Hell, I'd even had a handgun in my possession, an inheritance from my dad, and hadn't reported it until one of my students was shot with a similar weapon and I had to surrender it for forensics evaluation. Since it was against the terms of my parole, Rick had held it for me after the ballistics didn't match the weapon used.

If Santiago Santos wanted to turn me in for parole violations, there were plenty of ways he could do it.

I wished I could take Rochester with me, for the comfort of his company, but I was sure dogs wouldn't be allowed in the Bucks

County Courthouse in Doylestown, where the regional office of the Parole Board was located. I left him on the first floor of the townhouse, with the gate up blocking the stairway to the second floor. The tile was strewn with his toys—his squeaky blue plastic ball, the frayed rope we played tug-of-war with, a miniature piano keyboard that played different squeaks depending on where the dog bit down.

I have no idea how Doylestown became our county seat. It's a medium-sized town in the center of the county, in the middle of an ocean of waving stalks of corn. It has no distinguishing features, and it's far from any highway. I negotiated a series of two-lane roads to the outskirts of the city, then found the round glassy rotunda of the courthouse.

I parked and took the elevator to the seventh floor. My heart raced as I opened the door to the Parole Board's office. I checked in with the receptionist, ten minutes early for my nine o'clock appointment, and took a seat on a hard wooden bench in the waiting room.

As the time ticked away without any summons from Santos, my tension level rose, as I imagined all the reasons why he was keeping me waiting. He couldn't be on the phone to someone in California; it was too early in the morning for that. But suppose he was reviewing my records, picking away at details?

The walls were painted institutional green, and the only decorations were mounted posters explaining parole board rules. Other parolees came and went around me, from young men with tattoos up and down their arms to a cheerful woman in her forties, to a heavyset man in his sixties with a grizzled beard and a VFW ball cap. I couldn't help wondering what their offenses had been. Drugs? Theft? Assault? I knew from Rick that those were the most common crimes, after DUI violations. Bucks County was not exactly a hotbed of crime, though our proximity to Philadelphia, and to Trenton across the river in New Jersey, put us somewhat at risk.

At nine-forty-five I called Mark Figueroa to reschedule our eleven a.m. appointment at Friar Lake. "Can you make one o'clock?" I asked.

"Sure. The store's closed on Mondays so I've got the whole

day free."

"Thanks, Mark. I appreciate it."

I hung up and debated going up to the receptionist to ask when Santos would be able to see me. But I held back, unwilling to make a fuss.

By the time I was called, at ten, my tension level was through the roof. I was worried about what Santos might say, irritated about rescheduling the session with Mark, and nervous that I'd accidentally say something that might compromise me.

"Steve! Sorry to keep you waiting, but you know how it is in government. Come on back."

Santos was a stocky Puerto Rican guy a few years younger than I was, and I'd always felt he was fair and truly interested in helping me. But at the same time, he'd been very strict whenever I'd come close to a violation, and sometimes I found his attitude patronizing, as if I was some kind of common criminal. Which I guessed I was.

"No problem," I said, trying to calm down, as he led me into a warren of cubicles, and motioned me to sit in the visitor's chair across from his desk.

"You had an attitude problem when we started working together," he said, as he sat down. "I'm not sure you've overcome it, but you've managed to stay under my radar for two years, and the state says I have to set you loose."

I didn't know how to respond to that, so I said nothing.

He sat back in his chair and picked up a yellow rubber squeeze ball emblazoned with the Doylestown Hospital logo, a series of piggybacked triangles. "I have a feeling you've been flying loose with some of the conditions of your parole, but I could never catch you." Santos gripped the squeeze ball. "That doesn't mean you won't get caught again, though."

I was about to protest, but he pushed his chair back abruptly and stood up. "Let's get this over with." He dropped the squeeze ball to his desk, where it bounced a couple of times then fell to the floor.

I followed him to an office with a floor-to-ceiling window overlooking Court Street. A middle-aged black woman sat behind a cluttered desk, wearing a navy business suit with a scarf around her neck. She had a stack of file folders in front of her.

"Steve Levitan, this is Barbara Aurum, my supervisor," Santos said. "Mrs. Aurum has to sign off on all our parole completions."

"Pleased to meet you," I said. As I shook her hand. I got a closer look at her scarf. "Is that the Paris metro system?"

She smiled. "I admit, I'm an absolute Francophile. If I could, I'd live in Paris."

"Sounds good to me," I said. At least she was pleasant, I thought. If Santos wanted to make trouble for me, would she let him?

She picked through the pile of folders and found mine, then opened it. We were all quiet for a moment or two as she scanned the contents.

"All your paperwork looks to be in order," she said, when she finished. "Santiago says you've landed a long-term position at Eastern College. Congratulations."

"I've been very fortunate. I went to school there myself, and many people there, up to the college president, have supported me."

"Excellent. That's the kind of result we're looking for." She looked at Santos. "Santiago? Anything else to add?"

My heart skipped a beat.

"Steve's made a solid transition back home from prison," he said. "He's put down roots, made friends, and rejoined the work force."

I waited for him to say something else, but he didn't.

"Then I guess we're ready to move on," Aurum said. She picked up a cheap ballpoint pen emblazoned with the Quaker State Bank logo and signed the form. Then she looked at me. "Don't take this the wrong way, but I hope our paths never cross again."

It felt like I let go of a breath I'd been holding for months. I was going to be free. I could finally put my past behind me. I smiled and looked at Barbara Aurum. "At least not professionally," I said. "I'm a bit of a Francophile myself. You never know, we might meet up at the Eiffel Tower one day."

"That would be very nice." She stood and we shook hands, and Santos led me back toward the front.

As we reached the door, he stopped. "You may be a smart

guy, Steve, but remember, there's always somebody smarter than you are. If you let your ego get ahead of you in the future, you'll end up in the same trouble you were in back in California, and I know you don't want that."

I was too happy to argue or complain, so even though I didn't want another lecture, I just said, "I'll do my best."

We shook hands, and I walked out of the office without the leash that had been holding me back.

9 – The Real World

"Lili? It's me. I'm free!"

I'd waited until I was out of the courthouse building, standing in the shade of a maple tree that was beginning to turn golden, to call Lili.

"Congratulations!" she said. "But I had no doubt you'd do fine."

"I had a couple of nervous moments. I'm glad it's all over." I looked at my watch. "I wish I had time to swing by the college and celebrate in person with you, but I've got an appointment at Friar Lake with Mark Figueroa, and I've already pushed it back once."

"No problem. I have a class soon anyway. I'll talk to you tonight."

We hung up, amid mutual endearments. Traffic moved past me on Court Street and attorneys and clients eddied in and out of the courthouse, but I felt removed from it all.

I looked at my watch, and realized that with the meeting with Mark postponed, I had time to head home and pick up Rochester, who usually went to work with me.

I didn't often leave him home alone. At two years old, he was still a big puppy, and puppies are destructive when they're bored. I had given up on dragging Rochester into the metal crate I had used when he was younger; he hated it, and he used to bark and rattle the bars like a prisoner in a black-and-white movie. Only when I'd been behind bars I'd never protested, just kept my head down and took each day as it came.

When I opened the front door, I braced myself for disaster. But he had been a good boy, only shredding one of his tug ropes, resulting in red and white strands all over the tile floor. Within seconds, seventy pounds of Golden Retriever hurled at me, huge front paws aimed at my midsection. "Easy boy." I ruffled his head. "I missed you too."

He backed away and romped around the downstairs. "Yes, I

know, you need a walk." I grabbed his leash and tried to get him to sit so I could hook it up.

No matter how strict I made my voice, Rochester was too intent on playing to obey. I finally had to grab the fur behind his neck and immobilize him with my body. As soon as I let him go he raced for the front door, dragging me behind him.

He dashed for my next-door-neighbor's oak tree and peed copiously. Then he darted ahead, continuing to pull me along. When I finally got him back home, he was eager to jump in the car. I loaded him into the front seat and he stuck his head out the window all the way up along the River Road to the turn off to Friar Lake.

My office was in a small stone building that had once been the abbey gatehouse. The college's director of physical plant, Joe Capodilupo, was in charge of the renovations to the buildings and grounds, and his first project had been renovating the gatehouse to serve not only as a construction field office, but eventually as the office for the conference center.

The architects had designed a warm, welcoming lobby with a desk and comfortable chairs. Hunter green walls, dark brown leather sofas, crown molding and pointed arches over the windows completed the look, which was masculine, academic, and ecclesiastical. A scale model of the project was on the low table by the front door, along with a stack of glossy brochures. Lili had taken the photos and I'd written the text.

There were two offices off the lobby and a large conference room where we kept the full-sized plans of the property. As Rochester and I walked in, Joe stepped out of his office. He was a gruff, heavyset guy with white hair and a white beard, and he looked like he'd have been at home with the Benedictines if you slapped one of those black robes on him. He was accompanied by a tall, good-looking guy in his early thirties. Though he was nearly a head taller than Joe and his hair was dark, I spotted a family resemblance immediately.

"Morning, Steve. Let me introduce you to my boy, Joe Junior. He just started as the superintendent of the construction crew here."

"Call me Joey," he said, as I reached out to shake his hand, which was large and calloused. He had a faint tracing of five o'clock shadow, hipster sideburns, and a diamond stud in one ear.

"Good to meet you." I introduced Rochester, who slobbered all over the knee of Joey's faded but neatly pressed jeans. He reached down to ruffle the dog's ears, and Rochester had a new friend.

"When the decorator fella gets here, we'll take a walk around," Joe said. "In the meantime, Joey's got a lot to learn."

"My dad's been saying that since I was about five," Joey said. "See you later."

I went into my office, put down my messenger bag, and turned on my computer. The office was a change from the one I'd had at Fields Hall on campus, with its high ceilings, ornate moldings, and French doors out to a garden where I could take Rochester for quick walks. At Friar Lake, I had a picture window view of the abbey chapel, a Gothic pile that needed serious rehabbing. The property sat atop a low tree-covered mountain, and there were plenty of places where I could let Rochester off his leash to run.

I began to go through my emails, deleting all those that had no importance to me, including what was probably the fifteenth message from a textbook rep inviting me to sign up for the digital lab for freshman comp. I'd tried writing back to let her know that I wasn't teaching that term, but the message came from one of those "do not reply" addresses, and I'd long since lost her business card.

I'd just finished when Mark walked in. He was in his mid-thirties, exceedingly tall and skinny, wearing a tight black T-shirt and close-fitting black jeans.

"Sorry I had to push things back," I said, standing up to shake his hand. "I hope it didn't wreck your schedule."

"No problem." Rochester lunged for him, but Mark intercepted. "Black pants, puppy! I don't want blond hairs all over them."

I grabbed the dog's collar and tugged him back as Mark stepped into my office. "If you like the samples I've brought we're ready to place some orders," he said. "I can get a good deal on the dormitory carpets from the manufacturer."

"Sounds good." We sat down and went over the samples, then looked at the delivery schedule for some of the other finishes.

When we were done, Mark sat back in his chair and asked, "So, did you hear about the fuss at the Meeting House during Harvest Days?"

"I was part of it," I said. "Or at least Rochester was. He's the one who spotted the dead man's foot."

Rochester perked up at the sound of his name, but when there were no treats forthcoming, he went back to sleep.

"Creepy," Mark said. "Do the police know whose body it is?"

"I saw Rick Stemper yesterday, and he doesn't have much to go on yet. He's pretty sure it's a guy, but he doesn't know how old he was, when he died, how he died, or even how he got stuck in the building."

"What do you mean?"

"The body was between a false wall and the exterior clapboard," I said.

"Yeah, I've heard of false walls in other Quaker buildings."

I looked at him. "How would you hear that?"

"I did an independent study paper in college on colonial architecture, and one of the building types I focused on was the meeting house. I'll bet that wall was built to hide runaway slaves," he said. "Back in the 1850s, the Quakers got involved in the anti-slavery movement, and there have been rumors that their Meeting Houses were used in the Underground Railroad."

"Oh, yeah. I remember Rick saying something about that."

"You think this body could be that old?"

"Nah. The foot Rochester found was wearing a sneaker. Converse, like the ones we wore as kids."

Joe stuck his head in my office, and asked, "You guys ready for a walk around the property?"

I shelved any further thoughts of Quakers and slaves as Mark and I followed him out to the lobby, where Joey was lounging by the front door.

"I'm Joey. You must be the decorator," Joey said, reaching out to shake Mark's hand.

"Mark. But I'm not really a decorator. I just have better taste than Steve has."

Joey looked at him and smiled. "I can see that."

I was about to protest when Joe said, "All right, enough

flirting, you two. We've got work to do."

Flirting? A dozen thoughts rushed through my head. Joey was gay? His father knew and was comfortable enough about it to make an offhand comment? Or was that some kind of construction site trash-talk?

Joey opened the door and ushered us out. "Gotta listen to the boss," he said. We filed out and walked toward the chapel, a few hundred feet away. The Friar Lake property also included a dormitory wing, a kitchen, and several outbuildings. The contractor Joey worked for had nearly finished clearing out the interiors for renovation and was ready to start on the next phase.

We walked through the old dormitory, and it was a revelation – the walls enclosing the tiny monastic cells were gone, as was the outdated plumbing and the exposed electrical wires. The floors had been stripped down to the original oak, and light streamed in through the multi-paned windows.

"Now you can see how this is going to shape up," Joe said as we walked. "There will be a covered walkway along the inside of the courtyard, and each one of the suites will have its own entrance."

It was exciting to be there at the birth of something totally new, and I was eager to make my own imprint. We continued walking through the property. By the time we'd finished with the last outbuilding, it was nearly two and I knew Rochester would be getting antsy back at the office. "I've got to get back to work," I said. "I'll talk to you once you have those numbers, all right, Mark?"

"Sure. I need to get to the store myself."

We all shook hands, and Mark and I walked back to the office. "He seems like a good guy," I said, probing to see what Mark thought. "Joey."

"I've sworn off men," Mark said. "After that disaster with Owen." Mark had briefly dated a guy who worked for him during the summer, a situation that hadn't ended well.

"Going to be tough to work with him if he's interested and you're not," I said.

"He's only interested because he doesn't know me."

"Well, aren't you cheerful?" I said as we reached the parking lot.

"He's probably not even gay," Mark said. "When his dad said we were flirting? That's the way construction guys talk."

Well, I'd thought that at first, too, until I saw the way Joey looked at Mark. "Uh-huh," I said. "You can believe that if you want. See you later."

I found Rochester bouncing around in my office. I took him outside and let him loose for a run around the back side of the property, away from all the construction work.

As he neared the edge of the woods, he startled a doe and fawn beneath a pine. The doe was darker, body poised like a bow string; beside her, the tan and white fawn nibbled at the grass, oblivious to danger. At some unspoken signal, they leapt away, but Rochester didn't follow; he'd found some more interesting smell in front of him.

While he sniffed, I called Rick Stemper. "I had my exit interview with Santiago Santos this morning. My parole is over."

"Congratulations."

"Do you still have that laptop I gave you after the intervention?" I asked. "The one that used to belong to Caroline Kelly?"

"You mean the one with all the illegal hacking software?"

"Just possessing those tools isn't a crime," I said.

"Yes, I still have the laptop. I have a meeting at The Chocolate Ear at four-thirty but I could meet you over at my house after that."

"A meeting about the case?"

"Remember Hannah Palmer, the clerk of the Meeting? Her sister is the unofficial historian of the property, and Hannah set up an appointment with her for me this afternoon. Why don't I call you when I'm finished?"

"Sounds like a plan. Any news on the bones?"

"Not yet. The county ME passed the remains on to a specialized FBI unit. They're going to extract DNA from the bone marrow and the teeth, which we can use if we ever find somebody to match them to. They might even be able to do a facial reconstruction based on the skull."

"The FBI? Cool! I've seen a couple of episodes of that show about the forensic anthropologist. They're always figuring out who the body belongs to and how the murder was committed."

"And they do it all in an hour," Rick said dryly. "Including commercial breaks. It takes a lot longer when you live in the real world."

I hung up as Rochester and I circled back to the office. In addition to helping with the interior renovation of the site, I was also responsible for designing a schedule of programs we could run. I'd been meeting with various faculty members on campus, reading brochures from similar operations, and brainstorming my own ideas. That afternoon I worked on a program about Jane Austen.

We had a great professor in the English department who specialized in women writers, and I knew there were a ton of Janeites out there, as fans of the novelist were called. I thought we could combine a series of discussions about Austen's books, led by Professor Christine Jackson, with some fun experiences, like a costume tea party, an examination of Austen fan fiction, and an afternoon of music from Austen's era directed by a musicologist, along with some demonstrations of the types of dances featured in the novels.

I spent the afternoon working out the details for that program. Around four, Lili called. "I really wanted to celebrate with you tonight," she said. "But one of my adjunct photography professors has the stomach flu, and I have to take over her class."

"What time will you be finished?"

"She scheduled a field trip to take photos of Leighville after dark, so I won't be done until late. And after herding a dozen kids all over town I'm sure I'll be exhausted. Would you hate me if I just went home and went to sleep?"

"I'd never hate you," I said. "Don't worry, we'll see each other later in the week."

"Thanks for understanding," she said. "Love you."

"Love you too."

Well, that sucked, I thought, as I hung up. I had pretty much made my decision about having her move in, and I'd thought we would talk more about it that night. And I'd been looking forward to sharing my happiness about the meeting with Santos with her, too.

I looked at the clock. Well, if I couldn't hang out with Lili, Rick was a solid second choice. I could head down to Stewart's Crossing and catch him as his meeting with Hannah Palmer's sister was ending. Especially after what Mark had told me about the Quakers helping runaway slaves, I was curious to know more about the history of the Meeting.

And if I happened to get to the café a few minutes early and added myself to his appointment… what was he going to do? Call me a party crasher? He'd called me a lot worse in the past when I'd snooped in his investigations.

10 – War Hero

My aged BMW sedan was the last relic of my life in Silicon Valley. I could still remember the thrill of buying it right after Mary and I moved out there from New York. It was the first car I bought new, and when I financed it for five years I never dreamed I'd still have it for so long. It got me and Rochester from point A to point B, and sometimes that was as far as I wanted to go.

Rochester loved to ride in the car. He plopped his big golden butt on the passenger seat and pressed his nose against the window. "What's the matter, haven't figured out how to operate the switch yet?" I asked. I pressed the one on my side of the car and the window slid down. He stuck his head out, and the gold fur on the back of his neck fluttered like a bunch of Tibetan prayer flags. I bet that if I showed him how the switch on his side worked, he'd master it quickly.

Rochester and I pulled up in front of the café as Rick approached on foot from the police station, a half a block away. When I opened his door, Rochester jumped out to greet him, licking his hands as if he'd dipped them in doggie treats. "What are you doing here?" he asked me.

"Lili has to work tonight and I thought maybe we could get a beer together after you're finished, celebrate my release."

"Or you thought you could insert yourself and your dog into my meeting." He shook his head. "I ought to make you get right back in your car and leave."

"But then you'd just have to tell me what you learned," I said. "Better I should get it first hand, right?"

"Who says I'd have to tell you?"

"Because you're a dedicated police officer who recognizes the importance of using all the resources available to solve crimes and protect the people of Stewart's Crossing."

He laughed. "And you're a major bullshit artist. Fine, you can stay."

Rick and I staked out a round wrought-iron table on the sidewalk. I waved at Gail's mother Lorraine through the window, and she came out to greet us. "We're going to be four," I said. "Including Rochester, that is."

"I always include him," she said, scratching his head. He opened his mouth in an exaggerated yawn, then settled to the ground.

"Café mocha for me," I said. "One of Gail's special biscuits for the hound."

Rick ordered an iced tea, and Lorraine promised to have everything out right away.

"Do you know Hannah's sister?" I asked Rick when she'd gone.

"Don't think so, but you never know in StewCross. Her name's Tammy and she must be a few years younger than we are. Hannah says she described me."

"Not too accurately, I hope, or else she might not show up."

He held up his middle three fingers and said, "Read between the lines."

We were both laughing when a huge SUV pulled up at the curb in front of us, and a tall, leggy blonde in a pink and white sundress stepped out. She was in her late thirties and almost fashion-model beautiful, with a smooth face, demure lipstick, and a flash of white teeth. A silver heart on a matching chain rested above the cleft of her breasts.

"Hi, Rick!" she said, waving as she closed the door.

"Crap," Rick whispered to me, and it looked almost like he was blushing. "I know her. That's Tamsen Morgan. Her son plays in the Pop Warner league I help coach."

Rick jumped up, knocking his metal chair backwards. "Hi, Tamsen," he said to her. "When Hannah called you Tammy I didn't realize that we already knew each other."

"Hannah's almost the only one who calls me that anymore," she said. "And it's funny, I never knew your last name – the kids all call you Coach Rick. When my sister told me I was meeting with Detective Stemper I had no idea it was you." She raised her eyebrows. "Though she did say you were very handsome. I should have guessed—there aren't that many handsome men around

Stewart's Crossing."

"Excuse me?" I asked. "There are other guys present at this table."

Tamsen turned her smile on me. "Yes, who is this good-looking fellow?" She stuck her palm out to Rochester, and Rick guffawed.

"That's Rochester the crime dog," Rick said. "And the human attached to him is my friend Steve. You don't mind if he joins us, do you?"

"Not at all." Tamsen and I shook hands. Lorraine came out with our drinks and Rochester's biscuit, and Tamsen ordered a coffee for herself. "God knows I need the caffeine. I have to pick up Justin in half an hour and he'll keep me running until bedtime." She sighed. "Sometimes I wish he was more like his cousin Nathaniel, who can actually sit still for more than five minutes. But then, when Nathaniel wants something, he's relentless. He wants a dog right now, and he won't let up until he gets one. Justin has a bit of ADD – he jumps around from one thing to the next. If I ever take him to a Meeting I have to let him run around in the back of the building."

"Justin's eight," Rick said to me. "He's very energetic."

"He's a holy terror," Tamsen said. "Not exactly an exemplar of the Quaker ideals of peace and serenity. He's his father's boy through and through."

Her words reminded me of the two children that Mary had miscarried. We never asked their sex, because we thought at the time it would make them less real to either of us. No such luck.

"Your husband must be glad to have a son," I said, picking up my coffee.

"He was so proud when Justin was born. I think he showed baby pictures to every soldier in Iraq. And then he was killed outside Fallujah four years ago."

I put the coffee down without drinking. "I'm so sorry."

"We met in college. I was a shy Quaker freshman and he was a sharp-looking junior in ROTC. You can imagine what my parents thought of my dating – and then marrying – a soldier. I moved away from the Friends until after his death, when they welcomed me back."

Lorraine delivered Tamsen's coffee. After a sip, she said, "Oh, that's good," and sighed with pleasure. Then she looked at Rick. "Hannah said you had some questions about the history of the Meeting?"

"Did she tell you about the body we found behind a false wall along the north side of the building?" Rick asked.

"Yes. It really shook her up. She's so devoted to the Quaker ideals that she felt it as a personal violation." She took another sip of her coffee. "So, here's a capsule history. The first Friends arrived in Stewart's Crossing in the early 1800s. At the start they met in a field down by the river. God is everywhere, you know."

I glanced over at Rick, who was staring at her like she was the only woman left on earth.

"The Meeting House was built in sections, as you might have guessed from the different materials," Tamsen continued. "The center section with the fireplace was first, in 1825. The north wing was built in the 1850s, and the center section opened up to one big space, and the minister's gallery on the south side was enlarged, too. The kitchen didn't come until later, around the turn of the century."

"Rick said he learned something about the Meeting House being a way station on the Underground Railroad," I said. "And then another friend of mine suggested that the false wall might have been constructed to hide slaves."

"I've heard about false walls at other Meeting Houses. But I didn't realize that ours had one until... well, you know." Rochester nosed at her leg, and she leaned down to pet him. "There's something else tickling around in the back of my mind. Let me think for a minute."

She closed her eyes, still absently petting Rochester. I noticed Rick had a sappy grin on his face as he stared at her. I'd have fun teasing him about that later.

Tamsen opened her eyes again. "I know there's something, but I can't seem to retrieve it."

"You mentioned that you let Justin run around in the back of the Meeting House," I said. "Did you do that yourself when you were a kid?"

"Oh, sure. Hannah and I knew every corner of that building."

Her mouth opened. "That's what I was trying to remember." She put her hand on my arm. "Steve, you're a genius."

Out of the corner of my eye I saw Rick frowning, and I thought, *Take that, Frank Hardy.*

"What did you remember?" Rick asked.

"When Hannah and I were kids, maybe eight or ten, the lock on the door to that storage closet was broken and we used to hide there sometimes. One day Eben Hosford discovered us, and he had a fit. I remember he told our parents that it wasn't safe back there, and he volunteered to repair the door and put on a new lock."

"That's the old hippie who sells soap?" I asked.

"Yes. Sometimes I find it hard to believe he's really a Friend. Despite the hippie exterior there's something very angry inside him."

"Do you think he knew about the false wall?" Rick asked.

She shrugged. "I remember how nasty he was, and how Hannah and I were mad that we'd lost our special hiding place."

"Do you know anyone who might have known about it?" Rick asked.

"Maybe one of our older members." She thought for a minute. "Steer clear of Eben, though. He's been very opposed to the reconstruction project, and he's gotten even crankier as he's gotten older." Her eyes lit up. "You know who you could talk to? Edith Passis. She was very active in the Meeting in the 1960s, before she got married. Do you know her?"

"I used to take piano lessons from her, back in the day," I said. Rick was looking moon-faced so I kicked him in the shin. "Rick knows her, too. He helped her out when her identity was stolen last year."

Tamsen looked at Rick. "Well, well. Good with kids and kind to elderly ladies."

"Don't forget the handsome part," I threw in, and Rick glared at me.

Tamsen laughed. "I've got Edith's number in my cell. Want me to call her for you?"

Maybe it was the meeting with Santos that morning, which reminded me of my incarceration, but for a moment I thought she meant prison cell. But as soon I realized my error, I said, "That would be great," before Rick could protest. She dug a phone out of her shoulder bag and pressed a couple of buttons.

"It's Tamsen Morgan, Edith," she said. "I'm here with Rick Stemper from the police, and his friend Steve. They want to ask you a couple of questions about the Meeting House. I'm going to put you on speaker." She pressed a button and laid the phone on the table.

"Hello, Edith. We don't want to bother you," Rick began.

"No bother at all. This is about what you found on Saturday, isn't it? There's no time like the present. Can you come over here? I'm not busy, just noodling around at the piano."

All throughout my youth, Edith had given piano lessons to the talented and the tone-deaf; I fell squarely into the second category, though Edith and I had both endured about three years' worth of lessons, only ending when I was able to substitute Hebrew School. I knew she still gave the occasional lesson at her home, though she had stopped teaching advanced students at Eastern a year before.

"We're downtown," Rick said. "Give us about fifteen minutes."

Tamsen she picked up the phone and as she ended the call she must have noticed the time. "Gosh, I've got to go," she said, then drained the last of her coffee. When she stood up, Rick and I jumped to our feet, too. Our mothers would have been proud of our manners.

"Thank you for coming over," Rick said. "I appreciate your insight."

"It was my pleasure. It's nice to see you when you're not surrounded by a horde of pre-adolescent boys." She shook hands with both of us. "I'll see you on Saturday?" she asked Rick.

"Sure. I'll be there."

I noticed Rick watch her walk back to her SUV. "Put your tongue back in your mouth," I said to him when she was out of hearing range. "You're not Rochester."

"I wasn't looking at her."

"Sure you were. And she seemed to like you, too." I raised my voice to sound like a child's. "She called you handsome!"

He glared at me. He pulled a couple of bills out of his wallet and tucked them under his iced tea glass.

"So. You going to ask her out?" I asked.

He shook his head. "Her husband was a war hero. I can't compete with that."

"He's dead, Rick. And she's still alive, and she's beautiful, and she's interested in you." I beeped my car open. "You want me to drive us over to Edith's?"

"Only if you drop this. She said I was handsome. Big deal."

I batted my eyes and put a seductive curl in my voice. "See you Saturday?"

"Jerk." He opened the back door of the BMW and ushered Rochester in, then sat in the front as I got in and started the car. "We'll have to drop your dog somewhere, though. I'm not taking him over to Edith's."

Rochester knew we were talking about him and he looked up. "What, you think he'll want to play the piano?" I asked.

"With your dog? I never know."

11 – Making a Difference

It was closer to drop Rochester at Rick's house, so I headed that way. "Who was the friend you mentioned to Tamsen?" Rick asked as we drove.

"I told you, I talked to Mark Figueroa today. He's doing some work for me up at Friar Lake." I repeated my conversation with him to Rick, and he took a couple of notes.

Rick had bought the sixties ranch house where he grew up from his parents when they retired to a trailer park in central Florida. After he and Rascal began agility training, he set up a small course in his fenced-in backyard for practice. We left Rochester back there with Rascal, both of them running and chasing each other around. Then we drove the extra mile to Edith's.

She still lived in the same house, a cheerful red Cape Cod a few blocks from the house where I grew up, in the Lakes neighborhood south of downtown Stewart's Crossing. She opened her front door as I parked in front of the house.

"Come on in. Would you like some lemonade?"

"No thanks, Edith," Rick said. "We only have a couple of quick questions."

She led us into her living room, still furnished as I remembered from my lessons. The black baby grand piano rested by the front window, where other houses might have a dining room. Rick and I sat on a comfortable old couch, Edith across from us in a big wing chair with a paisley slipcover. The smell of lemon furniture polish hung in the air, and dust motes danced in the late afternoon light streaming in from the picture window.

"How can I help you?" she asked.

"You've probably already heard that there's a false wall along the north side of the Meeting House," Rick said. "That's where the body was found. Hannah and Tamsen didn't know it was there, but Tamsen suggested you might know more."

"I did know about it, way back when," she said. "But I have to admit I'd forgotten all about it until Saturday."

"Was it common knowledge back then, among the members?" I asked.

"I don't think so." She leaned forward. "Before and during the Civil War, the Meeting was a stop on the Underground Railroad."

"We've heard that from a couple of sources," Rick said.

"I believe that the escaped slaves hid behind that false wall to avoid bounty hunters." Edith paused. "And then in the 1960s, our Meeting was part of a network of Friends groups that helped young men avoid Vietnam. They stopped with us for a day or two until we could arrange transport for them to Canada."

I looked at Rick. "That matches the time when the sneaker was manufactured. That could be the body of a draft dodger."

"Let Edith finish her story," Rick said.

"You know, of course, that one of the tenets of Quaker belief is non-violence. Very early in the Vietnam conflict several Quakers organized an action group to try and affect public opinion through pacifist campaigns. We collected relief supplies for the wounded in North Vietnam and for the Red Cross on both sides."

"You weren't some kind of Hanoi Jane, were you, Edith?" I asked jokingly, remembering the outcry against Jane Fonda's actions at the time. An image of a younger Edith in one of her mod outfits, posed against a cannon like the ones in Washington Crossing Park, flashed through my head.

"Not at all. I picketed at a few rallies in Philadelphia, but most of what I did was volunteer as a draft counselor with the American Friends Service Committee. We helped hundreds of men gain conscientious objector status and other exemptions and deferments." She shook her head. "Many of these young men had been abandoned by their families and friends because they refused to fight in what they saw as another country's civil war, where we had no business interfering. When they learned that we cared about them and were willing to help them, many of them broke down in tears."

Edith pulled a tissue from her pocket and dabbed at her eyes. "It was very emotional work, you know, because it was literally life and death for some of them. When we were able to arrange for someone to serve in a hospital or non-profit instead of going to war, it was the most fulfilling thing."

I looked at Edith. When I was a kid, I'd been impressed with her 1960s style – thigh-high boots, tie-dyed T-shirts and big dangling earrings. As her student, I was in awe of her musical knowledge and her endless patience with my stumbling efforts. When I reconnected with her after my return to Stewart's Crossing, I'd seen her as a sweet elderly lady.

Now I was looking at her in a new way. How amazing to have been able to make such a difference. In my years as a college teacher, in New York, California, and back at Eastern, I'd been privileged to mentor a few students and feel like I'd helped them. But what Edith had done was in a whole other league.

"We had another role, much more clandestine, and that relates back to the false wall," Edith continued. "From our Meeting, there were only half a dozen of us involved. John Brannigan, the headmaster at George School at the time, was our leader."

George School was a private day and boarding school in Newtown run by the Society of Friends. Many wealthy parents in Stewart's Crossing sent their kids there to avoid the hoi polloi in the public schools.

"John was quite dashing, you know, so all the girls wanted to be involved, but he only picked the most sensible ones."

I looked at Edith in mock surprise. "You were sensible back then?"

She laughed. "Oh, yes. I was quite the demure Quaker girl." She sat back in her chair. "I remember that John organized us in 1966, because it was right after I graduated from Trenton State. We had a very secret rendezvous at the edge of one of the playing fields at George School, under the trees. He explained what he needed and asked us if we were willing to be a part of it."

"How did the process work, exactly?" Rick asked.

"John would get a phone call from someone at another meeting. I never knew where the calls came from. He kept that very secret. A boy, sometimes more than one, would be heading past us on his way to Canada. John would arrange to pick the boy up – sometimes at the train station, sometimes in Philadelphia or somewhere out in the country. The boy might stay here in

Stewart's Crossing for a day or two, and then be escorted on to another Meeting closer to the border."

"They hid behind that false wall?" Rick asked.

"Yes. Some of the boys had already been drafted, and we were afraid if they were out in public they might be arrested."

She looked from me to Rick. "Do you think the body you found might be one of those boys? Because I don't see how that could be. No one stayed with us for very long, and surely we'd have noticed a body in that narrow space."

I struggled to remember the years of the draft, and the Vietnam conflict. I knew that United States involvement in Southeast Asia began in earnest during the Eisenhower administration, when the first military advisers were sent to Saigon. But I hadn't been born until 1967, and by the time I was aware of the world around me Henry Kissinger had already negotiated the cease-fire in Paris and the US had withdrawn all its troops.

Rick must have been thinking along the same lines, because he asked, "When was the last time that empty space was used?"

"I wish I could remember. But it was so long ago, after all. More than half my life." She smiled ruefully. "And I only played a very small part. I wouldn't want to mislead you by just grasping at a date. But the draft ended in January of 1973, I remember that."

Edith sighed. "I'm sorry, the old brain doesn't work as well any more. But I'll play some of the music from back then—that often helps me remember things."

"Tamsen mentioned that in, I guess, the early 1990s, the storage closet that led to the false wall had a broken door, and that Eben Hosford fixed it," I said. "Was he part of your group back then?"

She shook her head. "No, John only recruited girls because he thought the police would be more lenient with us if we were arrested. And Eben wasn't a Friend back then. I don't know when he joined the Meeting – I was already married to Lou, and as you know, going to synagogue with him. I have to admit I was surprised to find Eben in the congregation when I returned, after Lou's death. He's not exactly a gentle soul."

I was disappointed. I'd been hoping that Eben Hosford had a

connection to the group smuggling the boys through Stewart's Crossing, but it looked like that wasn't the case.

"George School has an archive of John Brannigan's papers," Edith said. "You could check there and see who the last boys were to pass through Stewart's Crossing."

"That's a great idea, Edith," I said. "And maybe there will be some records of who the other people were who were involved in moving the boys around, and who might have known about the false wall."

"Is there anyone else you can remember who knew about that empty space?" Rick asked.

"So many of the members who were around back then have passed on, or moved to Florida," Edith said. "It's all the same to me – they go to God, or to one of His waiting rooms. But you can't think that one of the Friends was responsible for this death. That's so against everything we believe."

"Sadly, people betray their ideals all the time," Rick said. "Sometimes for good reasons, sometimes for bad. Someone could have been using that space for years after the war was over, for a hundred reasons. Hiding, smuggling, storing. You name it."

"It really is awful," Edith said. Her hands were trembling, which surprised me. As a pianist, her hands were part of her livelihood, and I knew she was religious about practice and almost obsessive about warding off the effects of old age and arthritis, taking various supplements and acupuncture treatments so that her fingers remained strong and steady.

I wondered if her hands shook was because she was upset – or because she was nervous about the secrets that had been hidden for all those years. Could it be that she knew more about the boys passing through Stewart's Crossing than she let on? .

12 – Good Reasons

I waited until Edith's front door was closed to ask Rick, "Do you think Edith is worried about all this stuff coming to light? I mean, she probably broke a bunch of laws back then."

"There's a statute of limitations on everything but murder," Rick said. "And public opinion about Vietnam has changed dramatically since then. If she didn't kill the kid, or help cover up his death, she's got nothing to worry about. You made a good point about that false wall, though. The body doesn't have to belong to one of those boys. I've been going through missing persons reports and I haven't found any good matches."

"You could get a list of all the members from the early seventies on and see if any of them knew about the space," I suggested. "I can help with that, if you want."

"I appreciate it. But it's my job." He turned to me. "So. You said something about celebrating your release from parole. I've got beer at my house but nothing to eat."

"How about hoagies?" I asked. "We could stop at DeLorenzo's."

"It's not the same since those new people took over. But I could suffer through a sandwich. You can drop me back at my truck, and I'll meet you at my place."

I took his order, and after I let him off at The Chocolate Ear I circled around to Canal Street, where DeLorenzo's deli huddled against the back wall of the post office. I went into the shop, which had been owned by an Italian family for as long as I could remember. They'd recently sold to a Thai couple, who had stripped the floors, painted the walls and replaced the photos of Italy with panoramic shots of Bangkok. I missed the old place and hoped the hoagies hadn't changed.

I ordered the sandwiches with double meat so we'd have something to feed the dogs and drove to Rick's. Rascal and Rochester rushed over to the fence in a blur of gold, black and white fur, dissonant barks and yelps, and tongues lolling out like the unfurling of a red carpet.

I opened the gate and the dogs romped over to me. Both of them followed me inside, lured by the smell of turkey and roast beef. Rick was in the kitchen, opening bottles of an Oktoberfest ale from a local brewery. "Your stuff's in the dining room," he said, as I laid the bag of sandwiches on the Formica-topped kitchen table.

As far as I could tell all Rick had done in the way of redecorating after he bought the house from his parents was to install a flat-screen TV in the living room. But in high school we'd been acquaintances more than friends, bonded by a chemistry class we both had struggled through, so I'd never been to his home when his parents lived there.

He handed me a beer. "It's a sad commentary that I trust you more with your Dad's gun than with Caroline's old computer," he said. "How does Lili feel about your getting the laptop back?"

"I haven't told her," I said. "I just thought about it this afternoon. But she says she trusts me to make the right decisions."

We unwrapped our sandwiches, the dogs sniffing eagerly beside us. "And the gun?" Rick asked, as he peeled a slice of turkey off his sandwich and rolled it up.

"What about it?" I did the same with my roast beef.

"How does Lili feel about you having a gun in the house?" He fed the turkey to Rascal, then yelped and said, "Watch my fingers, you monster."

"Lili's fine around weapons. She's spent a lot time in war zones, and I know she's shot everything from a handgun to a confiscated Kalashnikov in the past."

"Yeah, I can totally see her behind a machine gun. Be careful if you decide you don't want her to move in."

I put my sandwich down. "You're kidding, right?"

"You know her better. What do you think? Is she the type to fly off the handle if things don't go her way?"

"I don't think so." I picked up my hoagie again. "But honestly, this came at me out of left field. I like things the way they are. Lili and I talk a lot, and we see each other during the week and on weekends. But we both have our space."

"Then tell her that. But be prepared for her to say that doesn't work for her."

Rick fed another tidbit to Rascal and Rochester nosed me for his, but my mind was elsewhere. When I met Lili, something clicked between us. I wanted to see her, date her, sleep with her. I enjoyed the time we spent together, and I believed that I loved her. I didn't want to lose her. But did keeping her mean losing something else?

I looked at Rick. "You think Lili would break up with me if I say no?" Rochester snuffled my leg and I fed him a scrap of roast beef.

"Every woman is different," Rick said, in a tone of voice that usually accompanied a lecture on the birds and the bees, "but every woman is the same, too. If she brought up living together, then she wants to. Right? She could have gone ahead and renewed her lease and never even mention it to you."

"Crap," I said.

He picked up his beer. "But you're not getting anywhere obsessing about it. This is supposed to be a celebration, right? You're free from the yoke of Santiago Santos's oppression."

I tapped my beer against his. "You're right. Only happy thoughts for the rest of the evening."

We talked about classmates and changes in Stewart's Crossing, and by seven-thirty we were cleaning up. I got my laptop and my dad's gun, still in its leather pouch, from Rick's dining room table.

I said goodbye to Rick and Rascal, and Rochester trailed reluctantly behind me as I walked out, sorry to be leaving his friend and playmate. I put the laptop and the gun in the trunk, just to be safe. After all, both of them were dangerous.

When we got home, I stowed the gun in the nightstand beside my bed, where it had been before Rick was forced to confiscate it. I'd kept the laptop hidden away in the attic – but without the threat of a surprise visit from Santos, I didn't have to anymore. I left it right in the middle of the kitchen table, a kind of "so there" at him.

Rochester was in a playful mood after his fun with Rascal. He hopped around me, trying to hump me from behind, and I had to wrestle him onto his side, burying my head in the golden fur behind his neck, raking my fingernails across his belly. He wriggled onto his back and every time I scratched the place where his left hind leg joined his body, he shook that leg like he had a tambourine grasped in his paw.

Though I had a king-sized bed, there wasn't a whole lot of room there for me, Lili and a seventy-pound dog. Could the three of us cohabit together? Would Rochester forsake me for Lili's charms? I hugged him tight despite his efforts to wriggle out of my grasp.

Eventually, though, he squirmed away, and jumped off the bed. I heard him go down the stairs and then his toenails click against the tile floor. I got up and followed him to the kitchen, and there, like one of the Sirens of Greek mythology, was Caroline's laptop.

"It couldn't hurt to do a little searching online," I said to Rochester, who was lapping water from his bowl. "Nothing illegal."

I turned it on and poured a tall glass of water for myself. Once it had booted up, I decided to see what I could find about missing persons. I discovered a whole site dedicated to Pennsylvania missing persons and unidentified victims. But there were only three males listed between 1962 and 1969, and none of them matched the details of the body.

The more I read, the more depressed I got. Not just at the sheer number, but at the personal stories behind them. The worst were the kids who had disappeared without a trace—the paperboy returning from a friend's house, the hitch-hiking teenager, the multi-racial girl with turquoise hair, the small-town toddler in yellow boots and rain slicker.

I couldn't imagine how those parents must have felt. I remembered my father's friend Des and his lost son in Laos, how his obituary said that he'd never stopped hoping his boy would come home. The chances were that every missing in child in that database was dead, but what parent could accept that without the chance to say goodbye?

I'd read newspaper articles about hidden websites where pedophiles connected to share sexually explicit photos and stories. Using my hacking skills, could I delve into those, find some evidence of a lost child, give some peace to a grieving family?

My fingers hovered over the keys. I knew how I'd get started, the software I'd initialize, the unsecured ports I'd search for.

Rochester came up and rested his sloppy wet mouth on my leg. "I'm not your napkin, dog!" I said.

That interruption was all I needed to break my trance. Instead, I logged into my online hacker support group, using an email ID I had created for that purpose, one that had no link back to me.

Each of our stories was different, but each was the same. We'd all given in to those itchy fingers at some time. Some of us had good reasons, or ones we thought were good; others did it for the thrill of sneaking in somewhere or exacting revenge on some foe.

We were all anonymous there, so that we could be honest with each other, or as honest as we could be, without fear of law enforcement. My ID was CrossedWires – a tongue-in-cheek reference to Stewart's Crossing as well as to the idea that all of us have a few wires crossed in our brains. Mine had led me to become a hacker.

I began to read the messages from other members. Stinger23 had written a long post about his hair-trigger temper, and how he'd felt a physical ache when he got angry and wanted to screw with someone's identity. Ilovekitkat was a teenager who had hacked into his high school's computer system to change his grades. He was smart, but not hard-core like Stinger23. He'd posted about his temptation to hack in order to impress a girl.

I'd shared my sad story when I joined. Mostly I logged in to remind myself of the trouble I could get into, but sometimes I added messages of support to those in difficulties or reminded those who were tempted of the consequences they could suffer.

By the time I had finished reading through all of them, the urge to break in online had passed, and I spent some quality time playing tug-a-rope with Rochester. I knew I'd never be fully "cured" of my desire to hack – but I also knew it was important to those I loved that I keep trying.

13 – Thoughts of Heaven

Tuesday morning, I was on my way up to Friar Lake, Rochester riding shotgun, when Rick called. "You busy this afternoon?" he asked.

"No more than usual. What's up?"

"I called George School and spoke to the headmaster. I asked if Brannigan had left any papers there that might help me out in the investigation. He passed me off to his secretary, Vera Lee Isay, who it turns out was Brannigan's secretary, too. She's very twitchy, though. She finally admitted that after Brannigan died in 1995, she boxed up all his personal papers and put them into storage."

"Do you need a court order to look through them?"

"Not if the person in charge of them gives me access. As soon as I said I was looking for information about what Brannigan did during the Vietnam War, she closed right up. I had to convince her I wasn't interested in going after him, just that I wanted information about the boys who he might have helped."

I turned onto River Road for the drive up to Leighville. The swamp maples at the river's edge were a bright gold, and I glimpsed bits of gray-blue river through the branches.

"She sounds like a kind of lioness—been there forever, very protective of his memory. Finally got her to agree I could take a look – but only this afternoon. There's some kind of program starting tomorrow and she says she'll be too busy to supervise me. I'm afraid there's going to be too much for me to look through on my own. Think you can come up and give me a hand?"

"What time?"

"She asked me to wait until school was out. I guess seeing a police officer, even one in plainclothes, would be too upsetting for the delicate youth. So I said I'd be there at four."

"I've got a meeting at three," I said. "Should only take a half hour. I can take the back roads to Newtown and meet you, but I'll have to bring Rochester. I won't have time to take him home and I don't want to leave him at Friar Lake and have to go back for him."

"Sure, bring the dog. What kind of trouble can he get into? Dig up another body?"

"I'm assuming that was a rhetorical question," I said. "I'll see you at four."

"English teacher," he said, and hung up.

When I got to Friar Lake I had contracts to review and sign for the materials Mark Figueroa and I had discussed, and the morning went by quickly. One of the disadvantages of leaving the campus was the lack of lunch facilities out in the country, so I had begun bringing food for myself and Rochester. Around noon, I walked down to the conference room and opened the refrigerator.

Rochester was right behind me as I collected what I need for a dog and daddy lunch alfresco. I opened the exterior door and he rushed right to the picnic bench beneath a spreading pine tree. He barked once, and I said, "Hold your horses, dog. I'm coming."

When I got to the table, I poured food and water for him, then sat down to eat my sandwich of chicken salad on challah bread, with sea salt and black pepper potato chips. Rochester slopped up his water and downed his chow, and then sat beside me with an expectant look on his face.

"You just ate," I said. "Don't give me that look."

He slumped down to the ground, resting his head on the grass. I wasn't sure why I was still worried about making a commitment to Lili. I had certainly made one to Rochester, hadn't I? When I took my previous job at Eastern, in the alumni relations department, I made it conditional on him being able to accompany me. Rick had done something similar after he adopted Rascal. He couldn't take his dog with him to work, so he'd found that neighbor who could keep the Aussie active during the day.

I had begun to organize my life around Rochester, making sure that he was fed and walked, that his teeth were brushed, his toenails clipped, that he was bathed regularly and saw the vet when he had to, that he had toys to play with and lots of belly rubs.

In a strange way, I'd exchanged the restrictions of prison life for the constraints of being a doggie daddy, though there were a lot more benefits to life with Rochester. I bundled up my trash and took my big golden boy over to a secluded part of the hillside where he romped until his tongue hung long out of his mouth and he rolled on the ground beside me, in doggie heaven.

Then we went back to the office, where he slept beside my desk until I left him behind with a rawhide chew and walked out to the abbey for the three o'clock meeting Joey Capodilupo had requested. "What's up?" I asked, when I found him in the abbey.

"What do you want to do with all these pews?" he asked. "Architect's drawings say this is going to be a big open space, so I've got to pull them out. Shame to throw 'em in the dumpster. Chop 'em up for firewood?"

"Surely they're too good for that!" I looked at the pews, lined up in rows like the ones at the Quaker Meeting in Stewart's Crossing, and had a sudden memory of my own wedding to Mary, in a synagogue in Southern California we had picked because it was convenient, had lots of parking, and was willing to marry two people who didn't belong to the congregation.

I remembered my parents walking me down the aisle on either side of me, in the Jewish custom, then leaving me at the altar to wait for Mary's parents to deliver her. Would I ever wait for Lili that way, my heart in my chest as I saw the sanctuary doors open and her standing there in her white gown, looking radiant?

Probably not. Even if Lili and I did marry, it wouldn't be a big ceremony, and I was sure she wouldn't wear a fancy white gown. That was very far from her style. But I could see us doing something together someday – a ceremony on a beach in Fiji, a climb to the top of a (small) mountain in the Himalayas, a sunrise commitment during an African safari. Something unconventional, to set our relationship apart from those we'd had with others.

"Steve?"

I looked at Joey. "Oh, the pews." I leaned down and ran my hand over the back of one row. "They're in pretty good condition. And look at the carving on the ends. You don't see work like that these days. I wonder if they could be refinished and sold as seating."

"Looks like solid oak." He pulled a tape measure off his belt and measured the length. "Four feet long. I could refinish one of these in a couple of hours."

I must have still had marriage, or at least matchmaking, on my mind as I realized what the next step ought to be and turned to Joey. "You know what? I'll bet Mark Figueroa could sell them in his shop. Why don't you work something out with him? You could refinish a couple of them to use here at the center, and in exchange you could have the rest to sell."

Joey smiled. "That's a great idea. I'll give him a call."

I went back to the office and let Rochester loose for a quick run. I watched him dash toward the trees, loving his athletic grace and the times when all four of his paws were off the ground. I realized he was chasing a squirrel, who scrambled up the trunk of a pine and disappeared in its boughs.

Rochester put his paws up on the trunk and barked, but the squirrel didn't respond. Then he dropped back to the ground and started to dig.

"Rochester! No digging!" I yelled. He looked up at me, then went back to clawing the ground.

I jumped up and strode across to him. "Did you not hear me say no?" I tugged at his collar and he raised his head and looked at me, all guilt and contrition.

It struck me then that I'd been feeling guilty myself for so long – over the loss of my unborn children, the failure of my marriage, all the bad decisions I'd made, including the one to break into those credit bureaus, and my inability to be there for my father in his last days because I was in prison.

I let go of Rochester's collar and he smiled up at me, all traces of guilt passed. I had to do the same thing, I thought. Move on. Stop letting the past hold me back. And get on the road to my meeting with Rick at George School.

14 – The Annex

As I headed inland on Durham Road, past farms and small towns and isolated gas stations, Rochester leaned out the window, the wind streaming through his glossy blond hair. I wished I felt as happy and confident as he appeared but I had too many things to worry about, from Lili to my work at Friar Lake to the body in the Meeting House..

As I pulled up beside Rick's truck in the George School parking lot, I saw him standing by the front door of the administration building with a sixty-something woman in a severe black pants suit, her brown hair pulled up into the kind of top knot that I thought had gone out of fashion in the 1960s. She looked like a grim schoolmarm who'd rap your knuckles with a ruler as soon as look at you.

But she softened immediately as Rochester resisted my attempt to get his leash on and rushed over to where she and Rick stood. "What a beautiful dog!" she said, kneeling to pet him. Rick raised his eyebrows behind her as I walked up.

"Sorry," I said. "Come here, you monster. Get your leash on."

"Oh, he's fine," she said. "What's your name, Handsome?"

Boy. First Tamsen Morgan, now Vera Lee Isay. I was either losing my looks or losing my touch. "His name is Rochester." And because I thought she'd appreciate it, I said, "After the hero of *Jane Eyre*. Though I didn't give him the name – he came to me with it." I hooked the leash to his collar and he looked reproachfully at me.

"Funny, you don't look dark and brooding," she said to him. "More like sunny and charming." She stood up. "I want your assurance that anything you do will not blacken Mr. Brannigan's good name. He was a wonderful man who did great things for this school."

"I'm investigating a murder, ma'am," Rick said. "I can't make any promises. But I'm not interested in digging up anything that doesn't relate directly to the death I'm investigating."

"Did you work for Mr. Brannigan back then?" I asked.

She nodded. "I was hired as his secretary right after I graduated from high school, and I've never left."

"When did Mr. Brannigan start to work here?" Rick asked, as he pulled a small spiral notebook out of his pocket.

"Let me see," she said. "He was born in, oh, 1920, I think, and graduated from Haverford College. He served in the war after that."

"I thought Quakers were pacifists," I said. "How could he have done that?"

"Pacifism doesn't mean acceptance of violence, or simply standing by," she said. "Mr. Brannigan was very passionate about the need to help people less fortunate than ourselves. He volunteered with an ambulance corps in England sponsored by The American Friends Service Committee. It was a difficult time but he was a very brave man."

"And then?" Rick asked.

"Then he came here. He married and lived with his wife in Newtown until she passed. Soon after that the previous headmaster retired, and Mr. Brannigan stepped in."

"When was that?"

"I believe that was 1966," she said. "His secretary retired two years later."

I could tell by the way she spoke about Brannigan that she'd had a bit of a crush on him. I could imagine her as a young woman, working with a man she admired.

"Were you aware of the work he did helping draft evaders?" Rick asked.

She crossed her arms over her chest and glared at us. "We called them draft resisters," she said. "It was a moral decision. Mr. Brannigan couldn't stand aside while young men were forced to serve in a conflict they didn't believe in."

"Even though he had served himself?" Rick asked.

"World War II was a very different conflict, with the fate of the world at stake. In Vietnam, we were meddling in a foreign country's civil war to protect American business interests."

She stopped speaking and glared at Rick. "Maybe this isn't a good idea. Mr. Brannigan worked very hard to find alternative means of service for boys who qualified as conscientious objectors. Helping them leave the country was his absolute last resort. Those young men have moved on in their lives, and I doubt they'd want their past dredged up."

I looked at Vera Lee. Could she be protecting something other than Brannigan's reputation? Suppose our victim had discovered what Brannigan was doing and threatened to expose him. What if Brannigan committed the murder to protect the boys, and his volunteers, and she'd helped him cover it up?

There I went again, imagining situations without any basis in proof. The immediate problem was that Rick and Vera Lee appeared to be at a standoff. I had to focus on getting us into that Annex.

"I get your concerns," I said. "Rick and I both grew up in Stewart's Crossing, and we had many Quaker teachers. We both understand the ideals of the Friends movement, and how sometimes those ideals can cause conflict."

I could see in her eyes that she was following me.

"But that body belonged to a living, breathing person, who died, possibly at someone else's hands. We have a duty to him, to find out who he is so that his family can know what happened to him."

A group of teenaged boys ran past, kicking a soccer ball back and forth between them. I saw Vera Lee watch them, and then when she turned back to us her demeanor had softened. "The boxes are in the Annex," she said, and pointed to a square brick building with a couple of small windows. "It's right over there."

"I'll put Rochester in the car," I said.

"Oh, no, you don't have to do that," she said. "You can take him into the Annex. We're only using it for storage right now."

At least she still liked the dog, I thought. Rochester stopped to pee on a tree as Vera Lee led us to the Annex. She unlocked the door and flipped on the light switch. "I'll pull out the right boxes for you."

We stepped into the cool, dim room, lined with rows of metal shelving, and each shelf groaned with cardboard storage boxes. I could see why Rick had thought he could use some help. A long aluminum table rested against the wall by the door, with two folding chairs leaning beside it.

Ancient wood file cabinets took up one wall. "Those are student records in there," she said. "All those are off limits."

"Of course," Rick said.

She walked over to one wall and started scanning the boxes. "Here they are," she said. "When Mr. Brannigan passed, I boxed everything up by decade. There are six boxes for the seventies."

Rick began taking boxes off the shelf and handing them to me, and I placed them on the folding table as she supervised. Rochester sat on his haunches beside her. "The door will lock behind you," she said. "Make sure to turn out the lights when you're finished."

We agreed, and Vera Lee let the door close as she walked away. I assumed that we had convinced her she didn't have to supervise us the whole time we were there.

"What exactly are we looking for?" I asked Rick, as he pulled the lid off the first box.

"Anything related to moving those draft dodgers through Stewart's Crossing. Their names, where they came from, where they went. Anybody who helped Brannigan, had contact with the boys, or might have known about that false wall at the Meeting House."

Rochester sprawled on the concrete floor beside me. I lifted the lid off the first box and began flipping through faded bills and copies of personal correspondence. Brannigan had been a social studies teacher, like my own Mrs. Shea, and I wondered if that was a field that attracted Quakers. In addition to running the school he had taught a senior seminar each year, focusing on the Civil War, and I scanned through his syllabi and class notes.

The bottom of the box was lined with books. I pulled the first one out of the box, an ancient text Brannigan had annotated. I quickly went through a few more, then lifted them all out and stacked them on the floor.

Rochester got up from beside me and began prowling around the room. He stopped beside a box on the far wall, and kept nosing at it and scratching it.

"What is it, boy?" I asked. "Is there something in that box?"

"Probably dog biscuits," Rick said.

"You never know with this dog. Could be a clue to the identity of the dead body." I pulled the box, from 1992, off the shelf and popped it open. "We won't tell Vera Lee that we looked in here."

Rochester was right on top of me, sticking his big nose into the box. "Back off, dog," I said, elbowing him aside.

I found a folder of Brannigan's research on the Underground Railroad, particularly those stops in Pennsylvania. He had written several pages about the Meeting House in Stewart's Crossing and how it had been a way station for escaping slaves. At the end of the folder was a diagram of the Stewart's Crossing Meeting House – including the location of the false wall.

"You think Vera Lee would let us use the copy machine in her office?" Rick asked.

"Don't need to." I pulled my cell phone out of my pocket. "You have one of these, don't you? She said we couldn't take anything away. She didn't say we couldn't take pictures."

"You're awfully sneaky," Rick said. "But you're right. She gave us access to the building, didn't stick around to watch us, and didn't say we couldn't take pictures. I could make that argument with the D.A. Of course, my only witnesses are an ex-con and a dog."

"Take the pictures," I said.

There was nothing else of use in the box, and after Rick photographed the diagram and the pages of Brannigan's notes, I repacked the box. "At least we have evidence beyond Edith's word that Brannigan knew about the existence of the wall," Rick said.

The bottom was scattered with dry crumbs, but I wasn't going to let Rochester eat them. Who knew what they could be. He stared at the box as I put it back, but then padded back to my chair and settled behind it.

"You didn't believe Edith?" I asked Rick.

"Not that I didn't believe her. But it's always good to have corroborating evidence."

I went on to the next box. Rick and I worked in silence until we had each gone through three boxes.

"You find anything at all?" he asked me.

"Nothing." I stood up, dislodging Rochester from his position behind my chair, and stretched. "What they were doing was illegal, after all. It wouldn't surprise me if he destroyed all the records after the war. If he even kept any records at all."

"Crap. Another dead end. We'd better get these boxes packed up again."

Rochester was nosing around the stack of books on the floor, and he swiped his paw at them, and they tumbled into a haphazard pile. "Rochester!" I said. "How are we going to know which books go back into which boxes?"

"I doubt it matters," Rick said.

I leaned down and picked up the book closest to me. It was a personal journal, the first few pages filled with newspaper clippings about the Vietnam War. "Look at these," I said. "Maybe there's something in one of these articles."

"You read while I pack," Rick said.

I sat and began to read. It was fascinating to see the news through the lens of history, and I admit I got too caught up in the articles.

It must have been a half hour later when Rick said, "All right, professor. I'm ready to go."

I flipped through the rest of the articles. After the last one, the next page was written in what looked like a foreign language. "This is weird," I said, showing it to Rick.

"What language is that?" he asked.

It took me a moment to figure out that what I was looking at was a substitution cipher, a means of encrypting information by substituting a different letter. I had done some of those puzzles as a kid, and enjoyed them.

I explained the basic principle. "This looks like a simple one, because he's maintained the integrity of the units," I said. "See here? This single letter? Probably either 'A' or 'I.' And the three letter word there – maybe it's 'and,' or 'the.'"

"Why go to all this trouble?" Rick asked.

"It was the sixties, and people were paranoid back then," I said. "Remember, they were smuggling kids out of the country to avoid the draft. I'm not surprised he was careful."

"If we have to solve this cipher, we'll be here all night," he said.

"Time for the camera phone again," I said.

I held the book flat while Rick took high-def pictures of each of the ten encrypted pages, then emailed them to himself and to me. We replaced the journal in the last box and walked outside. It was full dark and the air had cooled. Rochester hurried to a bush to pee again, dragging me behind him.

"Do you think you can decipher Brannigan's notes?" Rick asked.

"I can try. It'll be easier if I print the pictures out and then write on them."

We walked back to where we had parked. "Do you ever think about what you'd have done if you'd been eligible for the draft back then?" I asked.

"I probably would have gone. Maybe even volunteered, because that's what my Dad did for Korea. You know I wasn't the greatest student in high school. So it could have been a real option. How about you?"

"My parents were determined that I go to college, so I'd have done that, and had a deferment for four years. But after that? I don't know. My great-grandfather left Russia to avoid serving in the Czar's Army, so I have that heritage of draft resistance."

"I'm glad I wasn't a cop in the sixties," Rick said. "Talking to Bob Freehl about it, there were a lot of problems in families, between neighbors, everything from drugs to the war to guys with long hair." Bob was a retired cop who lived down the street from me, and I'd spoken to him occasionally about his work.

"Looking back, it's easy to see that the whole conflict was one big blunder, but back then? Would we have known?" I asked. "Would either of us had the strength of conviction that these boys did?"

"Don't forget fear," Rick said. "The guys who went to Canada were the ones who couldn't get CO status. They may just have been afraid of dying."

We walked the rest of the way back in silence. For one of those boys, that fear had been realized.

15 – Decoder Ring

I stopped at a drive-through on my way home, picking up a couple of plain burgers for Rochester and one of the pre-made salads for myself. He couldn't wait until we got home, though, and kept nuzzling at me, so I gave him one of the burgers when we were stopped at the single traffic light in Stewart's Crossing, at the corner of Main and Ferry.

"That's all you get," I said, snatching my fingers back before he chomped on them. "You can wait til we get home for the rest."

He wolfed down the burger, bread and all, and sat back against the front seat. He yawned, and his pink tongue rolled out. When we got home, I crumbled the remaining burger into a bowl of chow, and he ate his dinner as I ate mine. Then I turned on my computer and opened the email from Rick. I used a photo program to enhance the first image and then printed it out.

I began to look for patterns, as I'd pointed out to Rick. A single letter had to be either A or I, and the statistical frequency of "and" and "are" combined was a lot higher than "its." By that method, I was able to figure out and identify all the uses of the letter A – which was represented, in the cipher text, by the letter G.

It was a lot like working with computers, the same application of logic to a problem. It was something I was good at, and it was nice to find a legal application for those skills.

With all the "A"s accounted for, the other single instances had to be the letter I, which was represented by in the cipher text by F. I began compiling a list of letter parallels, working my way through the recurring words.

Lili called as I was working. She told me about the class the night before, how much fun it had been to be out taking pictures again. "And how was your day today?" I asked, leaning back in my chair.

"Another meeting with Peter Bobeaux. For a half hour he talked about falconry in the Middle East, how when he was working in the United Arab Emirates he knew people who used falcons, but he preferred a hunting rifle. It's a good thing I didn't have a rifle with me in the conference room. What did you do today?"

I told her about driving up to George School, and what Rick and I had found. "I'm still thinking about you moving in here," I said. "Rochester wants you to know that he's all for it." I hesitated then plunged in. "After living in close quarters in prison I really loved having my space. The whole house just for me. I know sounds selfish, but it was such a joy not to hear some other guy snoring or farting. It took me a long time to get accustomed to having Rochester around."

"I get that," Lili said. "After my divorce from Phillip, I took a bunch of assignments that kept me moving from place to place." Phillip was Lili's second ex-husband, a magazine editor who had cheated on her. "One of the first things I did was go to a tanning salon so I wouldn't have a tan line on my ring finger. I didn't want to talk to anybody, especially anybody who knew I'd been married. I just wanted to be on my own."

She took a deep breath. "But I got over it, and I know you will, too. And if it's not this year, then I'll sign another lease and we'll go on."

"Don't sign anything yet," I said. "Give me another few days?"

"I won't sign until they threaten me with eviction."

"You won't have to go that far," I said.

We talked about a few other things, and then, after mutual endearments, we hung up, and I thought that it would be nice to be able to have these conversations with Lili in person. To be that much more a part of each other's lives.

I went back to my puzzle. It was like solving a cryptogram in the newspaper, only there were a lot of short words I couldn't decipher at first. It was a long, slow process. I'd think I had one letter solved, but then using it in conjunction with another would create something that couldn't be a word or a name, and I'd have to wipe them out and start over again. Around eleven I got sleepy and Rochester nudged me for his bedtime walk.

What was equally frustrating, I thought, as we moseyed down

the darkened streets of River Bend, was that Brannigan's notes might have nothing to do with the case—the body could belong to someone who had no connection whatsoever to Brannigan or his efforts to help boys avoid the draft. But the only way to know if the information would pan out was to follow it to its natural conclusion.

Wednesday morning dawned rainy and dismal. I bundled up in a yellow slicker with a hood, left a towel by the front door, and took Rochester out for a walk. He nosed ahead, always in search of the next thing to catch his attention. He and I were a lot alike that way.

The dampness made the air seem chillier, but the dog didn't seem to mind. Goldens have two coats: a soft, water-repellent outer layer, and then short, downy hair beneath that serves as insulation, protecting against both cold and heat. It's great, I suppose, if your dog is regularly chasing after ducks. To me, it was a huge pain, because when Rochester got soaked it was a chore to dry him, especially when he chose to whack his wet, plumey tail against me.

He did his business, I cleaned it up, and then we hurried home to get out of the rain. By the time I finished toweling him dry, which he treated as a big game, he had transferred most of the water to me. I showered, dressed and ate a couple of croissants while Rochester wolfed down his breakfast chow. Before I left the house, I copied the images of cipher text that Rick had emailed me onto my flash drive.

The rain had intensified to a downpour by then. The Delaware was rising, and parts of the River Road were already under water. I was relieved when I turned inland that the country road to Friar Lake hadn't flooded yet.

As I drove up the winding road to the abbey, the rain sluiced down beside me. I made a note to move up the improvements to the road before the winter came and made it into an icy slide.

Rochester and I scampered from the car into the office, and he dried himself by rolling on the carpet in the lobby, waving his legs in the air like a dying cockroach. I went into my office, and after logging in and checking my email, I began to print enlarged copies of the rest of the cipher text.

I went back to the first page of Brannigan's notes. I was sure that I had figured out the ING pattern at the end of a couple of words – but using that logic, there were also several words that began with Ng, and there were no words in English that fit that beginning.

I was puzzling over that when I heard the sound of paper crunching. I looked up to see that I'd forgotten to flip up the plastic stop at the end of the paper tray, and my pages were tumbling to the floor. Rochester had his paw on one of the sheets.

Fortunately it wasn't one of the pages of cipher text, but a newspaper clipping that Rick had found that mentioned Brannigan. I tugged it out from under Rochester's paw and read the headline, about South Vietnamese president Nguyen Van Thieu.

"Of course!" I said to Rochester. "Brannigan is including Vietnamese names. Dog, you're a true Sherlock!"

That clue enabled me to figure out the last letter matches. The page, which was dated January 27, 1973, included some stuff about Thieu and his administration, but the interesting part read, "The Selective Service announced today that there will be no more draft calls. Men and women no longer will have to defy the law to follow their consciences. Though our active part in this service ended with the last two boys who passed through our hands, we can now turn our thoughts and prayers toward healing."

The phrase "the last two boys" rang in my head. Who were those boys? And had they both left Stewart's Crossing – or had one of them remained behind, hidden in the Meeting House?

I started working backwards, applying the cipher I had decoded to Brannigan's notes. I found a line that interested me – that Brannigan was writing this diary to preserve a piece of history, though he hoped no one would decode it until after the war was long past. The cipher worked fine for two pages, mostly political rants – but then it changed. I cursed out loud, causing Rochester to look up from his sleep.

My phone rang around eleven. "Are you building an ark up there at Friar Lake?" Lili asked. "Because it looks like we might need one."

"Is it pouring in Leighville, too?" I asked. "It was miserable driving up from Stewart's Crossing this morning." I looked out the window toward the abbey, an imposing two-story building of gray native stone in a Gothic style. Water was cascading from the roof, bubbling over clogged downspouts. Something else to be fixed. I made a note.

"It's gloomy and dismal here," she said. "But I went out this morning and took a bunch of pictures of the rain sheeting down through the trees. Very cool effect."

"That's my Lili," I said. "Finding sunshine even in a rainy day."

"If I could only find some sunshine in Peter Bobeaux," she said. "This afternoon we have a faculty forum about curriculum changes. I swear, he's like a dog who has to pee on every single thing in the humanities to mark his territory."

"Lovely image. I have some good news, though. I cracked one of Brannigan's codes and it worked on a couple of pages – but then he switched ciphers. I'm going to be decoding his notes until my eyes cross."

"Could be a good look for you," she said. "I'd have to see to be sure."

As we hung up, Joey Capodilupo came inside to dry out, shaking water from his rain jacket like Rochester did. We discussed gutters and downspouts, and then I asked, "You talk to Mark about those pews?"

He smiled. "Called him last night to see if we could talk about it over dinner. Took some pushing to get him to agree."

"To selling the pews?"

"That was the easy part, once I convinced him to have dinner." He paused. "You know anything about a guy named Owen?"

"Yeah. My neighbor's son. Worked for Mark for a little while. I think Owen took advantage of him – pretended to be interested, but all he wanted was to rip Mark off."

"He's out of the picture?"

"Definitely."

Joey smiled. "Good to know." He looked out the window, where the rain was tailing off. "Got to get back to work. See you later."

When he left, I went back to Brannigan's papers, moving backward and trying to find more information on the last two boys. I had a feeling identifying them would be the key to figuring out whose bones Rochester had found.

It looked like Brannigan had used a similar cipher, though with different letter correspondences. I found myself longing for a decoder ring like the ones you could get as a kid by sending in bubble gum wrappers. I even took a quick look online – but the ones I could find were too simple for my purposes.

It was hard to concentrate, because once the rain ended, the crew outside got noisy, the phone kept ringing, and there were emails to answer. Late in the afternoon, after the demolition crew was gone, I walked around outside with Joey to survey the water damage. Rochester romped along beside us, getting his paws muddy and his undercoat wet again from brushing up against bushes.

Back at the office, I was wiping the dog's paws and drying his fur once again when my cell rang. "Yo, yo, Rick," I said, putting on my best Jersey accent. "How's it hanging?"

"I got the results back on the bones. From damage to the skull, it looks like the cause of death was an impact with a blunt object. The victim was a Caucasian male of between seventeen and twenty-one, which fits the profile of a boy trying to avoid the draft."

"Nothing more than that?"

"Height was between five-eight and five-ten. Good dental care, including exposure to fluoridated water. Once we find a record of someone missing who fits that description, we can compare dental records. Now that I have that information, I'm going to dive back into the missing persons reports. How are you doing with decoding that diary?"

"I'm working on it. But Brannigan changes his code every couple of pages so it's going to take a while to crack it all. I've found one clue, though. Brannigan mentions 'the two last boys' they helped. I'm thinking that if there is a connection to the Vietnam era, then the bones have to belong to one of those two."

"It's a working hypothesis," Rick said. "I'll keep looking on my end. Let me know as soon as you find anything."

I promised that I'd get back on it as soon as I got home. I felt the same kind of thrill I had when I was on verge of breaking into a protected site. At least this was legal work.

16 – Breakthrough

I closed up the office and drove home. The streets were littered with downed leaves, and the bare trees showed the first signs of the approaching winter. River Bend smelled fresh, after the wash of negative ions from the rain. After dinner, I sat at my desk with the pages of Brannigan's cipher in front of me and thought about his determined opposition to involvement in Vietnam. Part of it came from his Quaker faith, but an equal part arose from his work as a teacher and headmaster. He could see no sense in educating young boys only to send them off to die.

I was fascinated by his passion, and by this brief exposure to a part of history I had lived through, but been too young to understand. I remembered the last traces of the anti-war movement in the 1970s, and the conflicts, even in a small town like Stewart's Crossing, between veterans' groups and hippies. Headlines about people spitting on men in uniform, songs like "Hey, hey, LBJ, how many kids did you kill today?"

Jerry Vandeventer, the son of the local vet, had gone to Vietnam and come back with what today we'd diagnose as PTSD. His father's office, Crossing Critters, was at the far end of the shopping center in downtown Stewart's Crossing, between the State Store -- Pennsylvania's state-run monopoly on liquor sales— and a little card and knickknack shop called Gertie's Gifts, where I often spent my allowance.

I remembered coming out of Gertie's once and seeing Jerry Vandeventer blast out of the State Store, yelling an inventive stream of curses about their refusal to sell him the vodka he wanted. Now I realize he must have been drunk, but back then I was amazed to see an adult act that way.

A heavyset black woman came out of the Laundromat on the other side of the State Store toting a packed basket of clean clothes. She shook her free hand and told him to shut the F up, because he was just a g-d baby killer.

He jumped on the hood of her car and began to kick cracks in her windshield with his steel-toed boots. She screamed, somebody in the State Store called the cops, and the vet came out in his white coat to try and calm his son down.

I hung back behind a column and watched until the cops got there. Then I got on my bicycle and rode for home as fast as I could. I found my mother in the kitchen, and I jumped up onto one of the bar stools around the table and began rattling the story off.

My mother shook her head. "It's very sad," she said. "Now you see why your cousin Harold waited to have that cyst removed from his back until after he turned twenty-six."

I had no idea what she meant then, but I could tell she didn't want to talk about the incident any more. It was only when I studied Vietnam in civics class in high school that I realized Harold's medical condition had rendered him 4-F and that he had waited until he was over the draft age to have it repaired. He'd gone on to have a successful career as an accountant, while Jerry Vandeventer had driven his truck into the Delaware a year or two later after another drunken binge. I felt bad about what both of them had to go through – worse, of course, for Jerry. His father had closed the practice soon after and moved to Florida. I guess those memories were too much for him.

I went back to the cipher, cracking the second code more quickly once I understood what Brannigan was writing about. I didn't find the information I was looking for on those last two boys – names, ages, hometowns -- but I learned a lot about the anti-war movement. One page I couldn't figure was a list of two-word pairs; one had a third word. I assumed they were proper names, and they had their own special cipher. Were those the names of the boys? Or the volunteers who had helped them? I pushed that list aside for the next day, when I'd be fresh. Deciphering names was a whole lot harder than ordinary text, because there were so many fewer patterns.

It was after eleven when Rochester nudged me for his bedtime walk. I knew I should have gone to bed after we returned, but I was too keyed up to sleep, too intent on looking for information on those two boys. I was sure there was something in Brannigan's notes, if I could only find it.

I was staring at the screen around midnight when Rochester came upstairs with his squeaky piano. He settled beside me and began gnawing on it, playing discordant notes. "You sound like me when I was studying with Edith Passis," I said.

I looked back at the screen. "That's it! Rochester, you've done it again. If this is a list of the volunteers John Brannigan recruited, then Edith's name will be here. I have to look for the right pattern to break the cipher."

I wrote E D I T H on a piece of paper, with P A S S I S under it. Then I looked for a first name of five letters and a last name of six. There were two matches. The third letter of Edith's first name was I, and that should be repeated in the fifth letter of the last name.

But neither of the two matched. Did that mean Edith wasn't really one of Brannigan's volunteers? But why would she lie about something like that? Or was the list something else? The boys who had passed through his care? His contacts at other Meetings? People in Stewart's Crossing who were sympathetic to the cause?

"Sorry, boy, seems like what I thought was a clue wasn't really," I said, reaching down to rub behind the dog's ears. "But it was a good try. I'm going to go back to the regular entries and keep decoding them."

He rolled over on his side and went to sleep. It was close to two in the morning by the time I found an entry about picking up two boys at the bus station in Philadelphia, Pete and Don.

"This is it!" I said, waking Rochester from his snooze. "This is the first time he's picked up two boys at once. Either Pete or Don has to be the dead boy." I hurried to finish deciphering the rest, then sat back to read what I had come up with.

"Each boy's story breaks my heart," Brannigan wrote. "Pete is from a poor family in West Virginia. He's smart enough for a college deferment, but his family is too poor to spare him even a penny. Don is a farm boy, from a small town outside Pittsburgh. He wants to stay at home and work the land, and he tried for the II C Agricultural Deferment. But he has three older brothers who work with his father so he was denied."

There was no mention of a last name for either boy. Either Brannigan was being overly careful or he just didn't know that information. He wrote of leaving them in the Meeting House in Stewart's Crossing overnight. He showed them the space behind the false wall, telling them to hide there if anyone came looking for them.

"When I returned to the Meeting House on that cold morning, Pete was waiting for me in the main room. He told me that he and Don had stayed up long into the night, talking about Canada. Don had decided he couldn't live in a strange country, and left at first light to hitchhike back home."

Brannigan continued, "I had a small amount of money put aside to buy the boys tickets on the train from Trenton to New York, and give them each a few dollars for food. But with only one boy to send on, I had enough to buy Pete a ticket straight to Montreal. I hope God will be with him, and the news we have heard about the ease of crossing the border is correct."

I was so excited that I had to get up and pace around the house for a few minutes. Brannigan had met Pete in the worship area of the Meeting House, which implied that Brannigan hadn't checked the space behind the false wall himself. Two boys had gone into that space – but only one had come out. The dead boy had to be Don.

Rochester must have thought I was going to eat something, or take him for a walk, because he kept following on my heels. I couldn't sit back down for a few minutes—that finding had electrified me and I had to wait for the aftershocks to fade – similar to what I felt when I'd committed a great hack, breaking in somewhere on line I wasn't supposed to be. I drank some water from the refrigerator and gave Rochester a tiny T-bone treat.

I walked over to the sliding glass doors that led out to my courtyard. A pair of headlights raked across the glass as some night owl passed by. The motion-sensor lights on the house across from me clicked on.

I stood there in the momentary glow. It was possible, of course, that Pete was telling the truth, and that once I found out Don's last name I would discover that he had left that Meeting House alive, and Rick and I would be back at square one. But something in my gut told me we were on the right track at last.

Rochester sat on his butt and woofed at me once. "I know,

boy, it's late, and we ought to go to bed. I can look for Pete and Don's last names tomorrow."

Suddenly I remembered the list of two-word pairs. Would Pete and Don be listed there? I galloped up the stairs to the second floor, two steps at a time, Rochester right behind me. I slid into my desk chair and pulled over the list. But no matter how hard I tried, I couldn't find a match for Pete, Peter, Don or Donald.

I looked at the clock above my computer. It was way too late to call Rick, even with news this important. There wasn't anything he could do until the morning, so I ought to let him sleep. Instead I composed a quick email to him with Brannigan's entry about the two boys, and hit *send*.

17 – Friends and Colleagues

Though he knew I'd been up late the night before, Rochester wanted to go for his regular morning walk, and he wouldn't stop licking my face until I got up to take him. As we returned, my cell rang and I had to scramble to get it out of my pocket.

"This is great, Steve," Rick said. "And you got all this information from Brannigan's notes?"

Was he worried that I'd hacked in somewhere? But where? Would he always assume the worst of me? I tamped down my irritation and said, "Yeah. The guy kept a pretty detailed journal. Do you think you can do anything with that information?"

"It's not enough to move forward, but it's a start," he said. "We know he was from a small farm town near Pittsburgh, with three older brothers."

"And you have a date of disappearance."

"Unfortunately there's no match to any of the missing persons reports I went through, even ones from years later."

"Are there any records from the Selective Service of guys who didn't report for induction?" I asked.

"Not that I've been able to find. Since those guys may still be alive, it might be a privacy violation to list them somewhere. Jimmy Carter issued an executive order in 1977 that terminated prosecution of any violators of the Military Selective Service Act and granted amnesty to any draft dodgers living in other countries. So there might not be any legal justification for the existence of such a list."

"But the list must exist," I said. "Even it's not public."

"Don't even go there," Rick said. "You are not hacking into any government database."

"Actually I was thinking of the Freedom of Information Act," I said. "But it would probably take too long to get the records that way."

"And it makes sense that our victim is not showing up on any missing persons reports," Rick said. "His family thought he was going to Canada. They wouldn't have reported him missing to the police."

"You get anything else?" I asked.

"Nada. I spent yesterday talking to members of the Meeting, but no one knew anything about the false wall or about Brannigan's group."

I heard him talk to someone away from the phone, then he said, "Listen, I've got to go. I'll talk to you later."

As I drove to work, I wondered if there was more information I could find based on what I'd learned from Brannigan's notes – legitimately. Don had come from western Pennsylvania, near Pittsburgh. Suppose he had been helped by Friends out there?

When I got to my office, I checked online, and there was a Friends Meeting in Pittsburgh, with a phone number. I knew I ought to ask Rick to follow up with them – but would they respond well to a police investigation, especially one so far removed from their own Meeting?

Before I could think too far ahead, I dialed the number. As the phone rang, I thought about what I could say that would get someone to talk to me. By the time a woman answered, I had an idea.

"I'm a professor at Eastern College in Leighville, outside Philadelphia," I said. "I'm doing some research on the involvement of the Society of Friends in the anti-war movement in Pennsylvania. Is there anyone in your Meeting who might have been there during the 1960s who I could speak to?"

"That was a long time ago." The woman's voice quavered, making her sound like she was about Edith's age, which was good – she might know something about the past.

"Were you involved with the Meeting back then?" I asked, my hope rising.

"Yes, I was. But I didn't have anything to do with those protests. I was already married and had my first child by then."

Oh, well, I thought.

"Amos Carter, though, he was a young firebrand back then. He might be able to help you. Let me see if I can find his number."

My hope soared again. "Here it is," she said, when she

returned to the line. She read me the number, which had a 267 area code. "He retired a few years back and moved to the eastern part of the state to be closer to his son."

"Thank you very much for your help, ma'am," I said. "I appreciate it."

I turned back to the computer and Googled the phone number she had given me. I got a long list of websites that indicated it was a cellular number assigned to a carrier in the Philadelphia area.

When I added "Amos Carter" to the search, only one result came up, but it was good enough. It was a list of the members of the Bristol Friends Meeting with their emergency contacts, and it was dated earlier that summer. That meant Carter was nearby, because Bristol was about a half hour south of Stewart's Crossing, along the Delaware. It also meant he was probably still alive.

It wasn't up to me to talk to him, though. This was Rick's case, though I hoped he'd keep me in the loop. So I called him. "I found a lead for you to follow," I said when he answered. I told him about Amos Carter, and the possibility that he'd been involved in helping the boy from western Pennsylvania escape the draft.

"Good job, buddy," he said. "You say he's in Bristol somewhere?"

"Think so."

"I'll call him right now."

"Great. Let me know what you come up with, all right? And if I can do anything else for you."

I had a committee meeting at the Eastern campus at three, so I bundled Rochester into the car and drove down to Leighville, following a Saab wagon with the bumper sticker "Caution: Farting Beagle." I made sure to stay a good distance behind it.

Even though I was an administrator, and wasn't working on campus anymore, my contract required me to participate in at least one college committee. The previous year I hadn't been hired full-time until January, so I had been placed on the graduation task force. This year I got to choose for myself, and I picked the technology committee, which worked with the instructional technology staff on questions like new computers for the lab, new software for testing, and so on.

I didn't mention my criminal history to anyone else on the

committee, though I did say that I'd worked in high-tech in Silicon Valley for ten years before returning east. I'd kept up to date with new developments, eyeing faster processors and expanded RAM with envy. And of course I was hyper aware of any new anti-hacking software, developments in protection, peer-to-peer file sharing, and the latest iteration, torrents. Since so many of these developments came from college kids, staying involved with technology at the college level was an opportunity to ride whatever tide was rising.

Lili was out at a class, so I got the key to her office from her secretary. Harrow Hall was a modern building, donated by an alumnus who'd made his fortune in pharmaceuticals, and at his request was shaped like a giant capsule, with wrap-around windows. Behind her desk, Lili had hung a montage of photos she had taken. A young Afghan girl played jacks with a female U.S. soldier in camo gear; the Baghdad skyline was lit by a tracery of what looked almost like fireworks; a tiny monkey, looking almost human, stared at the camera from the safety of a tree in a tropical rain forest. The grim beauty of a panoramic shot of a refugee camp in Darfur, taken from a helicopter.

Student artwork rested on easels and stands -- a woven tapestry, a rain-smeared photo of the college chapel, an iridescent black ceramic pot. I left Rochester there with an admonition to behave. Then I walked over to Fields Hall, where my office had been, feeling nostalgic for all that had happened since I returned to Eastern. I opened the door to the conference room for a lovely dark-skinned woman wearing a white jacket with a pleated back that hovered just above the waistline and snakeskin high heels. She was Marie-Carmel Etienne, and she taught in the computer science department.

We had met somewhere, so we said hello and walked in together. Oscar Lavista, the director of IT, was seated at the table speaking to Jackie Conrad, a friend of mine who taught anatomy and physiology. Oscar was a moon-faced guy with dark hair and a mole on his chin, a Florida transplant who had moved up in the department a few months before. Jackie was fifty-something, with an open, friendly face, framed with blonde curls, and she had a great sense of humor.

"Are we the committee?" I asked, as I sat down beside Jackie.

"Still waiting for our chair," Oscar said. A moment later the door opened and a balding man in his early sixties walked in. He wore a white business shirt, yellow power tie and the pants from a pinstripe suit, and had an unlit cigar in his mouth.

"I'm Dr. Peter Bobeaux, assistant dean for the humanities," he said, laying a leather portfolio on the table. "I'm the chair of this committee. But I'm new here at Eastern, so I'm counting on you to show me the ropes."

So this was Dr. Bobo, physician for the circus. Lili's nemesis, a man who according to Lili drowned his opposition in paperwork. Maybe this wasn't the right committee for me.

Bobeaux was about fifty pounds too heavy for his frame, and there was something overly authoritative about his bearing, but I tried to give him the benefit of the doubt. I wondered about the cigar, though; Eastern was primarily a smoke-free campus, though there were a few designated smoking zones outside a couple of buildings.

The meeting dragged. Despite his pretense at needing our advice, Bobeaux had a laundry list of complaints about Eastern's computers, culled from emails, questions and problems. The learning management system we used to deliver online courses was too slow, he said. We needed to look into a replacement.

"We're on a five-year contract," Oscar said. "It won't come up for bids for another four years."

"But the faculty are complaining!" Bobeaux said.

"The faculty complain about a lot of things," Oscar said. "Most of the things they bring up can't be fixed."

Bobeaux shook his head. "That's the wrong attitude to take, hombre."

Oscar pushed his chair back a foot. "I resent your use of Spanish to attempt to disenfranchise me," he said. "Don't think because I'm a Latino and you're white you can boss me around."

"Hear, hear," Marie-Carmel said. "We take a very dim view of discriminatory behavior at Eastern." She had a charming bit of a French accent and I thought I'd read somewhere that she was a native of Guadeloupe, in the Caribbean.

"I'm not... but I wasn't..." Bobeaux began. Then he caught

himself and stopped. He bumbled through a half-dozen other problems, each one shot down by Marie-Carmel or Oscar. I kept my mouth shut and my head down and occasionally I caught Jackie Conrad's eye and saw she was keeping mum like I was.

Finally Bobeaux dismissed us. "I have my doubts about the efficiency of this committee," he said. "I want to speak to President Babson before we reconvene." He glared at all of us. "And you can be sure that each one of you will be included in that discussion."

18 – Stages of Decomposition

Jackie Conrad and I walked out together. She pulled a little puppet from her pocket, a plush gray crab with a starfish attached on a long, nobby cord. "I was going to offer to lend Dr. Bobeaux one of these but I didn't think he'd appreciate the joke."

"A brain cell," I said, already familiar with the range of stuffed animals Jackie used to demonstrate concepts in her anatomy class. The fuzzy oval with tentacles was e-coli, and the little green blobs with eyes were gonorrhea microbes.

She turned toward Green Hall, where the science department was located. "How's that inquisitive dog of yours?" she asked.

"Rochester? Still getting into trouble. Say, Jackie, do you know anything about the decomposition rate of dead bodies? Like, for example, if you stuck one between a false wall and an exterior wall, how long would it take to start to smell?"

She stopped beside a commemorative bench donated by the Class of 1923. The campus was littered with those little plaques on everything from recycling bins to dormitory lounges. She raised the brain cell so that it dangled from her lobe like an earring.

"If I didn't already know you have a nose for crime, I'd be worried about a question like that," she said, and laughed. "A body begins to decompose as soon as the heart stops beating. It takes a couple of hours for the bacteria and other organisms to start decaying and releasing gases, which causes the smell. If this body was close to the exterior wall, the ambient temperature would affect it – slower in winter, faster in summer. But in general it would be about twenty-four hours or less."

"And how long would the smell persist?"

"Until the remains are skeletonized. We have five general stages to describe the process of decomposition: Fresh, Bloat, Active Decay, Advanced Decay, and Dry/Remains. The smell goes away by the dry/remains stage. Depending on the conditions, again, it could be as few as ten days to as long as a month or more."

"Thanks, Jackie. That's a question that's been bothering me."

"Is this about that body I read about in the paper?"

"Yup." As we walked, I explained about the sneaker and bone Rochester had found.

"They don't have any idea how long the body was there?"

"Probably since the 1960s," I said. "But I've been wondering why nobody would have smelled the dead body."

"Where in the Meeting House was the body?" she asked. "Near where the congregation sits?"

I shook my head. "In the back office area, behind a storage closet. But wouldn't you be able to smell it wherever in the building you were?"

"Again, a lot depends on the environment." We arrived at the tall, arched wooden front door of Green Hall. Ironically, it was probably the least "green" building on campus, and plans were afoot for new state-of-the-art labs.

I thanked Jackie, and walked to Lili's office. She was back from her class, and Rochester was sprawled on the wooden floor beside the wall of glass windows that looked out on the campus. He didn't even get up when I walked in. Traitor.

"How was your committee meeting?" Lili asked.

"Awful, as could be expected. Guess who's the chair? Dr. Bobo."

"You have my sympathy," she said, as I sat down in the chair across from her desk. "How are things out at Friar Lake?"

"You know Joe Capodilupo, right? His son Joey started on Monday as the construction super for the contracting company."

"Isn't that nepotism?"

"Joey works for the contractor, his dad for the college. And everything I've seen of Joe Senior says he's a real straight arrow." I smiled. "Joey, on the other hand, doesn't seem that straight. Since he seems like a good guy. I might be fixing him up with Mark Figueroa."

"You are such a *shadchen*, Steve," she said, using the Yiddish word for matchmaker. "First you're trying to get Rick to date this war widow, and now you're fixing up Mark. How'd you know this Joey was even gay?"

"I saw the way he and Mark were looking at each other. I did a little manipulating to push them together. Joey's going to refinishing the old pews from the chapel, and Mark will sell them at his shop."

Then I sat back in the chair and stretched my legs. "It looks like Rick and I made some progress last night on finding the identity of the body in the Meeting House." I told her what I'd discovered.

"You don't have a last name for either boy?" she asked.

I shook my head. "But I feel like we're making big progress." Suddenly my heart did a quick flip-flop, as I remembered the other question in the air: having Lili move in. If she did, my life was going to turn upside down, and so soon after taking on the new job at Friar Lake. It seemed like my life had become one big chain of changes, and I didn't like it.

I didn't tell Lili any of that, though. I stood and kissed her goodbye, and Rochester and I went back to my car. Dead leaves were accumulating around the bases of the trees, and the wind had a bit of a chill, a reminder that winter was coming.

As I drove down river, I thought more about how my life had changed since I'd come back to Stewart's Crossing. Progress had happened in fits and starts, from taking Rochester into my life to beginning full-time work for Eastern. Early that the summer Lili had mentioned that sometimes she didn't feel like there was room for her in my house, because I had so many of the boxes my father had left behind stacked in the living room and the garage.

I'd been determined to show her the opposite was true. And in addition to unpacking those boxes, I'd come to terms with some difficult things in my past, like my guilt over being unable to attend my dad's funeral because I was in prison. So lots of cobwebs were getting swept out.

I was passing through Washington's Crossing when my cell phone trilled with the *Hawaii Five-O* theme. "Yo, Rick."

"What did you tell that woman in Pittsburgh?" he demanded.

"Huh?"

"You spoke to a woman in Pittsburgh," Rick said, speaking slowly as if he was talking to a child. "She called Amos Carter and told him a professor was going to speak to him."

"Oh, yeah. That was just a cover story."

"And you didn't think to mention that to me?"

Rochester looked like he was about to launch himself out the car window at a passing cat, and I said, "No!"

"Excuse me?"

"I wasn't talking to you, I was talking to the dog. So? What's the big deal?"

"The big deal is that this guy was expecting a professor to call him, and when I said that I was from the police he got confused and he put his son on the phone. The son doesn't want him involved with the cops. I think he's afraid we're after him for something."

"You want me to call him?"

"No. I want you to go over there with me. You can spin your professor bullshit, and we'll see if that gets the son calmed down, and gets the father to talk."

"You're welcome for the tip, Mr. Ungrateful," I said. I looked at my watch. "When do you want to go?"

"I'm on my way to your house now. Should be there in about ten."

"Crap. I'm almost home, but I haven't fed Rochester or given him his evening walk."

"Get a move on, then."

19 – Difficult Times

By the time we reached our townhouse, Rick was pulling up in the driveway. I poured some chow in Rochester's bowl, put up the gate to the second floor, and made sure there was water in his bowl. "Back soon, puppy," I said, hurrying out the front door as he attacked his dinner with gusto.

Bristol is an old town, one of the oldest in Pennsylvania. It has three claims to fame: it was an early commercial center, and the Delaware Canal begins there, the one that runs through Stewart's Crossing on its way to Easton. And then there's "The Bristol Stomp," a 1960s song by the Dovells, which you still hear played all over Bucks County.

"You have an address for the Carters, I presume," I said, getting into Rick's truck.

"No, I figured we'd triangulate the cell phone signal when we get close," he said, slamming the truck into reverse and backing out my driveway. "Of course I have an address."

"Why are you so angry at me?" I asked, holding onto the door as he rocketed down Minsk Lane. "I'm just trying to help you."

"Investigation is my job," he said. "And yet somehow you manage to wiggle your way into my cases."

"I thought you wanted my help." He stopped to wait for the gates to River Bend to open and allow us out. "I can get out here if you don't want me along."

"I don't like needing your help," he said. "It makes me feel like I can't do what I'm supposed to."

"That's dumb," I said. "You don't do your own autopsies, do you? Collect the crime scene data? Prosecute defendants?"

"They're all part of the team," he said.

I crossed my arms over my chest. "And I'm not?"

"You're an amateur."

"And an ex-con," I said. "I'm always going to be that in your mind, aren't I? No matter how long we're friends, and how much I do to show you that I'm trying to change?"

"I didn't mean that."

"That's the way it came across. What would the chief of police say if he knew you were friends with a felon?"

"He can't tell me who my friends are."

"But if he knew that I was helping you with this case, he wouldn't be happy, would he?"

Rick sighed deeply. "He wants me to get this case cleared. So he'll have to live with how I do things. I'm sorry I snapped at you. I'm frustrated because I can't seem to get any traction on my own."

I didn't know what to say, so I didn't say anything. We took US 1, the highway that stretches all the way from Fort Kent, Maine to Key West, Florida, which my father always called Useless One, to its connection to Route 13, and headed for Bristol.

When I was a kid, we went that way all the time – my dad had friends in Tullytown, near the Delaware, and we often visited them. During summer school, I took swimming lessons at a pool down there, and once we ate dinner at a restaurant made from an airplane. It made me feel good to pass those bits and pieces of my childhood, reminding me of the connections that I had to my parents and my community.

The Carters lived in a brick duplex a couple of blocks in from the river. We parked on the street and walked up to the front door. Rick rang the bell.

A bulky fifty-something man with tattoos twirling around his arms answered the door. "Mr. Carter?" Rick asked. "I'm Rick Stemper, from the Stewart's Crossing PD. We spoke earlier today."

"I told you, my father doesn't want to talk to the cops." He tried to close the door.

"Mr. Carter, my name is Steve Levitan," I said. "I'm the one who spoke to the woman at the Friends' Meeting in Pittsburgh, who gave me your father's name and phone number. Rick isn't interested in arresting your father for anything. We just want to ask him if he can help us identify a young man who died back in the sixties."

The man crossed his arms over his chest. "How can he do

that?"

Rick explained about finding the body at the Meeting House. Carter shook his head. "I grew up a Quaker," he said. "My parents used to drag me and my sister to Meetings. Couldn't wait to get away from it. Joined the Marines, finally felt like I'd found a place I belonged." He sighed. "Come on in. He loves to talk about that old stuff."

He ushered us into the front room. The carpet was frayed, the furniture worn, but it was clean and welcoming. I liked the fact that there was a bookshelf against one wall, stacked with hard covers old and new.

"Pop!" Carter yelled. "Come on down here." He motioned us to chairs. "My wife's out at work, or I'd offer you something."

"No problem," I said. "Thank you for letting us come in and talk."

Amos Carter was eighty at least, and as frail as his son was robust. He had sparse white hair and he hadn't shaved for a couple of days. He wore a faded plaid shirt and jeans that were a size too large, gathered at the waist by a leather belt.

"These are the guys who wanted to talk to you," the younger Carter said.

Rick and I stood back up and introduced ourselves to Amos Carter, then we all sat. Rick looked at me, and I took the lead. "I understand you were involved in the anti-war movement back in the 1960s," I said. "I'm not a Quaker, but Rick and I grew up with lots of friends and neighbors who were, and I've always been interested in the Friends and the way they put their beliefs into practice."

Amos's voice was quavery but he didn't hesitate. "They were very difficult times," he said. "I was fortunate to be too old for the draft, but I felt it was my obligation to help those boys who didn't believe in the war."

"We found a body recently, which appears to be one of the boys who came to Stewart's Crossing on his way to Canada," I said. "We're trying to find his name so we can contact his next of kin. We think he came from western Pennsylvania, and that maybe he was helped along by the Meeting in Pittsburgh. That's why I called out there, and that's how I got your name and phone number."

"We helped a number of boys pass through," Amos said. "I don't know that I'll remember all of them."

"This boy's name was Don," I said. "He grew up on a farm, and had three older brothers. He tried for the farming exemption, but he was turned down. Unfortunately, that's about all we know."

"Don. Let me think." He frowned. "I'm afraid my memory isn't what it used to be."

When I got to be Amos Carter's age, I wondered, how much would I remember about things that had happened long before? Would I forget everything I knew about hacking? Would my ten-year marriage disappear? Would I remember having a dog named Rochester, and how much he meant to me?

Then Carter said, "I did take some notes back then. Maybe the information you're looking for is there."

He stood up, grabbing the arm of the chair for support, and walked over to the bookshelf. From the pattern of the wood beneath a shallow coat of white paint, it looked handmade, someone piecing together scrap lumber, with a strip of crown molding glued to the top of the highest shelf.

While Carter flipped through the books, I looked around the room. A fireplace already stocked with logs for the winter, a scattering of *Reader's Digests* and *TV Guides* on the coffee table, a big-screen plasma TV the only modern note. Above it hung an embroidered sampler with a picture of an evil-looking bulldog wearing a Marine drill instructor hat and the slogan, "I Love a Devil Dog."

"Semper Fiber," I said, without thinking.

Rick looked at me like I was nuts, but the younger Carter understood. "That's my sister," he said. "She makes those. I think they're crap, but what can you do? She's family."

By then Amos had found what he was looking for. He opened an old book with frayed binding that had once been navy blue. "Here they are," he said, pulling a few pages of lined white paper out of the back.

He handed the pages to me, and Rick looked over my shoulder. The first was a list of names, addresses and phone numbers of Quakers involved in the anti-war movement all over the state of Pennsylvania. Fortunately, Amos Carter hadn't felt the need to encrypt what he wrote.

The second and third pages were lists of activities, books and pamphlets. There were only four names on the last page, each followed by a date. The last two were *Peter Breaux and Don Lamprey, January 25, 1969.*

"Is that what you were looking for?" Amos asked.

"It is," Rick said. "Thank you very much."

20 – Art and Mortality

On the ride back to Stewart's Crossing, Rick looked at his watch. "Shoot, I've got to scramble to pick up Rascal from his doggie day care. If I leave him there past seven-thirty I have to pay extra."

"Why don't we get him and go to my house. We can order a pizza and look for information on Don Lamprey and Peter Breaux online."

"You think there'll be anything?"

I shrugged. "You never know. You can log into the police database remotely, can't you?"

"Yeah. At least I can see if either of these names is connected to a police record."

"And I can look for a Lamprey family in western Pennsylvania with four sons, one of them named Don."

I called and ordered the pizza, our regular large mushroom and sausage, and we picked up Rascal. It was my turn to pay, so I went into the pizzeria, where Rick and I had been going since we were kids with our families. It had changed hands a few times over the years. The new owners were a young Italian couple who bought their mozzarella from one of the last dairy farmers in the county and made their own sausage, from locally sourced beef and pork. As I stood in line, a very large man in a triple XL T-shirt that read "I Beat Anorexia" came in behind me.

I thought it was kind of funny. But as I was paying, a skinny woman came through the door. She walked right up to the man and said, "Your shirt is very offensive to all the girls and women who have fought eating disorders."

I wondered what she was doing in a pizza parlor if she had food issues, but I didn't say anything. The man said, "It's what you call ironic humor." He started to explain the irony, and I grabbed my pizza and hurried back to Rick's truck.

"While you were inside I started thinking about Vera Lee,"

Rick said, as he backed out of the space. "Why do you think she was so reluctant to let us see those records? Protecting Brannigan's reputation? Or something more?"

"I thought of that," I said, remembering my flight of fancy. "I didn't want to say anything because I didn't have any evidence. But if Brannigan was the one moving those boys around, he may have been the last one to see this kid alive."

Rick turned off Main Street toward River Bend. I noticed that the license plate on the car in front of us read ALL4JUAN, which reminded me of an Eastern student named Juan Tanamera, who'd been implicated in drug dealing at the college. Just because someone was a student or a teacher was no reason to eliminate him from suspicion.

"Suppose Brannigan killed Don himself – either accidentally or on purpose, and Vera Lee helped him cover it up." Thinking of the plate in front of us, I added, "Or the whole bunch of volunteers could have been involved. These were the last boys through -- maybe the kid was threatening to report them to the police, or to break up their smuggling ring."

"Not really a smuggling ring," Rick said, as he pulled into my driveway. "And if that was the case, then Edith Passis and Amos Carter wouldn't have been so willing to give us information. There must be something more between Vera Lee and Brannigan."

We carried the pizza inside and sat down at the kitchen table to eat. Rascal and Rochester were much more interested in the pizza than in each other. They clustered around us, waiting for crust or bits of sausage.

"You think maybe they were having an affair?" I asked. "Vera Lee and her boss? She might have been afraid that something we found would reveal that."

"Brannigan's wife was dead, and she was barely out of high school," Rick said. "So she probably wasn't married herself. And she wasn't wearing a wedding ring this evening."

"But still. He must have been in his forties by then, right? And with her almost the age of a student, that would be scandalous. If something like that happened at Eastern, even now, it would be a problem."

"But there's nothing that would keep you and Lili from

moving in together, right?" Rick asked. "No rules against fraternization?"

"If she was my boss, or vice versa, there'd be a problem," I said. "But there are lots of married couples and family members working at Eastern. I'm just not sure that I want to be part of one right now."

"Don't make any rash decisions. You know as well as I do that once you have a woman in your house it's hell getting her out."

"Didn't happen that way in my case," I said. "Remember? I'm the one who left. For prison."

"From what I've heard of your marriage, it was switching one prison for another, with a more pleasant roommate." He looked at me. "You weren't anybody's wife in prison, were you?"

"Nope. Got a couple of offers, but they accepted when I said no thanks. Especially when I added I could help them with their appeals if they let me keep my pants on."

"Smart guy."

"Yeah, but if I'd been smarter I wouldn't have been in there in the first place."

We ate in silence for a while, but as we were cleaning up, Rick asked, "Any chance you could keep Rascal Saturday night?"

"Shouldn't be a problem. Why?"

"I have a thing."

I laughed. "You have a date with Tamsen Morgan, don't you?"

"It's not a date." He looked embarrassed, which I thought was funny. "Just, you know, dinner. We'll probably talk about Justin and his football team."

"Uh-huh."

Rick took the pizza box out to the recycling bin while I washed my hands and then opened up my laptop. He had his own laptop in his truck, and he brought it in and logged into the police database while I searched for Lampreys.

At a genealogy websites, I found that Lori Lamprey, of Zelienople, Pennsylvania, had set up a family tree that included her father, Arnold, and his three brothers: Brian, Charles and Donald. Donald had been born in 1950, with no date of death shown. "Looks like we found him," I said, pointing to the screen.

I was able to save the tree as a PDF. "Let's see what we can find out about Mr. Arnold Lamprey of Zelienople, Pennsylvania," I said.

"Where the heck is Zelienople?" Rick asked.

I pulled up Google Maps. Zelienople was a small town about a half hour north of Pittsburgh. I found an address for Arnold Lamprey on Sunflower Road, and zooming in on the satellite view showed us it was a farming area.

"Looks like I've got a call to make tomorrow," Rick said. "Too late to call tonight – if they're farmers they're already in bed." He shook his head. "I hate having to notify next of kin. It's the worst part of the job."

We switched to Peter Breaux, who had presumably been the last person to see Don Lamprey alive, and thus was a person of interest. His birth certificate said he'd been born at Ruby Memorial Hospital in Morgantown; his parents were Reynard and Joy Breaux, with an address on Fairchance Road in Cheat Lake, West Virginia.

Rick took Reynard and I took Joy. We came up with our results at about the same time. Reynard had died first, in 1973, survived by wife Joy and son Peter. Joy followed in 1985, survived by son Peter. There were no other immediate relatives listed, and no matter where we looked, we couldn't find anything else about Peter Breaux.

"So he was alive in 1969, and then again in 1985," I said. "Where was he in between? And where's he been since?"

It was as if he'd disappeared into Canada, emerging only at the deaths of his parents, then fading back into the dust. "I'll have to go through channels on this," Rick said. "Get somebody up in Canada to search their records. Not going to be easy, especially if he doesn't want to be found."

For curiosity's sake, I asked Rick to do a quick search for Vera Lee Isay through the police database, and I did the same through my own sources – all legit, of course. She was born in 1950 and never married. She belonged to several pacifist and environmentalist groups. She was a member of the Stewart's Crossing Friends Meeting and served on the renovation committee.

"That's interesting," I said, twisting my laptop around so he could see. "You think Vera Lee joined this committee because she knew there was a body in the wall?"

"Or because she's the kind who volunteers for stuff," Rick said. "Who else is on that committee?"

I looked at the list online. Hannah Palmer, the clerk of the Meeting, was the chair. Besides Vera Lee, the only other name I recognized was Eben Hosford. "Edith pointed him out to me at the Harvest Festival," I said. "She said he's been very opposed to the renovations. I wonder why he'd join the committee."

"You know how committees work," Rick said. "Don't you have to serve on them at Eastern? If you want to screw up progress, you join the committee and then you argue every single point until the issue is dead."

I thought of the committee I was serving on, and had to agree with him.

He and Rascal left a few minutes later. I called Lili and told her about talking to Amos Carter and connecting Don Lamprey back to his family. "We can't be sure until Rick talks to his brother tomorrow, but it looks right."

"That's good," Lili said. "I'm glad we'll know who he is."

"The next step is figuring out how he died," I said. "But I can leave that up to Rick."

She snorted. "Like that's going to happen."

"You free for lunch tomorrow?" I asked. "It's going to be a slow day at Friar Lake, and I could come down to the campus. You have a studio class in the morning, right?"

"But it's done at eleven-thirty. I could meet you at noon. How about the Cafette? It's still warm enough to sit outside with Rochester there."

"That sounds great." I relaxed back against the throw pillow, and we chatted for a few more minutes. After she hung up, I stared at the cell phone as the screen displayed the call ending, then returned to the list of frequently dialed numbers. It was a visual testimony to the way I had begun to reintegrate myself into the world at large, and Stewart's Crossing in particular. Rick Stemper, Mark Figueroa, Gail Dukowski at The Chocolate Ear. A couple of folks at Eastern, including Joe Capodilupo. Tor, and Lili.

When I returned from prison and got the cell phone, the only number I had programmed in was Santiago Santos. I scrolled down to his name, and though I didn't delete his number, I did remove him from my list of speed-dials.

That was progress, I thought.

21 – File Search

After breakfast the next morning, I loaded Rochester in the car and we drove up to Friar Lake. Joey Capodilupo had set up a meeting with a guy who was going to redo all the gutters and downspouts, and I walked around with the two of them. I knew that Joey would be there to keep an eye on things until his crew shut down at three-thirty. "I'm going to head down to the campus," I said. "Call me if you need anything."

I closed my office, and Rochester and I drove to Leighville. Though dogs technically weren't allowed on the Eastern campus, nobody had ever complained about Rochester. He and I strolled through the grounds, trees turning color, students breaking out long-sleeve shirts, toting backpacks I assumed were full of books – though they could as easily have been carrying netbooks, laptops, tablets and other electronic gizmos. Rochester stopped beside a trash can and lifted his leg to pee, his nostrils quivering as he did so.

Old wooden picnic tables and benches clustered around the outside of the Cafette, an on-campus sandwich shop in a renovated carriage house. They were incised with initials of long-gone lovers and the wear of wind and rain. Lili joined us there, and Rochester tried to jump up on her, but she gave him a gentle push on his snout, then scratched behind his ears and told him he was a good boy.

"What about me?" I asked.

She reached up and patted me on the top of my head. "You're a good boy, too," she said, and laughed.

I looped Rochester's leash around the leg of an Adirondack chair painted in Eastern's colors of light blue and white and Lili and I went inside. The Cafette was a worn, homey-looking place, decorated with old college pennants and faded T-shirts. The multipaned windows at the far end were open and a light breeze ruffled the pages of an *Eastern Daily Sun*, the college newspaper, open on one of the small tables that cluttered the front of the room. The kitchen took up most of the back of the room, with a fireplace along one wall. The first cold day, there would be a fire there, and students lounging on the overstuffed chairs around it.

We both opted for the salad bar, chatting as we piled our plates with bibb and romaine lettuce, tomatoes, raw mushrooms, and diced green peppers. Lili added a bunch of other veggies to hers, while I opted for croutons, raisins and crumbled blue cheese. We took them up to the register, where the student worker on duty had a large silver ring pierced through the side of her nose. I had an urge to get Rochester's leash and see if I could hook it to her ring, but I resisted.

She weighed the salads, and Lili paid for them and the drinks. "My turn," she said. "Don't worry, I'll let you take me out somewhere nice this weekend."

"Not tomorrow night," I said. "We're baby-sitting Rascal so Rick and Tamsen can go out to dinner."

She began to sing, "Matchmaker, matchmaker, make me a match…"

The cashier looked at us like we were nuts. And she was the one with the big ring in her nose.

We walked back outside to Rochester. I fed him pieces of French bread while Lili and I ate. As we were finishing up, Lili said, "You're going to think this is weird."

"What's that?"

"You remember those pictures I took of the sneaker? I started fiddling with one of them, desaturating the color. Then I kept on fading it out a few degrees at a time until I had a series. I imported them into a movie program and timed the fade."

I understood the technical terms but I had no idea why she was telling me, or how I was supposed to respond. So I just said, "And?"

"And it's sort of beautiful, but creepy. Like a metaphor for life fading away. Though I would never say anything that explicit."

"Sounds interesting."

"Do you think it's too strange?"

"I don't think there's anything so strange, or so morbid, that you can't make art out of it," I said. "Look at murder mysteries and crime TV shows. They take awful stuff and bring it into our living rooms and bedrooms. And doing that helps us appreciate our own lives and our mortality."

"That's the way I feel, too," she said. "I took so many photographs of horrible things when I was a journalist, and there was always this fine line between exploiting the pain of the victims and documenting the events. Witnessing. There's something of that going on in the back of my head, too."

"Can you show me the movie?"

"I'd like that. You want to come over to my office now?"

"Sure." The three of us walked to Lili's office in companionable silence, and Rochester picked a good spot on the hardwood to sprawl. Lili and I sat in front of her desktop computer and she ran the movie for me.

It was creepy but oddly beautiful. The sneaker began in fully saturated colors, the blue canvas a vivid contrast to the white laces and sole. "The real shoe is a lot more faded," she said. "I upped the colors to start with."

Gradually, in frame after frame, the shoe's colors faded, and the background darkened. It was like watching a slow-motion shot of a flower dying.

She played me a couple of slow, dirge-like pieces of music that didn't add anything to the movie. "How about something from the sixties," I suggested. "Like in that scene from *The Deer Hunter,* where they played 'You're Just Too Good to Be True.' A song with a hard-edge but some melancholy."

"That could work. I can't use a real song because I'd have to buy the rights. But maybe I can find something similar on one of the royalty-free music sites." Her desk phone rang and she picked it up. "Dr. Weinstock."

She listened for a moment, then said, "But I can't do anything about it. It's a registration problem." Another pause. "Yes, I told her to go in and see you. I'm trying to notify you of the problem."

She hung up in frustration. "What's the problem?" I asked.

"I have a student in my art history class whose name on the roster is Jean Bean," she said. "When she handed in her first paper, she wrote her name as Joan. I asked her about the discrepancy, and she said somebody wrote the name down wrong when she first registered and she ignored it."

"But she can't do that," I said. "All her records will be wrong."

"You're preaching to the choir. I told her she had to make the change, but she didn't seem to care. So I called the registrar myself. You'd think with all the rigmarole students have to go through with registration and financial aid somebody would have caught this beforehand. But no. And they say she's the only one who can fix it."

She made a washing motion with her hands. "You know what? Not my problem."

"I agree," I said. "All you can do is figure out what name to call her."

"She's been answering to Jean. I asked her which she preferred and she said she didn't care."

"Students," I said. "Sometimes, you can't teach them anything."

"You got that."

I stood up. "Doing anything for dinner tonight?" I asked.

"Lean Cuisine. And then I want to go through some old rolls of film I've never had developed. My friend Adam says I can use his darkroom tomorrow."

"Adam? I haven't heard of him before." I felt a twinge of jealousy. Lili and I had never explicitly talked about being exclusive, but I'd always assumed we were, and that her desire to move in together was another step along the same line.

"He's a sweetheart. He does a lot of freelance work for magazines, but likes to experiment with new techniques, too. We met at an exhibit a few weeks ago and he mentioned that he had a darkroom in his basement. Then I ran into him when I was out with the students on Monday night, and I mentioned that I still had some rolls of film I never developed. He invited me to come over and use his darkroom, and we agreed on tomorrow morning. It'll be a lot easier to work there than in my bathroom."

I was dying to know more specifics about this Adam—how old was he? Did Lili think he was good-looking? I couldn't figure out how to ask without sounding possessive. Then I stopped myself. She had asked to move in with me, not Adam, even though he had film developing facilities in his basement. That had to reassure me. But I had to admit I didn't like the idea of Lili being alone in a dark room (or darkroom) with some other guy.

"I figured I'd come to your house after I finish at Adam's. If that's okay with you."

At least she wasn't having dinner with Adam, I thought. "Sure. I found this recipe on line for homemade dog biscuits. I'll make some of them while I wait for you, and then I'll have them when Rascal comes over."

"You really are puppy-whipped," she said.

I crossed my arms over my chest in mock anger. "And is that a problem?"

"Not when the puppy is as adorable as Rochester."

He heard his name and raised his head, and when we stood up he hopped to his feet. Lili leaned forward and we kissed. Rochester tried to nose between us but I swatted him away. When we backed apart she said, "I should be there about three or four o'clock."

"The only place I might be is out with the dog. But you have your key." I had given Lili a key to my house the second or third time she stayed overnight, and I'd added her to the permanent guest list at the front gate.

I hooked Rochester's leash and we headed for the parking lot. On my way home, Rick called. "I spoke to Arnold Lamprey. His brother went missing back in 1969. They assumed he'd made it to Canada, started a new life."

"They never wondered about him?"

"Their dad was a World War II vet, and his brother Brian served in Vietnam. The family didn't approve of Don's decision."

"It still seems cold."

"Well, Arnold's interested now. He's going to get his brother's dental records and send them to me so we can compare them."

"How about the other kid? Breaux?"

"I called the Mounties in Ottawa."

"Really?" I interrupted him. "The Mounties? They always get their man."

"They're the national police force for Canada, dimwit. I had someone check immigration and customs records. It took a while, but late in the day the guy called me back. No one named Don Lamprey ever entered the country. But Peter Breaux did, the day after John Brannigan's journal entry."

"Anything after that?" I asked Rick. "He have a driver's license, insurance card?"

"There are a number of other guys with that name. But none of them are the right age. Not even close."

"You think he went to another country from there?" I asked.

"There's no record of him leaving Canada, though my contact told me that he could have turned around and walked right back across the border, without anyone knowing. They only cracked down in the last couple of decades."

"So he basically disappeared after he crossed the border."

"That's about it," Rick said. "One more thing. I was curious about how come no one smelled the dead body at the Meeting, and once I knew when the boys were there I asked Tamsen to check the old records and see if there was any mention of exterminators or a bad smell."

"Did she find anything?"

"Yup. The heater broke at the beginning of February, and they couldn't afford to repair it until the spring. So nobody was in the building during the time the body would have smelled."

"You think someone broke the heater deliberately to keep people out? That would mean that the killer had to be one of the Friends."

"Or someone who had access to the building. Remember, when we were kids a lot of people never locked their doors. Anybody in town could have learned what was going on, and gotten into the Meeting, not just members." He sighed. "Anyway, I have to go to the gun range tomorrow morning and get some practice in before I requalify. Since I gave you back your dad's gun I should make sure you know how to handle it. Want to come along?"

"Sounds like fun. Can I drop Rochester off at your place to play with Rascal?"

We agreed that I'd meet him at his house at ten, and hung up. I wondered how a family could let a son go missing like the Lampreys had, and felt sorry for the kid, dying alone and unmissed.

Could the same thing have happened to me if I hadn't survived prison? Once my father was gone, the only person who kept in touch with me during that dark time was Tor—something I'd be forever grateful for.

Now, though, I had friends and a family again. It was up to me to manage to hold on to all of them, so that I didn't end up the way Don Lamprey had.

22 – Target Practice

Saturday morning after our walk, and after Rochester had wolfed down his chow, we played tug-of-war with a couple of different ropes, including a red-and-white striped one with a green plastic loop on the end that he kept trying to put his paw through. When he lost interest, I retrieved my dad's gun.

My father was born on a farm in Connecticut, and he had grown up around guns. He hadn't been a hunter or a target shooter, but he was a Civil War buff and had collected guns, rifles and other materiel from that period. Though my .22 wasn't historic, it had belonged to him and so it was one of the few real connections I still had to him. I took it out of its leather case and cleaned it at the kitchen table the way he had shown me, and it almost felt like he was looking over my shoulder as I applied the oil from an ancient squeeze bottle.

By nine forty-five the gun was clean and ready to fire. I got Rochester into my car and drove over to Rick's, where I let the dog loose in the back yard with Rascal. Then I joined Rick in his truck. "So how good are you with that gun, anyway?" he asked. "Do I have to worry you're going to shoot me?"

"My dad was pretty strong on the basics," I said. "Always know if the gun is loaded, and don't point it at anybody you don't want to shoot. That kind of thing."

"Good start."

I followed him into the gun shop, where I bought a box of ammo for the .22 while Rick filled out some paperwork for the police force that showed he was getting in the required hours to requalify with his weapon.

We got our ear protection and walked to the indoor range, where we laid our guns on the shelf, facing down toward the targets, and he watched while I loaded mine. Then he popped the magazine into his Glock and picked it up. He spread his legs and balanced himself, then raised the gun in a two-handed grip. He fired a series of six shots in quick succession, then lowered the gun.

He said something to me, and I lifted one side of the ear protection to hear. "Aim for center body mass." He pointed downrange. Five of his six shots had clustered around the target's heart; the sixth had hit the neck.

I readjusted the ear protection, then tried to mimic Rick's stance. My hands were shaking a bit as I raised the gun. Rick adjusted the position of my right thumb, then wrapped my left hand around the right. He pointed at the sight, and I raised the gun and tried to line up. I fired one shot and the kickback surprised me.

It wasn't the first time I'd shot, but it had been long enough that I'd forgotten what it felt like. I had hit the target high, somewhere on the cheek. I took a couple of deep breaths and raised the gun again, closing my left eye and focusing.

I fired the next five shots and then put the gun down, again facing forward, even though I knew it was empty. "Not bad," Rick said. I had hit three of my shots around the center of the chest; the other two had gone high.

He went through a couple of rounds, and I followed. My aim didn't get much better, but I did start to feel more confident. By the time we were finished, I felt that all the adrenaline my body could produce had drained away.

We didn't say much as we left the range. I guessed Rick was caught up in his own thoughts, as I was in mine. Could I ever shoot someone who menaced me? Or Rochester? I'd threatened it in the past, in the heat of the moment. But I hadn't had to carry through. And I knew that if I did shoot someone, even if it was justified, my felony conviction would make things difficult for me.

I was lost in memories when Rick said, "Assuming the dental records match, and the victim turns out to be Don Lamprey, I still have to figure out who killed him. I need your help to do some more searching for Peter Breaux. The Pop Warner kids are practicing this afternoon at the middle school and I've got to be there to coach."

"And to see Tamsen," I said.

"Give it a rest, Levitan. I already told you I'm having dinner with her tonight. Do you think you can do some searching for me this afternoon?"

"Never tried anything in Canada. I'm sure there are some public databases. I'm assuming you don't want me to do anything illegal."

He looked over at me. "You even have to ask that?"

I shrugged. "Just saying."

He shook his head. "You don't change, do you? Even after prison, and parole, and all the things Lili and I said."

"Hey, you're the one who needs my help."

"You know what? Forget it. Forget I asked. I'll put together an official request and send it to Canada."

"Rick..." I began.

"No. Just no, all right?" He pulled into his driveway.

He was acting like a jerk, and I wasn't sure why. Did he think that asking me for help was admitting he couldn't do his job? Or was he nervous about his date, and taking out his irritability on me?

"Thanks for taking me with you this morning," I said. "I appreciate it."

"You're welcome."

Rochester came romping over to the fence, and I reached down and scratched under his chin. "You have fun, boy?" I asked. He woofed. "I'll take that as a yes."

Rick looked at me as I opened the gate to let Rochester out. "Remember," he said. "Frank Hardy is the older brother, and he can kick Joe's ass."

At least if he could still make jokes, he wasn't that mad at me. Maybe he was just nervous about his date.

In the year and a half we'd been friends, since reconnecting at The Chocolate Ear one day soon after I returned to Stewart's Crossing, Rick had dated occasionally. They were always women he didn't see a future with, casual affairs that were mostly about sex. Tamsen seemed different. He already knew her and her son, and I'd never seen him bashful around women before.

But Tamsen's husband had been a war hero, and those were big shoes to fill. So I assumed that's why he'd snapped at me, and tried to let it slide off my back.

While the dog biscuits baked that afternoon, Rochester and I spent some quality time on the living room floor with him jumping back and forth over me. When he heard Lili's car pull up in the driveway, he abandoned me faster than smoke vanishing to rush to the front door. He stood there, panting and sniffing, until she opened the gate to the courtyard, when he barked a welcome.

I opened the door for her, and kissed her on the doorstep. Then I snuggled my nose into her curls and sniffed. "New shampoo?"

She laughed. "That must be the darkroom chemicals."

I liked the fact that Lili had started leaving basic toiletries and casual clothes at my house. Even so, she always brought a wheeled duffle bag with her when she came to stay over. I took the bag from her and carried it upstairs. Rochester raced around between us as Lili followed me.

"It was strange to be in a darkroom again," Lili said. "It brought back a whole lot of memories."

"And Adam? Was he helpful?"

I was trying to mask my jealousy with curiosity but it didn't work. "He was developing his own work," she said. "Erotic nudes."

My mouth must have dropped open, because she laughed and said, "Male nudes. Adam's gay and he makes most of his money doing boudoir shots of gay men from New Hope." She raised her eyebrows at me. "He shoots straight men too, if they want gifts for their girlfriends. Or photos for dating sites."

I'm sure I blushed, because she poked me in the side and said, "Christmas is coming, you know."

I had to change the subject quickly before I said something that embarrassed myself even further. "I'm surprised you're still using film to take pictures. I thought everything was digital these days."

"I started shooting digital back in '96 or '97, when I was on assignment in South America, and it was a lot easier to upload files than to overnight film," she said. "But I kept shooting film, too, for years after that, because the results weren't as good for art photos."

I hoisted her bag onto my bed and she began to unpack her toiletries, a sexy nightgown I liked to see her in, and her clothes for the next day. Rochester rolled around on his back on the carpet, and I got down to his level to rub his belly.

"Good color negative film has terrific dynamic range, so you can capture a scene with bright highlights and deep shadows," she continued. "But over the last few years the technology has improved to the point that there isn't much difference, and I love the immediacy of digital – I can see right away if I've captured what I want, or if I've screwed up. I can shoot like crazy and then with a click or two delete anything not worth saving."

She looked over at me. "Sorry, didn't mean to lecture. I was usually good about labeling my film canisters but I must have gotten sloppy toward the end, so I had a bunch of film I'd never developed. It was interesting to see what was there."

"Which was?"

"Mostly junk. A lot of background for a story I never finished, some art I might be able to use. And some personal photos, including a bunch of shots in Darfur of this translator and his family. He was this very sweet guy, and we loved working with him. Only after we left the country did we realize he was lying to us the whole time."

She pulled a folder out of her bag and sat down beside me. "This is Jafaar," she said, showing me a thin, dark-skinned man with a receding hairline. "At least, that's the name we knew him under."

"What do you mean?"

"I was working on a story with Van back then," she said. Van Dryver had been a work colleague and a boyfriend; he had ended up with the *Wall Street Journal*, and continued to float around Lili's periphery. I'd met him a couple of times, while he was nosing around stories that involved Lili or me, and I didn't like him. His whole *I live in the city and I'm a globe-trotting journalist* persona grated on me.

"Jafaar turned up one day and offered to translate for us." Lili pulled out another picture, of a dark-skinned young woman in a Western-style T-shirt. She had a small child on her lap. Rochester nosed his way between us, eager to sniff the photographs.

"Jafaar introduced us to his family. We trusted him and worked with him for nearly two months. Then we finished up and moved on. A few months later, another reporter told us Jafaar had been arrested."

"For working with foreign journalists?" I asked.

She shook her head. "He was a leader in one of the rebel groups. We didn't believe it – but the authorities discovered his real name, and that he had faked a lot of his background, including the fact that the woman wasn't his wife, and the child wasn't his. He was using us to get access to the people we spoke to."

"That must have been tough for you to realize," I said.

She nodded. "I learned something from it, though. Don't accept people at face value. Each of us chooses how we present ourselves – and sometimes that façade is very different from reality."

I stood up, and offered my hand to Lili. I felt that we were starting, after six months, to begin to know each other well. We had established the basics, bringing most of the dark details of our lives out, and while I knew there was much more we would learn about each other, we were comfortable together.

"How was your morning?" she asked, as we walked back downstairs. I told her about going to the range with Rick, and how he'd gotten angry with me.

"I was joking with him," I said. "I know that he can't use any information I find illegally. And I had no intention of doing any hacking. But he jumped to conclusions. This is the second time he's gotten touchy about asking for my help. I'm not sure if that's what he's really angry about, or if it's the case getting to him, or maybe that he's nervous about his date with Tamsen."

"Probably the case. Rick doesn't seem like the type to get nervous around women." She leaned over and kissed my cheek. "I'm sure things will be fine. You guys are friends, and friends sometimes get cranky with each other."

"I know, I know. What else is new with you?"

"Dr. Bobeaux is getting on my nerves," she said as we walked into the kitchen. "Every other day there's a new memo about department procedures, or new forms we have to fill out. New committees. It's enough to drive you mad."

Lili began to spread her photos out on the kitchen table. "I want to look through these before dinner. Is that all right with you?"

"Sure. Despite what Rick said, I'm going to see what I can

find out about that kid who went to Canada."

She looked up at me. "Have fun and play safe."

"I will." I went upstairs to the office, but Rochester chose to stay on the kitchen floor beside Lili. I couldn't blame him—there was a greater chance of getting a treat down there than with me.

23 – Like Alaska

I hadn't done much to decorate the townhouse's small second bedroom; I was still using the desk that had been in my bedroom as a kid, which my dad had brought with him. I had added a collection of books about computers and technical writing, which I never used because the information was out of date; a golden retriever bobblehead Rick had given me; and a light-blue Wedgwood cylinder filled with pencils and pens, which my mother had always used for the same purpose.

I sat down at the desk and turned on the laptop I'd inherited from Caroline Kelly. It was nice not to have to crawl up into the attic and keep all my activities hidden. I'd discussed this with some of the other hackers in my online group, and we all felt that when we could be honest about what we were doing, we were less likely to get into trouble.

I started searching all the public databases for Peter Breaux. A few times I thought I'd hit something, but then I'd click through to the full record and realize it didn't match the teenager who had crossed the Canadian border in 1969.

It was frustrating to find nothing legal, yet I knew there had to be some records of this guy. He couldn't have disappeared into the air. It was nearly impossible to live without a driver's license, an electric bill, a cell phone, or some other connection to the rest of the world. And how could a nineteen-year-old in a foreign country have managed to leave no trail behind him?

Had he changed his name? A woman could have married soon after arriving in Canada, and then all the records would be in her new name. But a guy? If Peter Breaux had done that, there had to be records. Why weren't there?

I closed my eyes and tried to ignore the tingling in my fingertips, the temptation to pull out my hacking software and launch a cyber-attack on the government of Canada. That was a stupid idea, to start with, and I doubted I had the skills for it. But what could I do?

What if I was Peter Breaux's age, a smart kid from a poor place, on my own for the first time in Canada?

I went back to Brannigan's notes. He had bought Breaux a ticket to Montreal. Rick had already had the Mounties check legitimate databases for any record of him, but there must have been a network of draft resisters in Montreal. Brannigan wasn't naïve enough to send a kid there on his own. I went back to the headmaster's notebooks, but there was no name, no organization, no contact number.

Well, that's what the Internet was for. I Googled *American draft resisters in Canada in the 1960s* and got about seven million hits. Brannigan was a Quaker, though, so it was logical he'd have connections to the Friends in Canada. I added that to my search terms.

I discovered that Quakers had been going to Canada as far back as the Revolutionary War to avoid conscription, and that over 100,000 Americans had fled there during the 1960s, either out of conscience or fear. Canada was attractive to draft dodgers and deserters because it was easily reached and had no extradition treaty. Some resisters settled in rural areas, as part of the "back to land" movement popular at the time, while others worked for social justice in urban centers.

But what had happened to Peter Breaux? He must have gotten off the train and used whatever contact information he had for Montreal Friends, then disappeared underground. No matter how much I searched, no matter what I tried, I couldn't get any farther than that. It was incredibly frustrating.

Rochester came upstairs and sprawled on the floor beside me. "Any ideas, boy?" I asked, reaching down to ruffle his fur. "Because your daddy has hit a dead end."

He thumped his tail against the floor twice and whimpered. Had he reacted to the word dead? Did he even know what that meant?

But wait. What if Peter Breaux was dead, too? That might explain why he had disappeared so quickly. Suppose there was a serial killer preying on draft dodgers, picking them up at the train station and then taking them somewhere to be murdered?

The idea of a Quaker serial killer was far-fetched. But suppose something had happened to Breaux. People died in big cities all the time, by accident, suicide or murder. And if someone had stolen his ID from his body, then he might have never been identified.

But what about his mother's obituary? It indicated she was survived by her son, Peter. He had to have been alive then.

It was a conundrum. I needed to get up and stretch, talk out my ideas, so I went downstairs to find Lili, who was in the kitchen preparing dinner.

"I hope chicken piccata is all right," she said. "I knew you had chicken breasts in the freezer, and I brought lemons and capers."

"Sounds delicious to me." While she sliced lemons, I explained the problem I'd come up against. "So how could he have disappeared in 1969, popped back up in 1973 and 1985, and then disappeared again?"

She dropped capers over the dish, then slid it into the oven. "How do you know he was alive in those two years?" she asked.

"He's mentioned in his parents' obituaries."

"That's it?" She shook her head. "That doesn't meant he was alive. It just means his mother thought he was."

"What do you mean?"

"I knew this photographer once. We were both working on stories in Uganda then. His uncle was MIA in Vietnam, and his grandmother refused to believe he was dead. She kept hoping, right up until she died, that he'd come back one day."

I remembered my father's friend Des, and his refusal to admit his son was dead. "So maybe that's the way Peter Breaux's mother felt," I said. "Too bad the Lampreys didn't feel the same way. It sounds like his parents wrote him off after he disappeared."

My regular search had come up empty and there was no way I could legally get into Canadian death records to look for a John (or in Quebec, Jean) Doe. Rick could do it, I thought. He could call someone in Montreal and have them look through the records of bodies that had never been identified.

"It's time to turn this project over to Frank Hardy," I said to Rochester. He looked up at me, and then rushed to the front door, barking madly.

"I guess he knows who you mean," Lili said, as we heard a set of answering barks. I walked over and opened the front door to Rick and Rascal.

"Hey," Rick said.

"Hey." The dogs rushed past me, heading for the lemon-smelling kitchen.

"Listen, I'm sorry I snapped at you this morning," he said.

I shrugged. "I made a stupid joke. But I appreciate that you're looking out for me. It's what Frank Hardy would do for Joe, right?"

"I don't think the Hardy Boys have gotten into computer hacking yet," Rick said. "Though I admit I haven't kept up with the series since I was about thirteen."

"Let me guess," Lili said. "That's about the time you discovered girls?"

We both laughed. "So we're chill?" Rick asked.

"Like Alaska." I made a fist and raised it to him, and he bumped his fist against mine.

I noticed Lili was looking closely at Rick. "Wait right there," she said, and she hurried toward the kitchen.

"What's that about?" Rick asked.

"No idea. But hey, I did come up with something. Maybe a wild goose chase, but you never know. Think back to when we were nineteen—not very worldly, right? We could have made a single bad decision back then, changed the whole course of our lives."

"Teenagers are still doing that. Where are you going with this?"

"Imagine Peter Breaux getting off the train in Montreal. He had to have a phone number or an address or something—Brannigan wouldn't have sent him forward without a contact in Canada. But let's say somehow he got off track, and he got hurt."

"Ah. Or died."

"Exactly. And if someone stole his ID, or he'd already ditched it, then nobody would know who he was."

"That would explain how he dropped out of sight so quickly," Rick said. "But what about the obituaries?"

I explained what Lili had suggested, and he nodded in agreement. He had clearly dressed up for dinner with Tamsen – a white linen shirt with embroidery down one side, untucked, and dark dress slacks with a crease. But he'd kept his small notebook in his rear pants pocket. He pulled it out. "I'll get back to the Mounties on Monday. See if they have any unidentified bodies from that time who match Breaux's characteristics."

Lili returned with a damp towel. She walked up to Rick and pressed it against his hair. "You have a cowlick," she said. "Don't want to look like Dennis the Menace for your first date." Then she kissed his cheek. "You're a great guy, Rick. If she doesn't see that, then she's not worth bothering with."

His face reddened and he said, "I'll be back for Rascal by ten."

"No rush," I said. "We can keep him overnight if you need."

"She has an eight-year-old," Rick said indignantly. "And a babysitter."

He left, and I turned to Lili. "That chicken piccata smells great."

"You can make some garlic bread while I put together the salad." I opened a bottle of white wine and poured two glasses, and we drank as we ate, the dogs curled around our chairs hoping for scraps.

I felt the question of Lili moving in with me hovering around us, but neither of us said anything. I knew that if she did, we'd have dinners like this often, and that was certainly good. But I was still stuck on all the freedom I'd have to give up.

After we cleaned up, we took the dogs out for a long evening walk around River Bend. "It's going to be cold soon," Lili said, rubbing her upper arms as a chilly breeze swept past us. She'd put on a light sweater that obviously wasn't warm enough, so I wrapped my arm around her shoulders and pulled her close.

"You don't mind the cold, do you?" I asked. We had met in February, but we hadn't begun dating until the spring.

"I don't love it, but I like being able to stay in one place and watching the seasons change. I'm happy here and I don't think I'll leave, at least not for a long time."

Rochester tugged me ahead, in pursuit of a squirrel, and I yanked on his leash, but he still pulled me away from Lili. "As a department chair, you're administration," I said. "So you're not eligible for tenure."

"I don't care about that. I have some money put aside, and I can always freelance again if I have to, or pick up adjunct work somewhere." She looked over at me. "How about you? You think you'll stay in Bucks County?"

I knew there was a subtext to her question. If we moved in together, would our futures match? I thought carefully before I spoke. "I like the countryside, feeling like I belong here when I see people in the grocery store or at The Chocolate Ear that I went to school with. I'm happy here. Especially since I met you."

"You're such a sweetie," she said, and kissed my cheek. I felt a glow in the pit of my stomach that certainly wasn't heartburn.

"I look at Tor's life in the city, and one part of me says it's cool – the big apartment, taking Town Cars everywhere, eating out in fabulous restaurants. But the reality is that I'll never make enough money to afford that, and I don't think I'd want it even if I could."

"A lot of people age out of city living," she said. "It's great when you're young, and you don't mind a dumpy apartment, taking the subway and scrounging for change for a Saturday night. But I've done that, and I lived the adventurous life for ten years. I've seen enough third-world bazaars and gotten enough food poisoning to last a lifetime."

"But you still want to travel, don't you? Anyplace you'd like to go with me?"

"I want to visit those places I never got sent on assignment – Paris and Vienna and Sydney and Cape Town. And I think you'd be a great person to be with." She looked down at Rochester, sniffing around the base of an oak tree. "You think you could leave Rochester long enough to take a trip with me sometime?"

"Oh, sure. The old guy who takes care of Rascal takes dogs in overnight, too. I'd leave him there. And I'd be delighted to go traveling with you."

I took her hand in my free one, and we circled back to the townhouse. She and I curled up on the sofa to read, with the big dogs sprawled beside us on the tile floor. I gave them a couple of the biscuits I'd made, and they chewed happily.

I was happy too, I thought. I loved Lili and enjoyed spending time with her. Wasn't all of life a give and take, a compromise? If I was an adult, couldn't I do that? Sacrifice some of my freedom to do what I wanted in exchange for Lili's company?

Around ten, both dogs started to bark, and a moment later I heard a brisk knock at the door. I opened it to see Rick grinning broadly, and Rascal rushed past me, eager to jump on his daddy. "How was your date?" I asked, as I stepped back to let him and Rascal into the house.

"Great. We went up to Le Canal in New Hope. Talked for a long time, then went for a walk along the towpath before I took her home."

Lili joined us. "What's she like?" she asked. His cowlick had popped up again, but she made no move to smooth it down.

Rick looked like that was something he hadn't considered yet. But he said, "She's smart, and she's kind, and she has a great sense of humor."

"Those are good things," Lili said. "I'd like to meet her sometime."

"I assume you will, whether she ends up dating me or not." Rick reached down for his dog's collar. "Come on, you Rascal. Let's go home."

"I'm going to read for a while," Lili said when they were gone.

"I still have one page of Brannigan's diary that I haven't been able to decipher yet. I might take a crack at that."

I walked upstairs, followed by Rochester, and sat at my desk. Beside it was a low table piled with a jumble of papers to be filed, a collection of headphones, charger cables and other computer crap, and, to remind me of all I had lost, a framed photo of Mary and me, taken in Monterey, California right before our wedding. The two of us posed against the rocky shore in a photo snapped by a Japanese tourist. We both glowed in the fading afternoon light like God had special plans for us.

The cipher used on that single page didn't match any of Brannigan's others, and I was stumped. Rochester must have sensed my unrest, because he stood up and started pacing around the room, wagging his big tail. A moment later I heard a crash and looked over to see that he'd knocked down the photo of Mary and me.

"Thanks for the clue, puppy," I said. "But I know for a fact Mary was nowhere near Stewart's Crossing in 1969."

He woofed at me, then stared with doggie devotion. "What? Is there something else about the picture? There couldn't be. I haven't touched it in years."

He kept staring at me, so I unbent the clips that held the picture in place and slid it out. There was nothing there but the picture. I flipped it over and saw that Mary had written the date and both our names: Steve Levitan and Mary Schulweiss.

"Rochester, you're a genius!" I said. "Of course. Edith wasn't married to Lou Passis then." I'd helped Edith the year before when someone had committed bank fraud against her, and I had her maiden name filed somewhere on my computer.

Rochester curled around behind my chair, as if he was going to keep me at the computer until I finished my work. I hunted through a couple of files until I found that Edith's maiden name was Fox.

There was only one two-word pair with a 5-3 pattern. I filled out all the letters in her name, discovering that Brannigan had used the letter Y for E, and so on. Then I converted all those letters in the word pairs on the list.

The name below Edith's was the one with three words. First word _ e _ _; second one _ ee; third one i_ _ _.

It only took me a moment to realize it was Vera Lee Isay, Brannigan's secretary. How long had she worked for him? She told us that she'd been out of high school for two years or so before she became his secretary. She'd have been at least eighteen, old enough to drive boys around, get them supplies for their travels, or whatever else Brannigan asked. And if she'd been part of his group, no wonder she had been reluctant to help Rick and me once she learned what we were looking for.

I kept going. The rest of the names were unfamiliar to me, though since they were all female it was possible that I knew one or more of them but under a married name, as I'd known Edith. There were a couple of letters I couldn't figure out, but I thought I'd show the list to Edith and see if she could help.

I picked up the photo of Mary and me. It was time to put it

away, I thought, along with all the memories it represented. Maybe that was why Rochester had knocked it over in the first place.

"You are one smart puppy," I said to him. He rolled on his back, and I clambered down to the floor to scratch his belly as a reward.

24 – Confession

Sunday morning, I made veggie omelets for myself and Lili, and we lounged around eating and reading the paper. Around noon, Lili decided to go back to her apartment in Leighville because she was eager to scan some of the photos she had printed and begin working with them. I kissed her goodbye and promised to see her during the week.

Neither of us said anything more about her moving in, but I knew that her deadline was approaching. I just couldn't open the subject up, one way or another.

I spent some more time online, looking for information on Peter Breaux, but I kept drawing a blank. The only clues I had were his hometown and his parents' obituaries. I wondered if he had been at their funerals, or if he was only remembered in those notices.

Several of my high school friends had showed up at my mother's funeral, even though I was living in California and we'd been out of touch for years. Small towns were like that. People read the obituaries and paid their respects.

Had any of his old friends done that for Peter Breaux? Would they have seen him, spoken to him? How could I track them?

I looked for records of his high school, and found that there was a group for its graduates at one of the school reunion sites. But when I tried to get in to view its members, I got a pop-up message that it was restricted, and I'd need an invitation to view it.

That was like waving a red flag in front of a bull. My fingers danced across the keyboard, initializing my hacking software, going online and finding an unsecured port I could use to launch my attack. The site security was pretty good, but they allowed members to use very simple passwords, and within an hour I had a list of all the people who had graduated from Peter's high school.

It was only then that I realized what I'd done. Despite all my protests, and my attempts to stay on the straight and narrow, I'd hacked into a protected website without even thinking about it.

I stared at the screen, at the list of names that meant nothing to me. Why had I done it? Risked everything I cared about for something so ultimately meaningless?

Rochester came padding across the carpet to me. He put his paws up on the desk and looked at the screen, then he woofed.

"I know, puppy, I shouldn't have done it," I said. But I didn't close the window either.

He licked my face, and I laughed. "Does that mean you approve?"

He woofed once more and then settled to the floor beside me.

"And you're supposed to be looking out for me," I said. "Oh, well, in for a penny, in for a pound." I copied all the names and their contact information into a file, then logged off the website and shut down my hacking software.

Most of the alumni of Peter's high school had included their addresses and phone numbers. I picked up my cell phone before I could think too much about it, dialed *67 to hide my number, and began calling.

I introduced myself as an old college friend of Peter Breaux's, trying to get back in touch with him. A few people had no idea who I was talking about; a few others had known him long before but lost touch. Finally, I hit pay dirt – a woman who had graduated with him and who'd seen him at his mother's funeral.

"He was there?" I asked.

"He come in a few days before she passed," the woman said. "She was at the hospital in Morgantown, and he stayed with her there. Then he come back to town for the burial, and to close up the house."

"Did you talk to him at all? Find out where he was living?"

"He said Canada somewhere," she said. "I've forgotten exactly where." She paused. "Now who exactly did you say you were? You're not a bill collector, are you?"

"No, ma'am," I said. "Thank you for speaking to me." I disconnected quickly.

So Peter Breaux was alive at the time of his mother's funeral. I made a note of the woman's name and phone number, in case Rick had to call her to confirm.

There was something else in what she'd said, though. I sat back in my chair and went through the whole conversation. He'd closed up the house. Of course! Why hadn't Rick and I thought to check property sales records, or for the probate of a will?

I was ready to get right back on line, but I stopped myself. It was up to Rick to continue that search, legally. I dialed his cell.

"I have a confession to make," I said.

"Call Father Donelan at St. Ignatius," he said. "I'm no priest."

"But you are my confessor," I said. "I hacked into a database online."

"Christ, Steve."

"I know, I know. It was stupid. I didn't even think about it."

"And you want me to say that makes it all right?"

"No. I just wanted to tell you. And I'm going to tell Lili, too."

"There's a but coming," he said. "I can hear it in your voice."

"I found out that Peter Breaux was alive at the time of his mother's funeral. Did you ever check to see if she had a will probated, or if her house was sold after her death?"

He didn't say anything. I couldn't tell if he was writing, or just trying not to lose his temper. "I'm an idiot," he said. "No wonder I always need your help."

"I'm guessing the answer to my question is no."

"I kept searching for Breaux himself. I didn't think to look for anything under his parents' names. But I'm almost certain that the search I ran would have included probate records, so if he'd been listed in the will he should have come up. And I know for a fact there was no property under his name in that town."

"Maybe he never sold it, never changed the name on the deed," I said.

"I'll look into it. This doesn't make what you did right, you know."

"I know. Do you want the name and phone number of the woman who saw him at his mother's funeral?"

He groaned. "And that would be a name and number you got by hacking?"

That didn't seem to require an answer, so I didn't say anything.

"Email it to me. Just the name and number, nothing else."

"I have her address, too."

"Just the name and number," he said very slowly. "Thank you for finding the information, but don't ever feel like you have to do anything illegal to help me. Understood?"

"Understood."

I hung up and called Lili. I got her voice mail but my message wasn't one I wanted to leave without explanation, so I just said I was thinking of her. I went online to my hacker support group and typed out a message, and I felt a little better after that. But I was still unsettled by the experience and I looked around for something else I could do.

I remembered that I had wanted to go over the list of names with Edith and see if she recognized any of them, so I called and asked if I could come over.

"Only if you bring that adorable dog of yours," she said.

Great. My dog was the handsome one, and it seemed that wherever I went people were happier to see him than they were to see me.

It was a crisp, sunny afternoon, and the roadsides were cluttered with fallen leaves and osage oranges, bumpy yellow-green balls filled with a sticky white sap. I remembered collecting them as a kid for my mom, who piled them by our front door along with Indian corn and colored squash.

I pulled up in front of Edith's Cape Cod. "You behave in there," I said to Rochester as I hooked up his leash. He shook his big shaggy head.

"This is such a treat," Edith said, when she opened her door to us. "My family always had dogs when I was a girl, but Lou was allergic, and after he passed I didn't have the energy for a dog anymore." She reached down to pet Rochester's head and he licked her fingers. She giggled. "Come on in."

Rochester was eager to sniff everything in Edith's living room. "I have this list," I said. "I think it's the volunteers who worked with John Brannigan back in the sixties, but I can't decipher all the names. I was hoping you could help me."

I showed her the paper I'd written the names on, with the first letters capitalized so that they would look more like names.

Edith Fox

Vera Lee Isay
_ e _ _ y H o d _ _ i _ s
S a _ d y _ h i _ _ a d i a
E l l e _ _ o o d
De_ o r a h / A l l e_

"Do you recognize any of these?" I asked.

"Why, it's like a puzzle," she said. "Let me get my reading glasses on."

As she pulled them out of her case, I explained the principle of the cipher. "I was able to figure out your name and Vera Lee's," I said. "So I filled in those letters. The blanks represent the letters I haven't matched yet."

"This one is easy," she said, pointing to the third name. "Ellen Wood. My cousin. She passed away two years ago."

By filling in those letters, I had:

Edith Fox
Vera Lee Isay
_ e n n y H o d _ _ i n s
S a n d y _ h i _ _ a d i a
E l l e n W o o d
De_ o r a h / A l l e n

Edith looked over my shoulder. "Of course, the first name there is Jenny Hodgkins. She married one of the Scudders from Scudder's Falls. They retired and moved to Florida. I haven't heard from Jenny in, oh, ten years or so."

I filled in the J, G and K which didn't give us any new clues. "Can you recognize any of these others?" I asked.

Edith stared at them. "I'm sorry, Steve."

"How about thinking back to those days? Do you remember anything more about them? Anyone named Sandy or Sandra, or Deborah or Debbie?"

She closed her eyes and thought, then opened them quickly. "Of course! How could I forget Sandy Chizmadia? She married John Shea and I was a bridesmaid at her wedding."

"Wait, Sandra Shea? My social studies teacher?"

"Yes, she did teach for a while, didn't she? But then her husband was transferred somewhere. We kept in touch for a while, but then, you know how things go."

That left us with:

Jenny Ross

Sandy Chizmadia

Ellen Wood

De_ orah Allen

"So this last woman must be Deborah Allen?" I asked.

"Of course!" Edith said. "Debbie Allen. She married... who was it? I saw her at the Harvest Festival." She took off her reading glasses and put them down. "She makes these horrible crocheted toilet paper covers, with dolls on top. I didn't talk to her because I was afraid I'd have to buy one."

I remembered those dolls. Where had I seen them? I tried to recreate the Harvest Festival in my mind – walking around with Lili, helping Gail....

"Mrs. Holt!" I said.

"Yes, that's it. How in the world did you know that?"

"Lili and I helped Gail out that day," I said. "Mrs. Holt's table was next to hers. Those crocheted monstrosities are imprinted on my brain."

Edith laughed. "Debbie was a silly girl even back then," she said. "She was always contriving ways to meet the boys, volunteering to bring them food. She'd go on and on about how cute this boy was, how brave this one was to stand up for his beliefs. How tragic it was that they had to move to a foreign country."

"We were all young once, Edith," I said. "Do you have Mrs. Holt's number?"

"I think she's in the book," Edith said. "But should you be going to talk to her yourself? Or asking Rick to do it?"

"I was going to tell him," I protested.

She smiled. "You were always so curious when you were a boy, Steve. I remember when I was teaching you, you wanted to know everything – what wood the piano was made of, how the hammers made the sounds, was that real ivory on the keys."

"You remember all that?" I asked.

"Things come back to me now and then," she said. "Getting old is a terrible thing. But then you consider the alternative."

I knew all about that.

25 – His Girls

I thanked Edith for the help, and took Rochester outside, where I called Rick and told him what she had said.

"You say you know this woman?" he asked.

"Not really. Lili and I worked at the table next to hers at the Harvest Festival and we talked a bit."

"Close enough. I'll call her and see if we can come over this afternoon. Between you and your dog, you've got a knack for talking to civilians."

I walked Rochester up Edith's street so he could sniff some new smells and relieve himself, and by the time we got back to the car Rick was on the phone again. "I spoke to her and she said she has some errands to run in town. I suggested meeting her at The Chocolate Ear, and she agreed. Two o'clock."

That gave me and Rochester an hour to kill. "That's good. I'll see you then."

I wanted to enjoy the fall afternoon and give Rochester a walk, so I parked at the VFW Hall at the far end of town and we strolled to The Chocolate Ear. Mark Figueroa was sitting at a table outside, reading the *New York Times* and nursing a cappuccino.

"How's it going?" I asked, settling into the chair across from him. Some red and gold leaves from the maple above had already fluttered to the ground.

"Well, if it isn't Cupid," he said drily. "Planning to shoot any more arrows today?"

"I don't know what you mean," I said, feigning innocence.

"You're trying to hook me up with Joey Capodilupo. I told you, I don't need your help to find a date."

"He seems like a nice guy," I said.

"Yeah, they all seem like that at first."

I remembered that like Rick with Tamsen, Mark had had a date the night before. "Did you go out with him last night?"

"Yes. And we had a good time."

"So why are you busting my balls?"

"Because he's going to turn out to be a jerk, and I'll have to work with him. And I don't need this kind of drama."

Rochester put his head on Mark's lap and for once Mark didn't complain about dog hairs. "I should get a dog," he said. "A Rottweiler or something that could keep men away from my door."

I stood up. "Well, you can practice with Rochester. I'm going inside to see what kind of pastry Gail has."

"Get me a napoleon," Mark said. "Maybe if I get fat Joey will leave me alone."

I laughed. Mark was six-five at least, without an ounce of fat on his bones. I doubted a dozen napoleons would make much difference.

When I walked inside, I saw Gail and Declan sitting at a table by the wall, deep in conversation. None of the other tables were occupied. "I guess this is why I couldn't get service outside," I said.

"Oh, gee, I didn't even see you come up," Gail said. "I'm sorry."

I waved my hand. "Love comes first."

She blushed. "What can I get for you?"

I ordered a cappuccino and a chocolate croissant for myself, a biscuit for Rochester and a napoleon for Mark. Gail disappeared into the back. "How are things going?" I asked Declan.

"Very well, thank you," he said. "I'm hoping to spirit the chef away to dinner when she closes down."

"Good luck with that. Gail works hard."

"I'm discovering that," Declan said.

I went back outside, and Gail delivered my order and Mark's napoleon a couple of minutes later. I shook my finger at her. "Remember, nobody ever said on her deathbed I wish I'd worked more."

"I know. But it's hard running your own business. If I want to go off with Declan I have to close down, and I need to squeeze every bit of revenue I can."

"It's not like you're bombarded with customers," I said. "And what time do you usually close, anyway?"

She looked at her watch. "In about an hour."

"I'm supposed to meet Rick here in…." I looked at my watch. "A half hour. If anybody comes up after that we'll tell them that you closed."

I paid her for the coffee, the croissant and the biscuit for Rochester, and she went back inside. I delivered Mark his napoleon, and we sat together for a few minutes, eating and watching traffic along Main Street. When he finished, he said, "I've got to get going. I have a new assistant at the store and I've already left her alone too long."

A few minutes later, Rick took his place. "You know anything about this Holt woman?" he asked, as he slid into the chair and then scratched behind Rochester's ears.

I shook my head. "Just that Edith said she was silly back then. Which matches her hobby, I guess." Rick had never seen the toilet paper holders, and I was describing them when a Mini Cooper pulled up. I recognized Mrs. Holt; she had straw blonde hair with an unnatural brassiness and skin so tight it had to have been artificially augmented. I stood up to greet her. "Mrs. Holt? I'm Steve Levitan. We met at the Harvest Festival, when my girlfriend and I were helping out at Gail's table."

"Oh, yes, I remember," she said. "Gail's pastries are so delicious!"

I introduced Rick, and he offered to go inside and get a coffee for her. "And one of those delicious pastries, if you like."

"I adore her rum balls," Mrs. Holt said, and she giggled girlishly. "And there's something so naughty about asking for them, don't you think?"

"Coffee and a rum ball," Rick said, and he went inside.

I introduced Mrs. Holt to Rochester, and she smiled nervously. "I'm not much of a dog person," she said.

"Don't worry, he's very attuned to people," I said. "He won't bother you."

And he didn't. He stayed on the pavement and continued chewing his biscuit.

"The detective said you had some questions about the 1960s," she said. "What's this all about?"

"Why don't we wait for Rick to come back," I said. "I'm sure he'll want to ask the questions. I agreed to join him because I mentioned that I'd met you at the Harvest Fair."

Rick came out a few moments later, balancing two Styrofoam cups of coffee and a paper plate of rum balls. "Gail said to tell you last call," he said to me. "She's closing up."

"I'm good."

He sat between us and turned to Mrs. Holt. He explained that the bones found at the Meeting House belonged to one of the last boys who had passed through en route to Canada.

"Not Peter!" she said, her mouth opening.

"You remember him?" Rick asked.

"Oh, yes. I made a point of meeting all the young men we helped. I wanted them to know that someone at home would be thinking of them. I often went over to the Meeting House to talk to them."

"Did you talk to Peter and the other boy with him?" Rick asked.

"Well, just Peter," she said. "The other one wasn't very friendly. And he was too restless to sit around. He went out for a while, and Peter and I sat in one of the offices at the back of the Meeting House and talked, oh, for hours."

"What can you tell me about Peter?" Rick asked.

"He was a very bright boy. He desperately wanted to go to college but his parents didn't have a spare nickel for him, and they didn't have such big scholarships back then as they do today. The best he could have managed was to go part-time, and that wasn't enough to keep him out of the service."

She picked up her coffee and sipped, then bit into one of the rum balls. Since Rick had brought a plate of them, I took one myself, ignoring his dark look.

"Did Peter have any plans once he got to Canada?" Rick asked.

"Just to go to school. We had heard, you know, that there were people at the universities in Canada who were sympathetic to draft resisters. He had a couple of names of people at various schools."

"And the other boy, Don? Did he get back while you were still there?"

She shook her head. "I only saw him the once, very briefly." She sniffed. "He asked me where people who smoked dope hung out."

"Did you tell him?"

"Of course I didn't have any habits like that," she said. "I was a very good girl. And my, I was only about eighteen or nineteen. I had heard rumors, though, about hippies who camped out in the woods behind the Meeting House. I told him that's all I knew."

She picked up another rum ball. "These are so delicious," she said.

Behind us, I saw Declan flip the "Open" sign on the café's front door to "Closed."

"Those were such special times," Mrs. Holt said. "John Brannigan was so handsome and dashing, and he kept telling us what good work we were doing. He called us his girls, you know." She looked at her watch. "Well, I'm afraid I must dash. Have to get Sunday supper on the table."

"Thank you," Rick said. "You've been very helpful."

She left, and I picked up the last rum ball on the plate. "It's another piece of the puzzle," I said. "Don left the Meeting House looking for dope."

"But he had to have come back alive," Rick said. "There's no way you could get a dead body in there."

"They could have argued," I said. "Don and Pete. Don sounds like a slacker, and Pete a smart kid. Maybe things got physical, and Pete killed Don."

"You're jumping to conclusions again," Rick said. "I'm not saying that's not what happened, but we still have more pieces of the puzzle to fill in."

I remembered what Edith had said, that even as a kid I was curious about everything. That curiosity had gotten me into trouble in the past, and I hoped it wouldn't do so this time.

26 – Husband of the Year

When Rochester and I were back in the car, I decided I needed to see Lili in person to tell her what I'd done. So instead of heading for home, I drove up the River Road to Leighville. I stopped at the Genuardi's outside town and bought a fall bouquet, asters and chrysanthemums in shades of red, yellow and brown.

Lili rented a second-floor apartment in a converted Victorian a few blocks from campus. The owners had restored it to its former glory, cleaning the small stained-glass windows, refinishing the pine floors, and painting the crown moldings. She had decorated it with an artist's eye, though she didn't display her own work. There were a couple of art-quality photographs and a few pen-and-ink drawings by undiscovered geniuses, but most of the apartment was simple and uncluttered, with classic Craftsman-style furniture and hand-knotted wool rugs from Mexico.

"This is a nice surprise," Lili said, when she opened the door. I handed her the flowers and we kissed. Rochester pushed past me into her living room, intent on something.

"What brings you up here?" she asked, as she led me inside. "You want to have dinner? I'm making spaghetti sauce to put up for the winter. It should be ready in a half hour or so, and I can boil up some pasta."

"First I have something to tell you," I said.

She looked at me. "It's all right. I shouldn't have even brought it up."

I was confused. Brought up what? I'd just gotten there. Rochester circled around twice and settled on the rug in front of the sofa. Oh, moving in together. I'd forgotten about that when I got caught up in my hacking angst.

"You may be changing your mind," I said. "Come on, sit down with me."

We sat on the sofa, slightly turned so we were facing each other. "I made a mistake today. I'm sure it's not the last one I'll ever make, but it reminded me that I still have a long way to go to be the guy you deserve."

Her eyes were dark and her voice serious. "What did you do?"

"I hacked into this reunion database online, looking for information on Peter Breaux."

She looked at me, and then burst into laughter.

My bafflement must have shown on my face, because she took my hands in hers. "Oh, sweetie, I know that no one gets over problems overnight. I thought you were…"

"What?"

She shrugged. "I don't know, confessing that you'd cheated on me or something."

"I'd never do that," I said. "I know that Phillip probably told you that, too, and it was a lie. But I'm not Phillip. I'm not wired that way. Even when things were at their worst with Mary, when we were sleeping in separate beds and she was telling me I was the most awful husband in the world, I never once considered cheating."

"Clearly you were never the worst husband in the world," Lili said. She leaned forward and kissed me again. "Not even in the top ten."

I kissed her and then pulled back. "In the top twenty?" I said, with mock irritation.

"Well, you did commit a felony and go to prison," she said. "So you're out of the running for husband of the year."

"I guess I'll just have to try harder." I leaned forward and we kissed again. I felt like the anvil that had been in the pit of my stomach had floated away, and I was very, very lucky.

That would have been a good time to bring up our moving in together, I guess, but I was worried Lili would see it as a bounceback after my hacking confession. I owed it to her and to myself to make sure I was saying yes for all the right reasons.

She sniffed the air. "My sauce," she said, and jumped up. Rochester was right on her heels, hoping there was food in the offing.

I followed them both. "Taste this," Lili said, offering me a wooden spoon with some rich orange-red sauce on it.

It was delicious, and I told her so. "I use fresh tomatoes, but I dehydrate them first to concentrate the flavor. Why don't you set the table while I put up some pasta?"

We ate dinner with Rochester at my feet, and then went into Lili's bedroom, where we cuddled together and then read for a while.

I didn't stay over, because I didn't have clothes with me for the next day, but I drove home in a much better mood than I'd been in on the way upriver.

Monday morning, I took Rochester for his walk around eight. As we walked, I noted the arrival of the maids and the nannies. Some came in their own cars, while others walked in from one of the bus stops along Main Street. We passed, as usual, an obese Russian man in his sixties, wheeling his tiny grandchild in a stroller, as well as a number of other dogs and their parents. The Camerons, who spent winters in Florida, were having their gutters cleaned, in preparation for their departure, and Bob Freehl was standing in his driveway supervising the work of an exterminator.

I felt like a slacker, when so many people around me were either already at work, or on their way there, and I still had an hour before I had to be at Friar Lake. Not for the first time I blessed my parents, first generation Americans who had worked hard so that I could get an education and qualify for a skilled job. Peter Breaux hadn't been so lucky, and I was sure that many of those maids and yard workers were intelligent, often educated in their home countries, but their immigrant status or limited language skills restricted them to manual labor.

I was very fortunate to have my job, and I knew it. Every day when I arrived at Friar Lake I marveled at the way I'd landed on my feet, that I had a job that was interesting and challenging and paid enough for roof and kibble.

The morning was busy, as Mondays often are, but at lunch I had some free time to think back on the case. I pulled up the list of the ten members of the renovation committee from the Friends Meeting website and printed it out. As I remembered, the only three I recognized were Hannah Palmer, Vera Lee Isay and Eben Hosford. But I was curious about the ones I didn't recognize. Could any of them have a connection to the case?

Two of the other members were Realtors in town; two others

were school teachers, one at General Lucius Stewart Elementary and one at Pennsbury High – both schools I had attended. I couldn't find anything on the other three, so I looked them up in the white pages online. They all lived in Stewart's Crossing, which made sense.

As I was typing I realized I didn't know Vera Lee's address. I'd assumed she lived in town because she belonged to the Friends Meeting. But a quick search, and a look at Google's satellite view, revealed that she lived in a small stone house in Lahaska, about a half hour north of the George School campus in Newtown. Why would she be involved with the Stewart's Crossing Meeting, when there was another right in her home town?

The quick answer was that she knew more than she was telling about the body behind the false wall, and that by belonging to the Stewart's Crossing Meeting, and serving on the committee, she could keep abreast of any developments.

I looked up Hannah Palmer's number and called her. "It's Steve Levitan," I said. "We met at the Harvest Festival."

"Oh yeah. Rick's friend."

Interesting. I guessed Hannah and Tamsen talked a lot. "I wanted to ask you about one of the members of the renovation committee. Vera Lee Isay."

"I don't know her that well," she said. "She used to belong to another Meeting, and she joined ours just about the time we began the renovation. She volunteered to be the committee secretary, which was a blessing, because she keeps excellent minutes."

I thanked Hannah, and hung up. Vera Lee's recent interest in the Stewart's Crossing Meeting House was suspicious, and I sent a quick email to Rick. I tried to come up with a way I could casually run into Vera Lee, perhaps with Rochester, who had charmed her. But I couldn't see walking the dog around the George School campus, or showing up out of the blue at her home. I'd have to leave following up on her involvement with the Meeting to the professional.

27 – The Whole Story

Rick called a couple of hours later. "Arnold Lamprey's on his way to Stewart's Crossing," he said. "He wants to see where his brother died. And he wants to thank you for uncovering the remains. You think you could join us at the Meeting House? He's going to be there in about an hour."

"I'm getting ready to leave the office," I said. "I can meet you. Did you get my messages, about Eben Hosford and Vera Lee Isay?"

"Yeah. I'm tracking down Eben Hosford so I can talk to him. He lives off the grid, though. No voter's registration or driver's license, doesn't own any property. I'll give Vera Lee a call tomorrow."

I locked up, and Rochester romped over to my car, tugging me with him like the tail on a kite, and then stuck his head out the window all the way down to Stewart's Crossing. It was chilly but I didn't have the heart to pull him in. The sky was brownish-gray, and a skein of Canada geese flew overhead, heading south for the winter. We passed a building where the first "S" had been torn away from the "Self-Storage" sign, and I wondered if that was where Santa kept his elves when he didn't need them.

At the Meeting House parking lot I saw a dusty pickup with one bumper sticker that read "My other ride is a tractor" and another in the shape of an apple with "Support Your Local Farmers." I figured that had to belong to Arnold Lamprey.

I hooked up Rochester's leash and he went for a quick pee. As we turned the corner of the Meeting House I saw Rick standing where Rochester had found Don's sneaker. With him was a big-chested man in his sixties with white hair, and a younger woman who looked like a contemporary of Hannah and Tamsen.

Rick introduced us. Arnold wore a faded all-weather jacket with a corduroy collar, jeans and work boots. His hands were broad and calloused and his smile was genuine. He had brought along his daughter Lori, the woman who had created the family tree and given us the connection to the Lampreys.

She got down on one knee to ruffle Rochester behind his ears. Her blonde hair was pulled back into a ponytail, and it looked like she wore no makeup—though I'd learned from living with Mary that often meant a woman was just skilled at its application. In Lori Lamprey's case, though, I thought it meant that she was a no-nonsense kind of woman who could castrate a bull as easily as create a webpage.

"Must have been a long trip across the state," I said.

"Didn't matter to me," Arnold said. "He was my brother, and we let him go for too long."

"I insisted that my dad bring me, too, because I know him, and I knew he wouldn't tell you the whole story," she said.

"Now, Lori, don't go rushing things. Let me have a moment here where my brother died."

Rick, Lori and I stepped away. "What's the whole story?" Rick asked her.

"I want to see how much my father is willing to tell you. But you'll understand when we're finished."

A chilly breeze picked up, scattered dead leaves around the broad horseshoe-shaped lawn. A low-riding car passed by on Main Street, bass thumping, and high above us a jet left a white contrail across the sky. The late afternoon had a lonely, almost funereal feel and I was glad to have the comfort of Rochester's warm bulk beside my leg.

Arnold spent a few minutes in silent contemplation of the wall of the Meeting House, and then came back to us. "I'm about dead on my feet," he said. "Anywhere in this town we can get a cup of coffee?"

We agreed to reconvene at The Chocolate Ear, where we sat at a table outside so that Rochester could stay with us. He sat between me and Lori, and she occasionally reached down to pet him.

"You know I had three brothers," Arnold said. "Each of us two years apart. Brian, Charley and Donny. Brian wanted to see the world, so he enlisted in the Army the day he turned eighteen. He was in one of the first divisions to leave for Nam, back in

1965."

"Did he come back?" I asked.

"In 1967, when Charley's number was coming up. Brian was healthy enough in body, but something inside him was broken. Had these nightmares, these black moods. Today they'd call it PTSD, but back then we didn't know what to think."

Arnold drank his coffee while the rest of us were silent. I thought briefly of Jerry Vandeventer, who'd suffered the same way.

There was a steady stream of traffic down Main Street, delivery trucks and SUVs, and I wondered where all the station wagons of my youth had gone. When I was a kid, every family with more than one child had one of those long wood-paneled numbers, and it was a treat for me to ride along with someone who had multiple siblings. Those were the days when all I knew of war came from bits of TV news. Now I was well aware of all its costs—from the soldiers who didn't come back, to the ones who did, to the people who reported on atrocities like Lili.

After a while, Arnold spoke again. "Charley saw what happened to Brian, and he filed for an agricultural deferment when his number came up."

"You said your dad was a World War II vet," I said. "How did he feel about that?"

"He came from that generation, said you had to pay your dues to live in a free country. He didn't approve when Charley got out of serving, but there wasn't much he could do. When Don came of age, he applied for the deferment, too, but he got turned down because the three of us were on the farm. Pop was pretty insistent that it was Don's duty."

Lori reached over and stroked her dad's upper arm. "There's more to the story," she said. "Go on, Daddy. Tell them."

"I hesitated because I didn't want to admit to breaking any laws," Arnold said. "But Lori here said I had to tell you, in case what my brothers and I did caused some harm to Donny. See, like I told you, when Brian came back from Nam, he had all those problems, and the only thing that made him feel better was smoking dope."

Rick and I leaned forward, listening closely. In the distance I heard the cawing of a crow and the blare of a car horn.

"Us being farmers, Brian had this idea. He got some marijuana seeds from a buddy of his fresh home from Nam and started growing them, first sprouting them in a corner of our greenhouse. Then come spring he planted those seedlings at the edge of a cornfield. Our pop never knew about them."

"But Don did," I said.

He nodded. "We had a real good crop that year. We harvested and dried it in big bunches. Then we separated out all the seeds and twigs and packaged it up. Brian used to take the bus into Pittsburgh every couple of weeks to sell to guys at the VFW."

He looked at us. "It wasn't about the money, you know. Just about helping those boys feel better after all they went through. We couldn't even spend the money, because all of us still lived at home and we didn't want raise any suspicions with our kin. Then come January, Donny disappeared. He had taken all the money we had, close to a thousand dollars, and all the marijuana, too. Brian was spitting mad. Took off on the bus to Pittsburgh after him."

Up to that point, Don Lamprey had been fairly anonymous to me. I thought of him as a teenaged version of myself, wondering what I'd do in his shoes. But hearing his brother speak, Don became more of his own person. Not a person I thought I'd like – but still a human being who had died.

Arnold drank some of his coffee before he continued. "Pop was plenty mad that Donny had run off, and even madder that Brian went after him. Brian didn't come back for a week, and he was a mess – drunk and high and I don't know what all. Had to keep him out in the shed for a day until he dried out."

"Did he eventually tell you where he went?" I asked.

"Just said he'd gone to Pittsburgh, looked around for Donny but couldn't find him. So he stayed with some friends til he ran out of money. When we never heard anything from Donny, we thought maybe Pop was intercepting the mail, or maybe that the boy was embarrassed about what he'd done and couldn't face us."

"You still growing the stuff?" Rick asked.

"No, sir. Soon after that, Brian left for California, and Charley and me had enough to do keeping the farm going." He looked at Rick. "I had to come and see this place," he said. "And to ask you a question."

Lori took her dad's hand and squeezed.

"Do you all think Brian could have tracked Donny down here, and killed him?" he asked. His voice wobbled, and in it I could hear the pain and dread that had to be in his heart.

"That's a big question, sir," Rick said. "You knew your brother. Was Brian capable of that?"

"Before he went to Nam I would have said no way at all. But the boy who came back – he wasn't my brother Brian. He wouldn't talk much about what he did over there, but I know that he killed people. Soldiers, but also ordinary people, old women and little children. He said that you never knew who your enemy was, so you had to protect yourself."

"You said Brian moved to California. You have a current address on him?"

He shook his head. "We tried to reach him when our pop died, maybe twenty years ago now. Phone number belonged to somebody else, mail came back 'addressee unknown.' Didn't have the Internet then, either."

"It's why I started that family tree you found," Lori said. "I wanted to know what happened to my uncles."

I looked at her. She wore a simple gold wedding band, and I imagined that she lived near her parents and looked after them. She was that type of woman.

"Did you find any records?" I asked.

She shook her head. "I tried a bunch of places but couldn't find a trace of him."

My fingers tingled. Here was a challenge. Could I find Brian Lamprey? Or discover what had happened to him? We all stood up. Arnold and Lori were staying at a motel out near the highway that night, heading back to Zelienople the next day.

"Thank you for meeting with us," Arnold said. "At least I know what happened to one of my brothers."

Rick and I watched them walk to Arnold's truck. Lori got into the driver's seat and pulled into traffic expertly.

"So Don wasn't such an innocent kid," I said as she drove away. "You think his brother could have tracked him down and killed him?"

"The crime scene team didn't find any traces of marijuana," he said. "So Don must have sold it before he went into that false wall."

"Or his brother tracked him down, took the dope and the money, and then killed him."

"That's a possibility. I know you – you're itching to see if you can find Brian Lamprey. But you've already screwed up once. Don't do it again."

I wanted to argue that if I could find Brian Lamprey, I might be able to give Arnold the same sense of peace that he'd gotten from knowing what happened to Don. But Rick was right – I'd already violated my promise not to hack once. Sure, he and Lili seemed to have forgiven me – but how many mistakes could I make before I lost them both?

It was safer to shift the conversation away from the last missing brother. "Maybe Peter Breaux found that Don had all that money, and killed him for it," I said. "Or maybe Don tried to sell the dope to someone in Stewart's Crossing, and that person killed him. And don't forget Vera Lee or Eben Hosford. There's something suspicious to me about her joining the Meeting just in time to serve on the renovation committee – and him being on that committee, too, when he's so opposed to the work."

"Don't let your imagination run away with you," he said. "I have a whole lot of possibilities to look into and I'm not going to pick any one theory until I have some evidence."

28 – Living off the Grid

As I drove up Sarajevo Court toward my townhouse, I spotted Bob Freehl, the retired cop, sitting on a folding chair in his driveway. He was a balding guy in his early seventies, wearing flip-flops, plaid shorts, and a T-shirt stretched over his belly that read "I'm Tired of Being My Wife's Arm Candy."

I had a flash of inspiration, and as soon as we got home I hooked up Rochester's leash and walked back down to Bob's. Rochester strained to rush up to him, and as Bob extended a hand, Rochester dropped to the ground and rolled onto his back so that Bob could scratch his belly.

"Hey, Bob," I said. "You used to be a cop in Stewart's Crossing, didn't you?"

"Long time ago," he said.

"Were you working here in the sixties?"

"You mean before the town got crapped up with all these city commuters? Sure."

When I was a kid, Stewart's Crossing was a small town surrounded by farmlands. The Lakes, where my family lived, was the only suburban development. Many of my classmates lived on farms, and when I took the late bus home from Pennsbury High we passed acre after acre of crops and cattle grazing. My parents were amazed, once I learned to drive, at how well I knew my way around those country roads.

By the time I left for college, I-95 had sliced through the hills and valleys, making it easier to dash into Philly. Gas stations and shopping centers sprung up at the interchanges, and hundreds of acres of farmland metamorphosed into developments of single-family houses, the same models repeated endlessly, skinny saplings the only landscaping.

I sat down cross-legged on Bob's driveway in front of him. The pavement was cold beneath my butt. "The sixties were a pretty wild time, from all I've heard," I said. "Any of that filter down here?"

He shrugged. "We had a couple of anti-war protests at the town hall," he said. "Used to be a bunch of hippies who camped out in the woods behind the Meeting House, and we rousted them a few times."

"Any drugs?"

"When the wind was right, you could almost get a contact high from driving down Main Street," he said. "Pulled a couple of 'em in for possession but never could find out who the dealers were."

Rochester got tired of being petted and jumped up. I scrambled to my feet. "Thanks, Bob," I said. "Always interesting to hear about life before I started paying attention."

Rochester tugged me forward, and I stumbled over my feet as I tried to keep up with him. "Who's walking who?" Bob asked.

"Only the dog knows, and he's not talking," I called back to him.

When I got back to the house I called Rick and told him what Bob Freehl had told me. "Maybe Don Lamprey smelled the smoke and went back into the woods there," I said. "Mrs. Holt told us that she'd mentioned that's where the hippies hung out. He could have tried to sell the dope he had with him, and gotten killed."

"How'd he get back into the Meeting House then?" Rick asked.

"Hey, you're the detective. I'm just the idea guy."

He snorted and hung up.

I wanted to look for information on Brian Lamprey that Lori might not have been able to find, but I knew that if I got started I'd be tempted to hack. Instead, I focused on Eben Hosford. I was intrigued by the idea that he was living off the grid. How could someone do that, in the twenty-first century, in a metropolitan area like the Philadelphia suburbs? I turned on my laptop and started searching.

Rick had checked property records and driver's licenses so I didn't bother with those. I also figured he'd looked for a phone account or one with PECO, the power company that supplied Bucks County, so I skipped those, too.

I didn't expect Eben to be on Facebook, LinkedIn, MySpace

or any of the other social networking sites, but I checked anyway. No results. I sat back in my chair. How could someone live without connections to the modern world? He'd have to be out in the woods somewhere, probably with his own well for water, a garden for food, and some kind of generator, probably solar or wind-powered.

But every inch of Bucks County belonged to someone, either a private owner or a public entity. He could have been camping out in the back of a park somewhere, but I doubted that. He'd have been caught years before.

So that meant that someone owned the property where he lived. A relative? I went to the property assessor's database and searched under his last name. Sure enough, there were a lot of Hosfords who owned property in Bucks County. I opened a mapping program and started to check each address, looking for a likely spot.

This was a good, legal project for my information skills, I thought. Unfortunately, the Hosfords were a farming family, and there were a half-dozen properties where he could have been living, a crazy old uncle or cousin camping out somewhere.

I sat back in my chair, thinking. Then I looked around for Rochester. He wasn't in sight, and he wasn't making noise. Not a good combination. Usually if he slept, he did so somewhere around me.

"Rochester!" I got up and started looking around the house for him, calling his name. He wasn't in the bedroom, either on my bed or beside it. He wasn't sprawled on the cool tile of the master bathroom.

I went downstairs, and from the staircase I saw him on the sofa, his gold coat a contrast to the dull brown upholstery. He'd kicked the throw pillows to the floor, and he had his paws crossed. He was licking something brown and square he had clasped between them. "What do you have in your mouth?" I demanded, as I jumped down the last couple of steps and hurried over to him.

"That's my wallet!" I said, tugging it away from him. As I did, my driver's license and credit cards spilled out to the floor. "You weren't planning to order some doggie treats online with my credit cards, were you?"

He hadn't hurt the wallet, just covered the leather with a thin layer of spit. I wiped it off on my pants, and leaned down to pick up the scattered cards.

Nobody's driver's license picture ever looks good, and mine was no different. My eyes were wide open, as if someone had poked me, and I had a five o'clock shadow and a cowlick. With my name beneath my picture it looked like a booking mug shot.

I rarely used my full name, Steven Jeffrey Levitan. I had been named for my mother's father, whose name in Hebrew was Shmuel Chaim. As was the custom then, my parents only used the initials of his name to provide me with an English one. And somehow, the "ch" in Chaim had translated into a J.

I was glad; there wasn't a single H name I liked. Howard? Hubert? Horatio? I was glad to have Jeffrey. One year when I went on a travel camp, I'd told everyone my name was S. Jeffrey Levitan – call me Jeff. Didn't seem like me, so I went back to Steve.

Brain flash. Had Eben Hosford done the same thing, discarded his first name and used his middle? I hurried back upstairs to the computer, after petting Rochester a couple of times and thanking him for the inspiration.

There were five Hosfords who owned an acre or more, where someone could live off the grid. One was in a woman's name so I skipped that for a moment. The other Hosfords were Jacob, Franklin, William, and Moses.

I did a quick experiment, searching for information on each man with the middle name Eben. The only match was Moses Eben Hosford, whose property was about a mile outside Stewart's Crossing, on the road to Newtown. I switched to the satellite view in the map application and zoomed in on the property address.

It was overgrown and I could barely make out the shape of the house in the middle of all the trees, a rectangle with a front step and a narrow driveway. What was visible, though, was a solar panel on the house's flat tin roof.

I was so pleased with myself. I'd found Eben Hosford without doing any hacking, just using my instincts and my basic knowledge. To keep from gloating, which I knew I'd do if I spoke to Rick, I sent him an email with Hosford's full name and address.

I thought briefly about searching for Brian Lamprey, since I was on a roll, but Rochester wanted to play, and the urge passed.

When I woke up Tuesday morning, I was still curious about Eben Hosford. I dressed for dog-walking and let Rochester have a quick pee in the front yard, then loaded him into the car. "Change in routine, puppy," I said, scratching his head. "But you'll like it, I promise."

I drove into downtown Stewart's Crossing, the streets full of early morning commuters, moms on school runs, and the elderly, who always had to have the first doctor's appointment, the first slot at the garage. I never understood that; why worry about waiting around when that's all you had to do anyway?

I turned inland at Ferry Road, passing the old Victorian library, long since converted to a community center; the pharmacy where we'd gotten our medications; and the Women's Exchange, where my father had once threatened to trade my mother in for a pair of twenty-five-year-olds (she told him at fifty he wouldn't know what to do with even one of them.)

About a mile from the center of town, I pulled into the parking lot of a strip shopping center on the right side of the street – karate dojo, beauty supply shop, Peruvian restaurant. It was too early for any of them to be open so I had my choice of spots.

"Let's go for our walk," I said to Rochester, and he tumbled out of the car. We waited for a break in traffic, then scooted across Ferry Road. Rochester sniffed and peed as we climbed a block of cracked sidewalk, skirting squashed osage oranges and downed maple branches.

At the first corner, we turned left into a neighborhood of old houses, two and three-story clapboard with broad front porches, hundred-year-old oaks and maples in the yards, the occasional Big Wheel or skateboard propped up against a wall. As we kept walking, the lots got bigger and the houses smaller. After about a quarter of a mile we got to our destination, the single-story bungalow owned by Moses Eben Hosford.

It was surrounded by a chain link fence with a padlock on the gate. Nobody had mowed the lawn for years. Small bushes and saplings had sprung up, and I could barely see the outline of the house behind a screen of trees. Fading paint that had once been green, broken downspout, one shutter hanging askew. An old bicycle leaned against the front wall of the house, and off to the side I saw what I'd always thought of as a wishing well – a stone cylinder with a hand crank and a peaked wooden roof.

I was looking through the chain-link when the door to the house popped open and Eben Hosford stepped out on to the porch with a shotgun in his hand. He raised it and it looked like he had me in his scope.

29 – Buried in Work

"Just walking the dog!" I called and waved, and urged Rochester forward. When we were far enough away I muttered, "Not exactly a friendly neighbor, boy."

We kept walking until we came to a cross street we could turn down, and then another that led us back to Ferry Road. As long as I was near downtown, I decided to stop at The Chocolate Ear for a café mocha to go and a biscuit for Rochester.

I turned on my Bluetooth and called Rick while I drove, and told him I'd done some recon on Eben Hosford's house.

"When are you going to recognize that you don't have a badge?" he demanded.

"Anyway, he's home now, if you want to talk to him. Looks like he gets around on a bicycle. Oh, and by the way, he's got a shotgun."

Rick grumbled a few more epithets as I pulled up a block from the café. "You talk to Tamsen since Saturday night?" I asked.

"I don't need your help, Levitan," he said. "Tamsen comes with a lot of baggage – the dead husband, the kid, the whole Quaker thing. We had a good time together, but I'm having second thoughts. I'm not sure I'm ready to jump into the deep end of the pool."

"You know how it was when we were kids," I said. "You close your eyes, hold your nose and jump."

Good advice for me, I thought. It was time I jumped into the pool with Lili. Close my eyes, reach for her hand, and jump. I loved her, and I could be myself with her, not always trying to be the person she expected. I had the benefit of cell phones and email and social media posts, things my father hadn't had access to when he was away from my mother, to let Lili know she was in my thoughts. And I didn't have to worry that she was sitting by the phone, waiting for me to call, for me to show up for dinner or drop by her office. She had her own life, and I liked that about her.

I just had to find the right time, and the right way, to tell her how I felt.

I left Rochester in the car and walked into the café. The lemon-yellow walls never failed to cheer me up, and I loved sounding out the names on the Art Deco posters for French foods: Orangina, Pates Baronis, Beurre de Normandie and Chocolat Escoffier. She'd ordered her pastry display case from France and chosen the chairs, tables, even the floor tile to recreate the ambiance of the cafés she loved.

Gail was manning the register, and there were a half-dozen patrons ahead of me. No one came in behind me, though, and I could see the relief on Gail's face when I got to the register.

"No minions this morning?" I asked, as she started making my coffee. She had a part-time waitress and help from her best friend as well as her mother and grandmother.

"Grandma has the flu and Mom's taking care of her. Ginny's youngest has pinkeye, which is contagious. And Mindy's back in school this term."

"How was your dinner with Declan on Sunday?"

"It was great. Too good, in fact, because it made me realize that I don't have time for a relationship. I'm up early every morning baking and by the end of the day I fall into bed." The door behind me jingled and a group of the red hat ladies trouped in, waving and calling hello to Gail.

"Poor Aunt Gail," I said to Rochester, when I slid back into the car next to him. "She works too hard. And now my matchmaking is falling apart. Aunt Gail, Uncle Rick, even Mark." I looked over at him. "You understand what I'm doing, don't you, puppy? I love Mama Lili and I feel so blessed with the way my life is going, I just want all my friends to be as happy."

He nosed me, whether in sympathy for my plight or because he wanted the biscuit. I wouldn't give it to him in the car because I didn't want to have to vacuum up all the crumbs, which put him in a mood. I left him in the kitchen with his bowl food, which he refused to eat as long as there was a biscuit in the neighborhood.

"Tough nuts, dog," I said, pointing at his bowl. "Eat your food."

I scrambled to get ready for work, giving Rochester his biscuit after I showered. Didn't help his attitude, though, and just to be as cranky as he was I wouldn't roll the window down for him. By nine-thirty, as we arrived at the winding road that led up to the abbey, we were both in a funk.

The road needed to be widened, repaved and landscaped before we opened, but we were waiting until all the heavy equipment was finished. I had to pull to one side, dangerously close to a stand of pine, in order to let a fire truck pass me, coming downhill.

"Don't tell me the place burned down," I said to Rochester, who didn't. I rolled down my window and sniffed the air. The breeze brought with it a smell of wood smoke but I had a feeling it was from something more than a fireplace fire. I pulled up in front of the office and looked down toward the far end of the property, where I saw Joey Capodilupo standing where the stable was. Or rather, had been. The ramshackle wood building with two big front doors was gone. In its place was a smoking pile of rubble. Another fire truck stood by as a couple of firefighters sprayed the debris with water.

I hurried down the gravel road to Joey, Rochester right behind me. "What happened?" I asked.

Joey had grime smeared on his forehead and along one cheek, and his T-shirt was soaked with either water or sweat. "Something ignited inside the stable," he said. "When I got here at seven-thirty the fire was smoldering, but it took off right after that."

"At least you saved the other buildings," I said.

"Yeah, but this opens another whole can of worms. You ever notice there's no fire hydrants up here?"

I looked around through a smoky haze that hung in the air and didn't see any. "That a problem?"

"It is if there's a fire. Fortunately this was a small one and they could put it out with the water they carry. None of these buildings are up to code, and we've already planned to install sprinklers. But now it's clear we need to have a couple of hydrants up here, too. That's going to require extra permitting and a new line from the main at the bottom of the hill. That's going to mean more money and more time."

"Crap," I said. At least that portion of the work would fall to

Joe Sr., not to me. "Any good news this morning?"

"We were storing the carpet rolls for the dormitory in the stable," he said. "It's all burned to a crisp, but it was butt ugly."

"I hope this is all covered by the college's fire insurance policy. And by the way, don't let Mark hear you say that. You know how sensitive these decorators are."

"Yeah. Too sensitive for me. Any way you can shift the job from him to somebody who has some taste?"

Ouch. Another matchmaking attempt fallen through, on top of all the damage. "You sure don't want me picking the finishes," I said.

He grumbled something under his breath that sounded like he didn't want Mark doing anything, but then his cell rang and he had to answer it.

The College president, John William Babson, showed up around noon to survey the damage, and he wasn't happy. I spent the whole day in meetings and on the phone, scrambling to help wherever I could. Long conversations with the college's insurance administrator, the fire chief, the company that supplied the carpet. All of them dull but required.

I got an email from the man who'd first hired me at Eastern, Lucas Roosevelt, the chair of the English department. He wanted my help with a computer problem, as he knew I was on the IT committee. The default settings on the computers in English department classrooms for paragraph indent and spacing didn't match what the department required of students. Verri M. Parshall, the previous IT director, had blocked his efforts to get that changed. Could I talk to Oscar Lavista and the committee on Lucas's behalf? I made a note.

Late in the afternoon, Lili called. "You want to come up to my place for dinner?" she asked. "I want to show you the movie I made of the sneaker with the music I found."

"I would love to come," I said. "Horrible day. I'll tell you about it when I see you."

By the time we left the office, Rochester was mad because I hadn't let him go anywhere near the burnt stables despite his eagerness to stick his nose where it didn't belong. I was dead on my feet and in no mood to jump into the delicate negotiations that would result in Lili moving in with me.

When Lili opened her door, the aroma coming from her kitchen was a tantalizing mix of sweet and spicy, which cheered both me and Rochester. "You smell like smoke," she said as we pulled apart after a kiss.

I followed her to the kitchen, where I sunk down at the table and explained about the fire at Friar Lake. "Nobody was hurt?" she asked.

"No, we were lucky." I sniffed the air. "What smells so good?"

"My mother's roast chicken with apricots and prunes," she said. "And don't make a face. It's delicious."

"At this point, sweetie, you could cook me shoe leather and I'd be happy to eat it."

She'd even bought a small bag of Rochester's chow, and she mixed it up with some diced chicken. He wolfed it down as we began to eat.

While we ate, I told her about my day, including my meeting with Babson. "He ought to be grateful it happened now," she said. "Imagine if you were already open for business."

"In that case, the ugly carpet wouldn't have burned up."

She raised her eyebrows. "Ugly carpet?"

"Joey Capodilupo thinks it's ugly. He also thinks that Mark Figueroa has no taste."

"Poor baby," she said. "Matchmaking not going so well?"

"Not at all." I told her about Rick's reluctance to get involved with Tamsen, and how Gail thought she was too busy to date Declan.

"Maybe you should stick to crime-solving as a hobby. You do a pretty good job of that."

"Thank you. I don't feel that way now, though. I've been able to give Rick a couple of clues, but I still don't think we're close to finding out who killed that boy."

She stood up. "I'll clean up in here. Why don't you go do some sleuthing. That always cheers you up."

"You are a treasure," I said. "A woman whose price is far above rubies."

She leaned down and kissed my cheek. "I love a man who

knows his literary allusions."

"I love you, too." I walked out to the living room, settled on the couch, and called Rick. "Did you speak to Eben Hosford?"

"Once I had his full name, I checked the computer database. Our town records have only been digitized as far back as the 1980s, and there's nothing under his name but a couple of building code violations. I haven't had time to go digging around in microfiche for anything before that. Drove up to his house but he wouldn't let me in the gate. Just stood on his doorstep with his shotgun next to him. Denied he was a part of Brannigan's circle. Denied he knew anything about that false wall."

I heard him sigh, then he continued. "I checked with Mrs. Holt and with Edith Passis. Neither of them remembered Hosford being involved, and both of them said Brannigan had only recruited girls to help him. Edith didn't even think Hosford became a Quaker until a year or two after the war was over."

"How about Vera Lee Isay?" I asked. "Did she know Hosford?"

"She says she didn't."

"Did you ask her why she joined the Meeting in Stewart's Crossing?"

"Yeah. She said she didn't want to be specific, but the Meeting in Lahaska wasn't serving her spiritual needs, whatever that means. She insists it was a coincidence that she joined just as the renovation was beginning."

"Can you get Hosford's fingerprints? See if they match any around the body?"

"The crime scene guys retrieved a lot of fingerprints, from the walls and the ladder inside that space. But I don't have anything that connects Hosford to Lamprey other than speculation, so I don't have any legal reason to request his fingerprints."

"What about the soap?" I asked. "Or the candles? I know Gail has bought from him. You could pick up what she has and get it printed. I'll bet his prints are on the inside of the packaging, so that would eliminate Gail or anyone else who happened to pick it up."

"I'll ask Gail. But look, Steve, sometimes we have to accept when a case reaches a dead end. The trail is dead. The autopsy results are inconclusive – somebody could have knocked Lamprey out with a blunt object, or he could have hit his head in an accident. I have no more clues and no suspects beyond Peter Breaux, and he's vanished."

"So you're giving up?"

"I'm moving on. I'm on the lookout for a Peeping Tom out in Crossing Estates," he said, naming a community of fancy homes in the suburbs. "Coordinating a DUI stop with the state police. And talking to the kids at Stewart Elementary tomorrow morning about what it's like to be a policeman."

"You'll let me know about the fingerprints?"

"Yes, brother Joe. Now I've got to go."

After I hung up, I thought about Arnold Lamprey and his brothers again. Was it enough closure for him to know that Don had died there at the Meeting House? Or would he always wonder how it had happened? I remembered those missing children I'd found about online, how their families, like that of my father's friend Des, had probably never stopped looking for traces of their kids.

I could always look for Brian Lamprey – but that was a dangerous slope to put myself on, because I could see how easily the search could lead me to unauthorized locations. One thing that I'd learned from my online support group was that when I was tempted to hack, I had to focus on something else—something that was equally important.

I looked at Rochester. "What do you think, boy?" I asked. "You ready to do this with me?"

He rolled on his back and wagged his legs in the air, his signal for a belly rub. I reached down and scratched, then stood up and walked to the kitchen, the dog on my heels. One of the lessons I learned in prison was that I had to face up to anything, or anyone, that scared me. If I didn't, I lost all power over that thing or that person.

Lili was just closing the dishwasher. I stepped up and said, "Yes, I said, yes I will yes."

She stared at me for a moment, then said, "The end of Molly Bloom's soliloquy from *Ulysses.* Are we playing literary trivia?"

"No, I'm telling you that I want you to move in with me."

I waited nervously for her response. Suppose she'd changed

her mind? Despite her reassurance, what if she was worried about linking her life to a convicted felon and an (sometimes) unrepentant hacker?

Then she said, "Just the kind of response I hoped I'd get. Positive and romantic and all tied up in a man who sees life through the lens of literature."

My heart skipped a couple of beats as joy rushed through my veins. I crossed the tile floor to her and took her in my arms, and we kissed. Rochester kept nosing between us and I had to push him away. This moment was all mine and Lili's.

When we finally pulled apart, I had a moment's hesitation. My life, and Rochester's, were going to turn upside down, and so soon after taking on the new job at Friar Lake. It seemed like my life had become one big chain of changes, and I didn't like it. But then I looked at the smart, sexy, beautiful, talented woman in front of me and knew I was making the right decision.

Rochester even seconded the motion with a woof – though that could have just been him wanting attention.

"You're sure about this?" Lili asked. "Because I don't want you to feel any pressure."

"I'm sure."

We went back into the living room together and talked through some details. "I like your couch better than mine," I said, putting my hand on it. "My parents had mine for ages, and when Rochester was a puppy he chewed on the legs."

We held hands as we walked around the apartment together. "Your dining room table is better than mine," I said. "But the chairs at my house are more comfortable than yours."

"I agree."

"And I think your desk will fit better into my extra bedroom than the crappy one I'm using, which I've had since I was a kid. And if we angle it right, there'll be room for both of us to have computers there and even work together when we need to."

I had a ton of kitchen stuff, inherited from my parents, but Lili had a few pieces she liked that I was sure we could make room for. "And I think you should bring all your art and your rugs," I said. "We'll move things around and rearrange until it all fits together."

"That's good," she said. "A lot of what I have is basic stuff I got at IKEA when I moved here. I'll either donate what I don't want to keep up or put it up on Craigslist."

"Whatever you want to bring, we'll make room for," I said.

I had grown up in a house full of clutter, and lived in tiny, cramped spaces in New York. When Mary and I moved to California I'd had the impulse to add layers – framed photos, books, occasional tables, potted plants and display cabinets. Mary had a design esthetic of Zen-like simplicity, though, and she fought me on each acquisition. Gradually I adapted, and the forced monasticism of prison life had become imprinted on me after that.

I had very little left from my life in California, and I'd grown accustomed to living with lots of open space, shelves empty except for books and a few knickknacks. Would all of Lili's stuff start to crowd me out?

Rochester nosed my hand, and I reached out to stroke his fur. As long as he and I were together, I could handle anything the world threw my way. Lili started talking about curtains and slipcovers and I flashed on the way Mary had taken over the decoration of our house in California.

Lili certainly wasn't Mary, though, and I had to find a way to get my ex-wife out of my head, or else I was going to doom my relationship with Lili. But how could I do that? In the past I'd always buried myself in computer work whenever something went wrong in my personal life. And see where that had gotten me.

30 – Scrawl

Lili had some papers to grade, so she went into her office and left me on the sofa. To keep from thinking too much about how my life was going to change once Lili moved in, I went back to the case, but there were no new clues I could follow. We had interviewed everyone still alive who'd worked with Brannigan. Despite his creepy behavior, there was no evidence against Eben Hosford unless Rick could match fingerprints from his soap or candles to the crime scene. Vera Lee Isay could have been involved somehow, but she was too busy protecting Brannigan's reputation to give us anything incriminating. And Peter Breaux had disappeared into Canada, never to be heard from again.

Rochester clambered up on to the sofa and nestled against me. He had a piece of paper in his teeth with the Eastern College letterhead, and I pulled it from him gently. "What are you, the postal person now?" I asked. It was a departmental memo from Dr. Peter Bobeaux announcing new procedures for petty cash disbursement. I was about to crumple it up when I looked at his scrawled signature.

It looked as if he'd written "Breaux" instead of "Bobeaux."

I remembered the problem Lili had had with her student, Jean or Joan Bean. Could the same thing have happened to Peter Breaux – a mix-up with the spelling of his last name? My brain started running. Lili's new boss was about the right age to have been a draft evader in the 1960s. He'd graduated from college in Canada. I'd assumed he was French Canadian, with a name like Bobeaux. But what if he wasn't?

I jumped up and went into Lili's office. She was sitting at the desk, logged into our online learning system. "I hate to interrupt you, but can I use your computer?" I asked.

"Sure." She pushed back her chair and stood up, and I slid into her place. "What do you need?"

"Give me a minute. I have so many ideas mashing around in

my head that I can barely type."

With Lili looking over my shoulder, I started at the Eastern website, where I found that Peter Bobeaux had received his bachelor's in French literature from Carleton University in Ottawa in 1973 – perfect timing for a high school senior fleeing the draft in 1969. I pointed that out to Lili.

"Oh, my," she said, and I could tell she was following my thoughts.

Bobeaux had gone on to receive his master's and doctoral degrees from the same university. From there he had taught at a number of colleges and universities, eventually landing in the United Arab Emirates, where he had been before coming to Eastern.

"What made you think of the connection?" Lili asked.

"Joan Bean, Jean Bean," I said. "Peter Breaux, Peter Bobeaux." I showed her the memo, and Bobeaux's scrawled signature.

"Why would he come back here, if he killed someone?" Lili asked.

"I don't know. But murder isn't a logical act, so I don't think you can apply logic to anything that happens afterward." I looked at her. "He has a temper, doesn't he? I saw him get angry in the committee meeting. Imagine somebody with his personality, a teenager with less impulse control, scared and nervous?"

"So what do you do now?"

My fingers itched to do some hacking. I wanted to check Peter Bobeaux's student records at Carleton and see if there was any indication of where he'd gone to high school. Maybe I could match that to where our missing draft dodger, Peter Breaux, had gone. I could make an excuse to Lili, head back to my laptop and its hacking tools. What the heck, right? Nobody had to know. I could be in and out of Carleton's database before anyone knew I was there.

Rochester suddenly sat up and placed his front paws on my thigh, sniffing at me, and that was enough to snap me back to reality. Nope. That was something I could get Rick to discover through official channels.

"I'm going to do a bit more searching on Peter Bobeaux," I

Neil S. Plakcy

said. "Nothing illegal. I want to see if I can find out where he came from before he started school at Carleton."

"I'll be in the bedroom reading. Come in whenever you're finished." She kissed my cheek and walked out of the room, and I let my fingers do the walking through the Internet. Everything I found tied back to that student at Carleton University, but I couldn't discover any records from before that time that matched him.

I called Rick again. "I have an idea I want to run past you." I explained about the way Peter Bobeaux scrawled his name, and the confusion over Jean or Joan Bean, and what I'd discovered about Bobeaux's background.

"You think he could be the same guy?" Rick asked. "But why would he come back to Stewart's Crossing?"

"He didn't," I said. "From what I understand, he needed a job, stat, and saw the one available at Eastern. He may not even have known that Leighville and Stewart's Crossing were in the same area. Or he may be some kind of psychopath who wants to revisit the scene of the crime. You pick."

"Spell the new name," he said, and I did. "Tomorrow morning, I'll call this university and check his credentials."

"More than that. See if you can find out where he grew up, where he went to high school, that kind of thing. If you come up blank, then we know we're on to something. Or else you find something that eliminates him."

After I hung up, I went into the bedroom, and Rochester and I spent the night at Lili's, where she and I further cemented our affection. When we woke up I said, "I hope you're going to bring these pillows with you, because they're a lot more comfortable than the ones I have."

"Always the romantic," she said, and she turned on her side to face me. "Think Rochester can wait a little while for his morning walk?"

I leaned over and kissed her. "My dog is very attuned to my moods. "He'll wait."

31 – Information Technology

By the time I got to Friar Lake on Wednesday morning, Joey's crew had cleared away the debris from the fire. A crisp breeze that rolled down from the higher mountains pushed away all but a lingering scent and moved puffy white clouds restlessly above us. I noticed that more of the trees were losing their leaves as autumn crept up.

My email box was full – a request for an update from President Babson, order confirmations for finishes that Mark and I had agreed on, and a raft of the usual academic business. The Faculty Senate wanted input on a resolution to ban student cell phones and the smoking of electronic cigarettes in classes. New parking decals were available for faculty and staff.

The last message was an invitation from Dr. Bobeaux, who had scheduled another meeting of the IT committee for that afternoon. I grumbled, because I preferred more notice for trips on campus. But a meeting organizer could view faculty schedules through the college intranet, and anybody could schedule an appointment with you as long as it didn't conflict with teaching. I'd have to drop Rochester at Lili's office, because I couldn't take him to the meeting and I wouldn't have time to drive him back home.

Around noon, Rick called. "You remember Hank Quillian from the FBI, don't you?"

I had met Agent Quillian a couple of months before, when my snooping into a murder turned up a website selling stolen goods. He was in his early thirties, with the kind of weathered, wary look I'd come to associate with ex-military guys. "Sure," I said.

"I got him to expedite a request for me. Peter Bobeaux got his GED right before enrolling at Carleton, and they have no records that would indicate where he came from or where he went to high school."

"I guess they were more lax back then," I said. "I can't

imagine a kid getting into Eastern today without a pile of recommendations, authenticated transcripts, and a laundry list of high school activities."

"It doesn't mean that he's the same guy as that kid who left the Meeting House in 1969, but it doesn't eliminate him from suspicion."

"What are you going to do now?" I asked.

"Keep checking. Hank's going to cross-reference immigration records for me and see when Peter Bobeaux entered and left Canada, but that's going to take more time."

I thought about telling Rick that I'd be seeing Dr. Bobo that afternoon, but I knew he'd caution me not to say anything. I figured I'd think on my feet, and see if any opportunity came up to ask Bobeaux about his background. I wondered if I could drop in a mention of my own application to Eastern, all the hoops I'd had to jump through back then. Maybe casually ask him if that had been the case when he applied to Carleton for his undergraduate degree.

I remembered Lucas Harriman's request, and I did some quick research on academic format for research papers. Every reputable site indicated that what Lucas was asking for was standard. I printed pages from a site I'd often used myself to bring to the committee.

I left Friar Lake at three and parked behind Harrow Hall. Lili's office door was locked, but I got her secretary, Matilda, to open it for me. "Don't destroy anything, Rochester," I said. Lili kept a couple of his toys there, and I retrieved a green squeaky ball and a blue-and-white rope to keep him occupied.

I was the last one to arrive at the meeting. I noticed that the collar of Peter Bobeaux's navy pinstriped suit jacket was a bit threadbare, but his white shirt was starched and gleaming, his red power tie spangled with tiny blue stars.

He had a whole agenda prepared for us. "Let's start with problems with the learning management system," he said. "I had lunch yesterday with Dr. Marshall, the AVP for Educational Technology, at the Faculty Club. He's very concerned about the way the system interacts with our college computers."

"I've complained to him myself several times," Jackie Conrad said tartly, "though not over lunch at the Faculty Club." The Club was a separate dining room at the rear of the college's new Howard M. Burgers Dining Commons, with separate entry and what was rumored to be higher-quality food than was served to the hoi polloi.

She crossed her arms over her white lab jacket. "My students are not able to access their exams, even though I know that I've set the dates and times correctly. And I'm tired of tech support simply telling me to go back and check my work."

"I agree," Marie-Carmel Etienne said. She was chic as ever in her tailored black suit and white cowl-neck blouse. She could have been a runway model as easily as a professor of computer science. "I've called a dozen times with problems and all I get is a run-around. My students are having problems uploading PowerPoint presentations because they're too large for the system to handle. That is ridiculous considering how much server capacity we have and what fast upload speeds we have."

None of the problems with the learning management system were anything we as a committee could handle, which was annoying. We went on to the monitors in teaching podiums, which were tilted too far down to be easily visible, then updates to Flash and Java which professors were prevented from installing. As we went through items, I couldn't manage to work in a reference to student applications or credentials, which was frustrating.

The last item on the agenda was identity theft. "I've been hearing of several cases recently where student passwords have been compromised," Bobeaux said. He looked down at the sheet in front of him. "Rachel Ritchie, a junior, had her entire schedule dropped. She said that an ex-boyfriend had access to her password and had done it to get back at her. Nelson Tarrazu was accused of sending suggestive messages through the college instant message system, and he alleges that he accidentally stayed logged on at a computer classroom and someone else sent those messages under his name."

"Those are user errors," moon-faced Oscar said. "There's no way we can prevent that kind of abuse." I had the feeling he'd worked too long for his predecessor, Verri M. Parshall, the Preventer of Information Technology. Then again, I'd worked in IT myself for years, and I knew that the habit of blaming users for tech problems ran deep.

"We could ask for double-secure logins," Marie-Carmel said. "You'd have to know a student password and some other piece of data."

Oscar shook his head. "If you know something as personal as someone's password, then you probably know any other piece of data we could use. And an outsider hacking into our system and stealing passwords could steal the confirmation data as well."

"Is someone breaking into our computers?" Bobeaux asked. "I haven't heard anything about that."

"There have been instances at other schools and colleges of hackers changing grades," I said. "I'd never done anything like that myself, but I'd read enough about it on hacker bulletin boards.

"Your identity is the most important thing you have online," Oscar said. "It's your responsibility to make sure you protect it. Not ours."

I saw my opportunity, and I jumped on it. "But how do we know who any student is, in the end?" I asked. "I've read about people who enter college or graduate school with false credentials, under assumed names. Every other week it seems you read about someone who's lost a job because he faked his graduation records."

Was it my imagination, or did Peter Bobeaux look directly at me? I looked back at him and smiled.

"I don't think we'll be able to solve this easily," he said. "We're done here."

"I have something to add," I said, and I thought that was fear I saw in his eyes. "A request from the English department."

The tension went out of his shoulders and I explained Lucas Roosevelt's request. "Other classes meet in those classrooms when English isn't using it," Oscar said.

"I'm not asking for anything specific to English," I said. "I'm talking about standard academic format." I handed around the pages I'd printed.

"Dr. Conrad?" I asked. "Would you have any objection to a science paper presented this way?"

She laughed. "Objection? I'd be delighted to have the formatting done for them."

Marie-Carmel Etienne agreed. "As you probably know, students have to take a computer proficiency test when they arrive at Eastern." I loved listening to her, all those "th" sounds rendered as zees. "Those who score below a certain range have to take a class in basic computer skills, where we teach them how to change the defaults in various programs. But a lot of students slip through the net and don't have these skills themselves."

"Even more reason why they should be learning them in class," Oscar said.

Jackie Conrad, Marie-Carmel, and I all began speaking at once, complaining that we had too much of our subjects to teach to get into such details.

Finally, Oscar held up his hand. "I'll look into it," he said.

"Excellent," Bobeaux said. "I'll expect some feedback by our next meeting."

We left the building, passing a hipster girl with Ray-Ban wayfarers and a white panama hat, carrying a trade paperback edition of *On The Road*. Her companion was a young guy wearing a hot pink polo shirt with a bright green T-shirt underneath, peeking out at the collar.

"College fashions," Jackie said.

"When I went to school here I lived in polo shirts and khakis," I said. "My roommate was a T-shirt and ripped jeans kind of guy so we never had confusion over wardrobe." I had a sudden memory. "The only problem we had was that we wore the same size and style of shoes—Sperry Top-Siders." I looked down at my feet, where I was wearing those very same shoes. "I guess people don't really change."

"Some do," Jackie said. "I wore sneakers in college and looked down at the old ladies who wore sensible shoes. And look at me now."

All the talk of shoes reminded me, as I walked back to Lili's office, of the faded Chucks Don Lamprey had worn. He never had the chance to see his style change with age, but at least I felt we were closer to figuring out what had happened to him.

32 – Gunshots

When I knocked at Lili's office door, I got no answer except the scrabbling of doggie toenails on the wood floor and snuffling at the door. I tried the handle and it was unlocked, so I pushed it open. "Lili?"

Rochester launched himself at me. "Yes, I know, you missed me," I said, as he put his paws on my thighs and sniffed me. "Where's Lili?"

I looked around the office. Lili was like my mother in that, like nature, she abhorred a vacuum. Every inch of wall space, other than the floor-to-ceiling windows, was covered with her own photos and the work of others, friends, students, colleagues and idols. Her shelves were stacked with big art books and souvenirs of her travels – South American fabric panels, an enameled vase from Turkey, wooden animals from Africa.

I finally saw a post-it on her computer screen. "Steve: Had to help a student with a darkroom problem. Talk to you later."

I wrote my own. "Auntie Em: I hate Kansas. I'm leaving and taking the dog." I added my name, a heart, and a couple of Os and Xs.

It was still daylight when got home, so I took Rochester for a long walk along the nature preserve and down toward the river. The current was strong, bubbling around rocks and splashing against submerged tree branches. Washington had made his famous crossing of the Delaware a few miles upriver from where we stood, on a bitter Christmas morning.

As a kid, I'd gone to the recreation of that crossing, Grace Kelly's brother playing General Washington, local fathers and businessmen dressed in colonial era uniforms rowing flat-bottomed Durham boats, letting the current carry them down toward Trenton. I didn't think, back then, of what a daring leap those soldiers had made, braving not just the ice-choked river but the Hessian soldiers garrisoned at Trenton, hoping that they'd be too wiped out from holiday celebrations to put up a good fight.

Now that I'd made a few dangerous crossings myself, I appreciated more what they'd done. I hadn't risked my life the way soldiers like Tamsen Morgan's husband had, but I had launched myself into the unknown a few times, stepping through the prison gates that first day, then stepping out a year later completely on my own. Coming back home to Stewart's Crossing with my tail between my legs, starting my life over.

I had come to understand how precious this life was, and how much the love of those around me mattered. When we reached Ferry Road, I tugged on Rochester's leash and turned him inland, toward home.

Darkness fell quickly as we walked inland. Cars whizzed by us in the deepening gloom, some drivers without headlights on. The pines and firs in the nature preserve huddled together, blocking my view of anything to the right or left. An owl hooted somewhere and a nearby car horn blared.

We had just reached the entrance to River Bend when I heard three gunshots, one after another, very fast. Rochester spooked and reared backward at me, knocking me to the ground.

Like many dogs, Rochester hated sudden, loud noises like thunder and firecrackers. He was even more phobic because he was there when Caroline was shot to death while walking him.

The gunshots made him completely nuts. While I was trying to get up from the ground, he was pulling on his leash as if he was going to tow me all the way back home. I scrambled forward on my hands and knees, tugging him toward me like he was a fish I was reeling in. I caught up with him by a big oak tree, and wrapped my arms around his neck. "It's all right, puppy," I said. "It's okay."

As I leaned back against the oak and sat on the sidewalk, holding his head against my chest, I realized that someone might have been aiming directly at me. Fortunately, we were blocked by the massive trunk, and I couldn't hear anyone coming toward us, on foot or by car.

My body started to shake but I struggled to hold myself together for Rochester's sake. He was already freaked out, and if he sensed I was scared that would only make things worse for him.

I took a couple of deep breaths, then felt my arms and legs. No blood, no pain.

I stayed there on the sidewalk, holding Rochester, until we both stopped shaking, then stood up. He immediately lunged forward, eager to get back home. I race-walked behind him, and as we got closer to the house my brain was able to work logically again. Why would someone want to shoot me? I'd put myself in danger a few times, but I always knew who I was up against. Now, I was baffled. Had they been warning shots? Scaring me away from investigating the body in the Meeting House? Was it someone Rick and I had spoken to in the course of the investigation?

From the speed of the shots, I figured they had come from a moving vehicle. Since there were only three, and I didn't know of any gun that could only shoot three shots before needing to be recocked or reloaded, I figured that the shooter and his or her weapon had probably gotten out of range by then.

As soon as we got inside, Rochester scrambled up the stairs and crawled beneath my bed, his place of refuge during storms or loud holidays. I sat Indian-style on the floor beside him, one hand petting his tail, the only part of him I could reach, and took a couple more deep breaths, trying to push the tension away. Once my heart rate and pulse had returned to normal, I called Rick.

"I think somebody shot at me this evening," I said, when he answered.

"You think?"

"Well, I'm not bleeding." I explained how I had heard the shots, and how Rochester had freaked out. "That's what made me think they were bullets, because of the way he reacted. Dogs have pretty acute hearing—I bet he can distinguish the sound of gun shots. Probably reminds him of when Caroline was killed." I stroked his tail once more. "He's under the bed now."

"Could it have been a hunter?" Rick asked. "That area along Ferry Road attracts wildlife, and you're close to the river there. Duck season doesn't start for a couple of weeks, but that doesn't stop some folks."

"I suppose it could have been." My voice started to shake, which I hated, but I couldn't help it. "But what if it was someone shooting at me or Rochester? Maybe Eben Hosford. He has a shotgun, I saw it."

"He's a Quaker," Rick said. "They're supposed to be non-violent, remember? Doesn't eliminate him, but still. Anybody else you might have pissed off lately?"

I reached for Rochester's head, but he scooted away. "I was in a meeting with Peter Bobeaux this afternoon. And I sort of tried to get a rise out of him." I stopped. "Oh, Christ. Lili told me that he used to hunt with a rifle when he was in the UAE."

Rick groaned. "What the hell are you doing meeting with this guy? Didn't I tell you I was going to handle things?"

"It wasn't a one-on-one. A committee meeting. We were talking about the possibility of identity theft at Eastern. I hinted that a student could apply under a false name. And that there were academics out there with faked credentials."

"I can't believe you were that stupid. You got to stop baiting suspects, Steve. You've had too many close calls already. Someday you're going to get hurt."

"Come on, Bobeaux is a college administrator. Not some homicidal maniac."

"Experience has shown that somebody doesn't need to be a gun nut to shoot at you, Brother Joe. You bring out the best in people." He took a deep breath. "Listen, I'm finishing up here. I'll get Rascal and come over. The dogs can play and you and I can talk."

While I waited for Rick, I called Lili. "I'm pretty shaken up," I said. I told her about the incident.

"But you're all right?"

"Yeah, I'm fine. More worried about Rochester. He's still freaked out."

"Who could want to shoot you?" she asked. "You're not teaching this term, so we can eliminate disgruntled students from the mix."

"Ha, ha," I said.

"Don't laugh. I read this article the other day – did you know there have been over fifty school shootings since 2010? I lock my classroom door five minutes into class and make anyone who's late knock to be let in."

"I talked to Rick and we came up with two choices, but neither of them sound reasonable. Eben Hosford and Peter Bobeaux. An old hippie Quaker and a college administrator. Neither of them sound like the kind to cruise down Ferry Street taking pot shots."

"Don't knock Peter out so quickly. He's said several times that he's a big NRA supporter."

"Yeah, I wish I had remembered what you'd said about his hunting habits before I baited him at the meeting." I heard Rick's truck pull up in my driveway, so I said goodbye to Lili and I left Rochester under the bed.

"I stopped at Genuardi's and got us both salads," he said, handing me a grocery bag. "We've both been eating too much rich food."

"You just want to be slim and handsome for Tamsen," I said, trying to lighten the mood despite the shivers I felt.

"I told you, I'm not sure I want to get involved with her." He sighed. "But she arranged for Justin to go home with one of the other kids after the game on Saturday so she and I can go out to dinner."

"Face it, you're hooked," I said, as Rascal shot past me and dashed up the stairs, following Rochester's scent.

"Moving on to the purpose of this visit," Rick said, as we walked into the kitchen. "Tell me exactly what happened. Where were you when you first heard these shots?"

I started with our walk back from the river, and noticed that my hands were shaking as I unpacked the food.

"After dinner we'll walk out there and you can show me where it happened. Tomorrow I'll go out and look for shell casings."

"Will you talk to both of them?"

"About what, Steve? I have no evidence to suggest that either of them had any motive to shoot at you. And honestly, knowing you, you could be snooping into a dozen other things without telling me." He pulled his salad toward him. "When you go online, you camouflage your identity, don't you?"

"What do you mean?"

"I mean, have you done something online that would get somebody mad at you, somebody who could track you down in the real world?"

"That's not the kind of thing I do, and you know it," I said. "All I ever do is look for information. And the only place I've been that I shouldn't have was that reunion database. I doubt that one of Peter Breaux's classmates has come after me."

He just shook his head. The dogs scrambled downstairs and began running around us in circles. Rick grabbed a piece of grilled chicken from one salad, broke it in half and fed a piece to each dog. "Now settle down, you vultures."

Rascal fell to the floor, looking up at his daddy, and Rochester did the same thing.

"When I spoke to Tamsen today, she said that Eben Hosford has been acting weird. There was a meeting of the renovation committee, and he's changed his tune—instead of arguing that they should leave the Meeting House as it is, now he says the building is cursed, and it ought to be torn down as soon as possible."

"You think our finding the body changed his attitude?" I asked.

"That would imply that he knew the body was there," Rick said.

"Which would imply that he put the body there," I said. Somehow, going back to the original crime and applying a logical analysis to it made me feel better. As we ate, we talked about ordinary stuff—where Rick might take Tamsen for another date, how I was going to manage getting Lili's furniture to my place and so on.

When we were finished, he packed up the containers and dumped them into my trash. "Let's take the dogs and go for a walk," he said. "You can show me where you were."

"I don't think Rochester will want to go back there," I said.

"He's a dog. He has an attention span of about sixty seconds, unless there's food involved."

I disagreed; I'd seen evidence that Rochester knew a lot more of what was going on than most people would give him credit for. We leashed the dogs and started walking toward Ferry Road.

It was completely dark, just the occasional house light or passing headlight. I'd always enjoyed walking Rochester at night, the two of us in our own little world, but after being shot at I felt differently. Every movement in a hedge, every door opening, every distant car horn made me jumpy.

We walked past the gate at the entrance to River Bend and I waved at the guard. A few feet farther ahead, Rochester planted his paws on the ground and wouldn't go any further.

"I told you so," I said to Rick. I tugged on Rochester's leash. "Come on, puppy, it's all right."

"You and your wacky dog," Rick said. "Give him to me."

We switched leashes, and Rascal took off toward Ferry Road, dragging me behind him. A moment later Rochester was rushing to catch up with his friend. Rascal and I stopped at the corner of Ferry Road. "This is where I was when I heard the shots," I said.

"And you say they came from behind you?"

"Uh-huh."

He handed me Rochester's leash. "Stay here." He left me with the two dogs and then, when there was a break in traffic on Ferry Road, he hurried across to the far side.

My heart beat faster though I wasn't sure why. I doubted that the shooter had been in the woods beside the road, and was sure he wouldn't still be there. Across from me, I saw Rick assume a shooting stance, raise his right arm and aim his flashlight at me, and I felt like a very exposed target.

"Don't shoot!" I yelled, only half in jest.

"Not going to!" he called back. I watched as he walked a few feet toward the river, repeated his stance with the flashlight, then back to where he was, then a few feet farther ahead and another repeat. Then when traffic broke he hurried back to me.

"I wanted to get a sense of the trajectory," he said. "It's too dark to waste time looking for bullets or shell casings but now at least I know what to tell the crime scene guys tomorrow."

I could tell Rochester was eager to get away from there. I was, too. We walked quickly back to the townhouse, and as we approached I saw Lili's car pull into my driveway.

"Hey, sweetie," I said, when I reached her. We kissed. "What are you doing here?"

"You sounded upset, so I thought I ought to come down."

I kissed her again as the dogs circled around us. "That was so nice of you," I said.

Rick and Rascal left a short while later, and Lili and I went up to the bedroom. Rochester got up on the bed and snuggled between us, and I stroked his gold flank and thanked him for pushing me down and out of the way of the bullets.

33 – Tough Situations

The summer heat suddenly returned the next morning, and by the time Rochester and I finished our walk I was soaked with sweat and he was panting like mad. I hurried through a shower while Lili poured granola for us.

"Even though I'm working at Friar Lake, it seems like I have so spend an awful lot of time on campus," I grumbled as I slid across from her at the kitchen table. "Joe Capodilupo needs to meet with me but he's too busy to come up to Friar Lake. Now that his son is the superintendent he never shows up."

"Don't worry, Rochester always has a home in my office," she said.

As if he knew Lili was talking about him, he rolled over on his belly beside her so she could scratch him while drinking her coffee. The domestic bliss hit me – soon, this would be our regular routine, with Lili living in my townhouse.

Would it someday be "our" townhouse? Would we get married, maybe buy a bigger house somewhere, with a yard for Rochester? I looked fondly down at my dog, who had a line of white spittle hanging from his mouth. I wiped it with a napkin and stood up to clear the table.

Lili suggested that Rochester ride up to Leighville in her car, since he was going to her office, and I agreed. After they left, I went up to my bedroom and dug out my father's handgun. If there was any chance that someone was shooting at me or my dog, I wanted to be prepared to defend us. I checked to make sure that it was loaded, and that the safety was on. Then I put it back in its zippered leather case, and stowed it in the bottom of my messenger bag.

I wasn't about to tell Lili or Rick. Both of them would worry, and I didn't have a carry permit for the gun, so I had to keep it in its case. I'd never felt I had to have it with me before.

It was odd driving up River Road without Rochester by my

side. I had become so accustomed to having him near me – what I called his Velcro behavior. He loved Lili, and she spoiled him almost as much as I did, but there were times when I looked around for him and realized he was with her instead of with me.

Sometimes I was grateful for the ability to back my chair up without worrying about running him over, to lie in bed and read without having him nuzzle me for playtime. But then there were times, like that morning, that I missed his company. I worried about that. He was a strong, healthy dog, but big dogs don't last as long as the little yappy ones. Goldens had a high rate of death due to cancer; they were prone to hip dysplasia, elbow problems, heart defects and eye problems.

I didn't know his exact birthday, because he'd been a rescue dog when Caroline got him, but I figured he was about two years old. How long would I have him in my life? Another ten years, twelve maybe? What would I do when he was gone? At least I hoped I'd have Lili with me. Despite all the affection I had for Rochester, I was coming to realize that I loved Lili more. Rochester's devotion was endearing and unconditional; but sometimes the love you have to work for, or deserve, matters even more.

I shook off those maudlin thoughts as I pulled up at the renovated carriage house where Joe Capodilupo's office was located. It was at the back of the Eastern campus, near the road that led down to Friar Lake. The quaint stone and shingle exterior was a contrast to the bland efficiency of the inside. To the left, beyond a receptionist's desk, was a series of cubicles and one big office, where I found Joe.

"How's my boy doing up there?" he asked, as we sat down. "Keeping everything going?"

"Yeah, he's very sharp," I said.

"I'm glad to see he's settling down. He had a rough time in his twenties – got married because he thought he ought to. Didn't think we'd love him if we knew who he really was." He shook his bald head. "Can you imagine that? That I wouldn't love my own son for something as dumb as who he wanted to sleep with?"

"He's lucky to have you," I said. "I've known guys with families that were a lot less accepting."

"Maybe it's working on a campus," Joe said. "You see all kinds of kids here, right? At least he doesn't have purple hair and a ring through his nose. Though I'd love him even if he did."

He pulled a manila folder over to him. "Now, about the fire at the stable," he said. "We have an opportunity to do something different with that part of the property, and the architect came up with some sketches. Let's see what you think."

We went over the ideas and then I left to walk to Harrow Hall. As I reached the front door, I spotted Peter Bobeaux in the wide, glassy lobby, but hurried up the curving staircase to Lili's office before he could say anything to me.

Rochester jumped up from his place beside Lili when I opened the door, and I ruffled him around the neck. "How's my boy?" I asked him, kneeling down to rub my face against his fur.

"I want to know what you meant by your comments yesterday."

I looked up to see Peter Bobeaux in the door of Lili's office. He was dressed in what I assumed was his regular uniform – another pressed white shirt, yellow power tie, and suit pants. All that was missing was the unlit cigar.

I stood up beside Lili, my left hand on the back of her chair. "About what?" With my right hand I reached into my messenger bag and unzipped the pouch containing my father's gun. I hoped I would have the courage to use it if I had to.

"You know what I'm talking about." Bobeaux stood there with his hands on his hips. "My credentials are completely valid."

I wrapped my hand around the pistol's grip. "If your real name is Peter Bobeaux," I said. "Not Peter Breaux."

It was like I'd stuck a pin into him, and he deflated.

"You'd better sit down, Peter," Lili said.

He sank into the chair across from her desk. I released my grip on the gun and pulled my hand out of the bag. "How did you know?" he asked me.

I pulled up Lili's other visitor chair, a spindle-back with the Eastern rising sun logo on it. "I'll get to that," I said as I sat, with the messenger bag on my lap. "Why don't you start. say, back in 1969?"

"I didn't want to go to Vietnam," he said. "Four boys from my high school had already come back in coffins. I just wanted to go to college, but my parents were dirt poor and it wasn't so easy to get scholarships back then."

"Were you a Quaker?" Lili asked.

He shook his head. "I was about as far from being a Quaker as you could be. I was in the color guard in high school. I used to go deer-hunting with my father in the fall. There was no way I could convince someone I was a pacifist. But one of my teachers was a Quaker, and I asked her for help. She connected me with a network that could smuggle me to Canada."

"Through Stewart's Crossing," I said.

"Yes. I didn't even know the name of the town back then, though. I got off the bus in Philadelphia and this man picked me up and drove me to the Meeting House."

"John Brannigan?" I asked.

"That was his name. He's not still alive, is he?"

"Passed away a few years ago. But a few members of his network are still alive."

"I should thank them," he said. "Once this is all behind me."

I considered him. He appeared to be relieved more than anything else. I couldn't see a weapon on him, and he didn't seem tense or angry.

"It had to be fate that brought me back here, though I didn't realize it at first. I was stunned when the college where I was teaching in Dubai closed its doors. I knew we were in the red, but…." He shook his head. "I assumed there would always be oil money to keep us going. But then one day there wasn't, and I was out of a job."

He turned to me. "It's tough to be unemployed at my age. I have another five years until I can collect Social Security. And who wants to hire someone for five years? I was lucky to find this opportunity. I'd have taken it even if I knew what I was coming back to."

I understood how he felt. I'd been in a similar situation myself when I left prison. Luck had brought me to Bucks County as well. I smiled at him and tried to look relaxed. "Why don't you tell us what happened when you got to the Meeting House?"

"There were two of us on the bus from Pittsburgh. Me and this other boy about my age."

"Don Lamprey," I said.

"I never knew his last name. We hardly spoke all the way across the state, both of us scared and caught up in our own heads. And he had a funny smell. At first I thought it was that he hadn't bathed in a couple of days, but then at a rest stop he pulled a joint out of his bag and offered to share it with me."

Bobeaux stood up and flexed his back muscles. "I'd never smoked it and I wasn't going to start. I changed seats for the rest of the trip. When we got to the Meeting House it was late at night. John let us into the building, and showed us the space between the walls. He told us to get some rest, and he'd be back for us the next morning."

He began to pace around Lili's office, dodging the student canvases against one wall and the pile of art books on the floor. "This girl came over to talk to us, but Don wasn't interested. He said that he was going out for a walk."

He was quiet for a moment, and I assumed he was remembering that night. "I don't remember the girl's name, just that she was kind of silly. We talked for a couple of hours, and then she had to leave to be home by her curfew. Don still wasn't back by then, and I started to wonder if he'd changed his mind."

He toyed with the watch around his wrist. "I sat up for a while longer and then dozed off. He didn't come back until the middle of the night. He said he had a bad headache and he went to sleep." He stopped by the door to her office, looked out the hallway up and down, then turned back to us.

"He stunk of the dope, and I guess I got a bit of a contact high. I slept, too, and when I woke up in the morning I climbed out of the closet to use the bathroom. When I got back I tried to wake him up, but he didn't answer me, and his body was cold."

"You didn't argue with him?" I asked. "Even innocently? Push him around?"

"There wasn't enough room in that space for an argument," he said. "We could both stand up, or we could both lie down. That was about it."

"Was there someplace he could have hit his head?" Lili asked.

"I couldn't see anything, but there was some blood congealed around his head, like he'd hit it or been hit there. I got scared. What if the police found him? I could be arrested for draft dodging, or worse, for killing him. I gathered up my stuff and climbed back out."

"You left him there?" I asked.

"He was already dead. There was nothing I could do for him."

Except report his death and give his family some closure after his disappearance, I thought. Then I remembered that Don Lamprey's family had hardly missed him.

"When John came back for me that morning, I told him that Don had decided to go home. I hoped he wouldn't look in the crawl space, at least not until I was gone. And I guess that's what happened."

He sat back down in the chair. "John took me to the train station in Trenton and bought me a ticket to Montreal, and I never looked back."

"How did you change your name?" Lili asked.

"That was an accident. When I got to the border I scrawled my name and the agent misread it. I knew I was on the run so I didn't challenge him. And I've been Peter Bobeaux ever since. I found a sympathetic admissions officer who helped me take the Canadian GED and get admitted to college. I did all the work for my degrees."

"You couldn't have been so successful if you hadn't," Lili said. I could tell that she'd already decided in his favor, even though at present we only had his word for what had happened that night. "You have an admirable teaching and administration record."

"Thank you." He smiled at her, and then he was silent for a moment.

"You have to understand, I was so scared back then. I was only a kid, and I had no idea what to do. I thought I'd put that poor boy out of my mind, but then my wife wanted to go to that Harvest Festival last month, and I recognized the Meeting House. When I heard someone say there was a body in the wall I hurried over there. I haven't been able to stop thinking about it since then."

Rochester got up and padded over to Bobeaux, then sat beside him, and Bobeaux reached down to pet his head. That decided me.

Rochester was a good judge of character, so if he liked Bobeaux the man couldn't be all bad.

"The detective investigating the case is a friend of mine," I said. "I'll give him a call and tell him you want to come in and talk to him."

Bobeaux nodded, and I called Rick. I handed my phone to Bobeaux, who explained who he was, and made arrangements to drive down to the police station in Stewart's Crossing.

After Bobeaux left Lili's office, I looked at her. "Do you believe him?"

"I do. I might have to start to like him, now that I know what he's been through."

"You don't have to go that far," I said. "He's still a blowhard." I reached for Rochester and scratched behind his head. "So then who or what killed Don Lamprey? He didn't curl up and die on his own."

"I can't help you with that," she said. "I teach art, not science."

I stood up. "Ah, but I know someone who does."

34 – Concussion

Before I left Lili's office, I checked the faculty schedules online. "Good deal," I said. "Jackie Conrad has office hours now." I leaned down to Rochester. "You stay here with Mama Lili."

She groaned at the nickname, and I laughed. If she was going to become Rochester's new mom, she'd have to get accustomed to being called silly names. I zipped up the gun pouch, put my messenger bag over my shoulder and walked out.

Everywhere I looked, students in T-shirts, shorts and flip-flops were taking advantage of what was probably the last warm day of the season. The guy walking in front of me had *If you can read this, thank a teacher*, on his back. Right below it, though, was *And if you can read this in English, thank a Marine*. Certainly not a shirt Don Lamprey or Peter Breaux would have worn.

As I walked to Green Hall, where the science faculty had their offices, I thought about what I needed to ask Jackie.

She had a student with her when I arrived, going over the function of the adrenal gland in preparation for an exam. When she was finished I asked, "Do you have a minute for a non-student-related question?"

"Absolutely. Come on in." As I sat, she asked, "How's that handsome dog of yours?"

I remembered that the first time I met her, she'd immediately figured out, from the hair on my slacks, that I had a Golden.

"He's shaken up at the moment," I said. "We had an incident last night." I told her about the shooting, trying to minimize its importance, but Jackie wasn't buying it.

"You think the person who killed that boy at the Meeting House is after you now?"

I shook my head. "He died over forty years ago, and we're not even sure that someone killed him. His death might have been an accident." I leaned forward. "Can you get a concussion somehow, recover, and then die from it later?"

"That's certainly not the kind of question I get from students. You think that might have happened to this boy?"

I nodded, and explained, without using his name, what Peter Bobeaux had told me. "I'm wondering if the guy could have gotten hit on the head somewhere, but then recovered enough to go back to the Meeting House and fall asleep."

"And never wake up," she said.

"And never wake up."

She turned to her computer and did some typing. "First of all, a concussion is basically a disturbance of brain function that follows a blow to the head. You said this other boy saw blood around the dead boy's head?"

"Yes."

"Was there an autopsy?"

"There wasn't a lot of body left after forty years," I said. "But there was some damage to the skull that was consistent with a head injury."

"You sound like you've watched a lot of cop programs on TV," she said drily. "Okay. So let's assume he hit his head somehow. Now, loss of consciousness is relatively rare in concussions – only about ten percent of the time. So it's likely he was still awake and functional after he got hit."

"Wasn't there an incident a while ago?" I asked. "An actress who hit her head while skiing?"

"I remember that. She went back home, didn't she? And didn't get treatment, and then died soon after." She did a quick search. "It says here that she suffered blunt trauma to the head, which is consistent with your victim. In a case like hers, 'blood from a damaged but still-pumping artery can quickly pool in the brain, creating pressure that must be relieved before irreparable damage is caused'."

She sat back. "They call this syndrome 'Talk and Die'," she said. "Patients can walk and talk, without realizing how serious their injury is."

"So that could have happened to this boy," I said. "He could have hit his head when he was out somewhere, and then gone back to the Meeting House. He told the boy he was with that he had a headache."

"That's consistent," she said.

"The boy with him said that he might have been smoking dope, too."

"That could have contributed to his unawareness of how serious his condition was," she said. "And as you and I have both seen, teenagers think they're bullet-proof. He probably just shrugged the headache off."

"So the question now is how he hit his head in the first place," I said. "He could have been out walking in the woods around the Meeting House in the dark. Or somebody could have hit him. Either on purpose or accidentally."

"There's your difference," she said, sitting back. "Between an accident and a murder."

The word "murder" reminded me that someone had shot at me, and that I had my dad's handgun in my messenger bag. I thanked Jackie and left Green Hall. Everywhere I looked I saw college students fooling around – pushing each other playfully, tackling in a pick-up football game, riding a skateboard. Had what happened to Don Lamprey been an accident?

It seemed like a good possibility. He could have gone out for a walk in the woods, knocked up against a branch and, despite the blood, thought nothing of it. He was nineteen, after all, and on the run from a different life-threatening situation.

But suppose he'd gone out to the woods for more than just a walk – to connect with a dealer who might buy the dope he'd stolen from his brothers. When I was a teenager, we had to sit through endless anti-drug movies and lectures. People who used drugs were bad, and those who sold them were even worse. Suppose one of them had knocked Don out, taken his dope and his cash?

The cash. According to his brother, Don Lamprey had stolen almost a thousand dollars he and his brothers had earned from their dope sales back in Zelienople. Where had it gone? Had it disintegrated? Or had whoever killed Don stolen it?

I stopped outside Harrow Hall and dialed Rick. "Follow the money," I said.

"I'm right in the middle of my conversation with Breaux or Bobeaux or whatever his name is. What are you babbling about?"

"Arnold Lamprey said that his brother stole nearly a grand from him," I said. "But there wasn't any money with the body, was there?"

"No."

"Ask Breaux about it. Did Don flash the cash around? Did Breaux pick his pocket after he was dead?"

"You have a ghoulish imagination," Rick said. "But I'll ask him."

When I got back to Lili's office, she was deep in conversation with a student, analyzing a black and white photo, so I grabbed my dog and waved goodbye. My car had been baking in the sun, so I had to turn the air conditioning on full blast and open the windows until it cooled down. Rochester stuck his head out his window, and I was tempted to do the same thing. Not only to cool down – but to blow away all the dark thoughts that kept popping into my head.

When I got back to Friar Lake I found an email from Mark Figueroa. He wanted to resign from doing any design work. No excuse given.

Crap. That might have pleased Joey Capodilupo but not me. Without Mark's help I'd be lost. I called his store. "Can we talk about this, please?" I asked.

"There isn't anything to talk about."

"Sure there is. How about we meet for a coffee at The Chocolate Ear. Say 5:30? I'll buy. Please?"

He sighed. "All right."

I hung up and took Rochester for a walk around Friar Lake, checking on progress. Plumbers had begun work in the gutted dormitories, electricians were in the kitchen, and the pews had been stacked to one side of the chapel.

It was interesting to see the way the basic structure of the old buildings had been preserved: slate roof, stone buttresses, stained glass windows in the chapel. Eastern's campus was the same way – old buildings repurposed for new uses, new ones constructed to fit into the overall look of the campus. Even the Meeting House in Stewart's Crossing was a mix of original construction and later renovation, so that the long-ago vision of those first Quakers was still evident to today's worshippers.

Rochester's discovery of the tennis sneaker, only two weeks

before, had shown us that what had happened back in 1969 could still have reverberations for the people who survived those years. I was still tempted to hack, and Rick's frequent references to those activities showed me he sometimes thought of me as an unrepentant criminal.

Our romantic histories were still with us, too. My ideas about women had been formed by my marriage to Mary, and I knew I was moving more carefully with Lili because of them. She had her own past love life – two ex-husbands and various other flings. Rick's marriage had imploded when his wife left him for a firefighter; Tamsen's husband died a war hero; and Mark had been treated badly by boyfriends. Even Gail must have had problems with that ex-boyfriend who'd roomed with Declan.

We all had our talents, too. Lili was an excellent photographer and teacher. Mark had design skills, Rick was a dogged investigator. Gail was a terrific baker, and Declan had managed to begin his career and get the work permit he needed to stay in the States. I knew I was a decent writer and a competent teacher – but what if my one true skill was hacking, which was illegal? How could I leave my past behind if it meant also giving up the thing I was really good at?

I wondered if we could put together a program that would explore some of the conflicts from the sixties, and the reverberations that were still with us today. Maybe a history professor could sketch out the timeline, and someone from sociology talk about the long-lasting effects of the war on our country.

I was once again excited about my job, and hurried back to my office, tugging Rochester along, so I could get back to work.

35 – Café Confrontation

By the end of the day, I had the outline of a program on "The 1960s and Beyond" prepared and I was researching recruiting faculty to carry it out. I was so caught up in ideas that it took me a minute to recognize that my cell was ringing.

"Hey, Rick," I said, the phone cradled at my ear, still typing possibilities.

"Finished up with Dr. Bobeaux, aka Peter Breaux," he said. "It's an interesting story. What did you think of it?"

"Lili believes him, and I guess I do, too. Did you ask him about the cash?"

"He swears he didn't know Lamprey was carrying any money. He said he had about a hundred bucks of his own, that's all. And when I pressed him, he started telling me all this stuff he did in Canada to make money before his scholarships kicked in."

"You want to compare notes on what he told you versus what he told Lili and me?"

"Yeah, that's probably a good idea."

We made plans to meet at The Chocolate Ear for a few minutes before my rendezvous with Mark Figueroa. "Hey, did you ever get a chance to look around for shell casings where somebody shot at me last night?"

"I sent the crime scene guys. Not sure if they found anything, but I'll check on it."

"I also talked to a professor at Eastern about concussions," I said. "I'll tell you what she said when I see you."

I kept getting program ideas that I wanted to put down, even as I knew I needed to close up and hurry to Stewart's Crossing. I settled for using my phone as a voice recorder as I drove, which confused Rochester, who kept turning to look at me each time I started talking.

Despite my delaying, I got to The Chocolate Ear first and staked out a table on the sidewalk. I left Rochester there and went inside to order, and by the time I returned with iced coffee for Rick and myself, and a biscuit for Rochester, Rick was there with my dog.

"Tell me what Bobeaux told you," he said, as I sat down.

I repeated it all.

"That's the same story he gave me," Rick said. "I'm not sure I believe him, but there doesn't seem to be any other choice."

"The details tie in with what we already knew," I said. "That he and Don arrived by bus, that he met Brannigan the next morning alone. You're sure he didn't take the money from Don?"

"If he did, he's a hell of an inventive liar," Rick said. "If he had an extra grand back in 1969, he could have lived just fine until school started in the fall and he wouldn't have had to clean toilets, pick weeds or any of the other crap jobs he told me were the only ones he could get."

"How about fingerprints?" I asked. "Did you ever check on those?"

"Yeah. The crime scene guys lifted dozens of different prints from the inside of that room, which is consistent with the story that a number of teenagers moved through there. Most of them couldn't be matched to anyone in the IAFIS system."

I knew from past experience that was the master fingerprint database maintained by the FBI. "How about Bobeaux's prints?"

"Yeah, we matched them to ones from inside the room. And I got an officer in Zelienople to go out to Arnold's house and open up a box of Don's stuff. Managed to get some decent prints there, and used them to eliminate a bunch of the unidentified ones."

He shook his head. "I don't get how Don Lamprey could go to sleep and not wake up. Where'd the bang on his head come from?"

"Bobeaux says that Don went out somewhere, and that when he came back he complained of a headache. Suppose he fell, or got hit, while he was out, and had pressure building up in his brain that didn't affect him right away." I told Rick what Jackie Conrad had said, about Talk and Die syndrome.

"That part makes sense," Rick said. "Say Don found the hippies and got high with them, then when he was walking in the woods in the dark, he tripped and hit his head."

I nodded. The neurons were firing in my brain, fast and

furious, and I remembered my thoughts after I spoke with Jackie. "That could make him disoriented enough to drop the cash and whatever dope he had let. But he was able to get back to the Meeting House and climb into the hidey-hole."

"I'm liking this theory," Rick said. "If we wipe out Dr. Bobeaux as a suspect, then what we have is a death that wasn't a murder, which is the end of my investigation. That will make the chief happy, and the mayor, too."

"But hold up a sec," I said. "There's also the chance that it might not have been an accident. Remember, the money is still missing. Bob Freehl told me that hippies used to camp in those woods, and that you could smell the dope from Main Street. Suppose Don smelled the smoke, and went looking for those hippies, hoping to sell them the dope he took from his brothers."

"And someone robbed him?" Rick asked. "I'd have to ask Bob if there were any reports of violence out there in the woods, or if it was just some happy love hippie thing."

"Bob said that the cops arrested those hippies a few times but could never make the charges stick. Would you guys still have those records? Maybe there's someone you could talk to."

"Like I told you before, that stuff hasn't been digitized," he said. "Boxes of paper and rolls of microfilm, in the file room at the back of the station. But maybe it's time I dug in."

"Want me to help?"

He shook his head. "Not with police files. Though I appreciate the offer." He stood up holding his iced coffee. "I'd better get back to the station. I'll call Bob, and then head to the records room. I've got a long night ahead of me."

Rick petted Rochester once more, then started back to the station. As I watched him go, I saw a tiny Fiat pull up down the block, and the guy who emerged from the front seat had a scruffy beard with a couple of dreads in it. He wore huarache sandals, knee-length shorts, and a T-shirt that read "Code. Ship. Repeat." Over his shoulder he carried a woven Mexican bag in bright red and yellow.

He reminded me of so many of the guys I'd worked with in Silicon Valley. Would I have turned out like him if I hadn't met and married Mary, who had tried to mold me into the kind of husband she wanted?

I doubted it. I'd been raised in the decades between the old hippie and the new hippie movements. I remembered the occasional tie-dyed T-shirt from my childhood, but the 1980s were the Reagan years, a conservative reaction to the looser sixties and seventies.

The clock had turned again, and what was old was now new. Eastern students and graduates were wearing tie-dyed T-shirts and granny glasses and dropping out of the rat race just like their predecessors had forty years before.

Rochester was nosing a copy of the Stewart's Crossing *Boat-Gazette*, our local weekly newspaper, that had fallen to the ground beneath my table, and I picked it up and started to read while I waited for Mark Figueroa to arrive.

The front-page headline was "Friends Renovation Stalled." Because the Meeting House had become a crime scene, rehab work had been halted temporarily. That recess allowed the critics of the project to complain again.

Were there other secrets hidden in that building? It was a couple of hundred years old, after all. And Quakers were human beings, so it was possible that all kinds of stuff could have gone on in the past, which someone didn't want dredged up.

The article quoted Eben Hosford, which surprised me, because he didn't seem like the kind of guy who was easy to get hold of. He wanted the Meeting dissolved, or merged with the one in Yardley or Lahaska. The building should be razed, and the site sold to real estate developers. I couldn't see Hannah Palmer or her sister or any of the other Quakers I'd met going along with that.

One of the disadvantages of small-town life is that we only have a weekly paper, rather than a daily, and thus our local news is often stale before it even arrives. I was sure that the fate of the Meeting House would take a long time to resolve, and that the *Boat-Gazette* would always be a few days behind. No wonder college students had a reputation for disdaining print media. The "real" story was more likely to be found in someone's Twitter feed, in Facebook posts or Pinterest images. They were more up-to-date, at least.

By the time Mark arrived, it was early evening and still quite warm. He went inside and got an iced tea, then joined me and Rochester outside.

"I'm sorry to leave you in the lurch, but I don't want to work with Joey," Mark said. "He says that I have a low self-image, and that's why I've been dating jerks. And then he had the balls to tell me that he thought the carpeting I picked out was ugly."

"So which one pissed you off more?" I asked. "His criticizing your taste in men, or in carpet?"

Mark glared at me, but then he had to laugh. "The carpet. I have damned good taste when it comes to design."

"I have to say I never liked the combination of green and brown," I said. "It reminded me too much of what comes out of Rochester when he's sick."

"This is really the limit," Mark said, in mock anger. "Now even a straight guy is criticizing my taste." He sighed. "I guess you have a point. It was a drab combination."

"But you could do better, right?" I asked. "You can show Joey Capodilupo that you do have good taste by finding a carpet that'll knock his socks off."

"Speaking of which, have you seen his feet? They're enormous."

"TMI," I said, holding up my hands.

Suddenly, Rochester jumped to his feet and started barking. "What's up with you, dog?" I asked, grabbing his collar. I looked up and saw Eben Hosford approaching.

"Can you hold him for a minute?" I asked Mark. "I know that Rick wants to talk to that guy."

I shoved Rochester toward him, still barking, and Mark leaned down to him and spoke directly into his ear. "Excuse me, dog? Can I help you with something?"

I pulled my phone out and texted Rick. *eben h @ gails*. Rochester stopped barking long enough to lick Mark's face.

Mark said, "Eww," and recoiled as Eben approached us.

"Ornery beast," Eben said as he passed, his open shoulder bag sagging with soap and candles. "You watch out I don't shoot him sometime."

I held my tongue, not wanting to scare the old man off before Rick arrived. But I felt in my messenger bag for my dad's gun, just in case. And I hoped Rick had kept his cell phone handy during his records search.

Eben went inside, and through the big windows I saw him showing some candles and soap to Gail. I sent her a mental message to take her time looking at the merchandise, giving Rick a chance to get there. But all circuits must have been busy, because instead I saw her shaking her head, and Eben began to pack up his wares.

As I looked at Hosford, my brain began to assemble all the information I knew about him. He was an old hippie, who had been around Stewart's Crossing in the sixties. He probably smoked dope and might have been part of the group that hung out in the woods behind the Meeting House.

He hadn't been a Quaker back then, but he had joined the Meeting soon after. Why? Because he knew what had happened to Don Lamprey and wanted to protect the evidence? Was he the one who had sabotaged the Meeting House heater so that no one would smell the decaying body?

And biggest question, could Hosford be Don's killer? I saw him finish packing up and head for the front door. Rick was still nowhere in sight.

I had to stall Hosford. When he walked out the door, I called, "Hey, Eben."

He looked over at me, and Rochester growled. I petted the dog and said, "You were around Stewart's Crossing in the sixties, weren't you?"

"What business is it of yours?"

"Did you hang around behind the Meeting House back then, smoking dope?"

"What I do or did is no concern of yours. You keep your nose out of my affairs."

"You probably weren't surprised when Rochester found that sneaker in the false wall at the Meeting House," I said. "You knew that boy, didn't you?"

"He was alive the last time I saw him!"

He reached into his shoulder bag and pulled out a short-barreled shotgun. He pointed it at me and said, "I told you, stay out of my business. Or you'll have a 12-gauge Mossberg in your face."

36 – Jailhouse Lawyer

I wrapped my free hand around the grip of my dad's gun, keeping it inside the messenger bag. Could I get the gun out, and get in a shot at Eben Hosford before he shot me? I remembered what Rick had said when we were at the shooting range together. Aim for body mass.

Shouldn't be too hard, with the man six feet away from me. But I was no kind of quick draw. I'd probably fumble the gun out of my bag, screw around too long with the safety, and end up with a bullet in my brain.

"Put the gun down, Mr. Hosford."

I turned and looked behind me. Rick was a few hundred yards away, approaching us carefully. He had his hand on the holster of his gun, still attached to his belt.

"I didn't kill him!" Hosford said, waving the shotgun. It looked like an old model, but still very threatening and effective. "He came around our campfire, looking to sell his dope, but none of us had any cash. He cursed us out and walked away. I got up and followed him through the woods."

My heart was beating like crazy, and Rochester growled and strained to go after Eben. I held onto the dog's collar with all my strength. Out of the corner of my eye I saw Mark Figueroa grasping the edge of the table, his eyes wide with fright.

Rick kept walking calmly toward us, keeping his hand on his gun in his holster. I was sure that a shoot-out on Main Street was the last thing he wanted. Cars moved past us quickly, oblivious to the drama taking place on the sidewalk. I was scared that one of them would blow a horn and startle Eben into shooting.

"Dumb ass came snooping around us in the woods, trying to sell some dope he said was excellent," Eben said defiantly. "But none of us knew him so we shooed him away. He could have been a narc for all we knew."

He cocked the shotgun and my heart raced. With my left hand

I gripped Rochester's collar; with my right I ease the gun upward, doing my best to keep one eye on Eben and one on Rochester. I'd seen the way the dog reacted when he thought I was in danger. This time, though, I was going to be the one to protect him.

"I was curious, so I followed him through the woods. Dumb ass didn't even have a flashlight, walked into the branch of a big old tree. Knocked him out."

I glanced to the side. Rick was moving forward carefully, his weapon still holstered, and still too far away to get a good shot.

"So you didn't hit him yourself?" I asked, to keep Eben talking, keep his mind focused on the past.

"Why would I hit him? I just wanted to see where he went. I had a few bucks, and if he wasn't a narc I was going to buy some dope from him. When he fell, I went right over to him, to make sure he was still breathing."

He waved the rifle. "Yeah, I stole the dope. And all the cash he had on him. But then I hung around in the shadows and waited to make sure he woke up. I wasn't going to just leave him there."

I didn't think that was the whole story, but at least Eben had demonstrated enough human feeling not to leave an injured man alone in the woods. "What happened when he did wake up?" I asked. "Did you two argue?"

Eben shook his head. "I thought he'd make a fuss when he found out he'd been robbed, that he might go for the police and accuse us dirty hippies. So I followed him as he wandered through the woods for a while, until he found his way to the Meeting House."

Traffic began to move more slowly on Main Street. I wondered if the drivers had noticed the armed man standing in front of the café, and I prayed that none of them would try to interfere – or that someone impatient at the back of the line would start honking and disturb our tentative equilibrium.

Eben stopped talking to rub his eyes, and the shotgun waved madly. "It was the middle of the night by then, and I was tired. I went on back to where we were camping and went to sleep, and I didn't think no more about it for a few days. But then I got kinda curious. What was that boy doing sneaking around the Meeting House in the dead of night? I knew this Quaker girl, Debbie, so I asked her if she knew him."

"Debbie Allen?"

He nodded. "She told me, all in confidence, she said, that he was a draft dodger supposed to be on his way to Canada. But he had changed his mind at night and gone back home instead."

He wiped his brow with the hand that wasn't holding the rifle. "I didn't see how he had gone anywhere when I'd taken all his money. I started to worry about him. What if he'd gone back into the woods after I left him, and passed out again? I combed every inch of those woods and couldn't find a trace of him."

With relief, I realized that Rick was only a few feet away, barely beyond the reach of the café's awnings. I released my grip on my gun – but I held onto the dog.

"We can talk about this at the station, Mr. Hosford," Rick said. "Now please, put down the shotgun."

But Eben was still too lost in the past to stop. "I started going to the Meetings with Debbie," Eben said. "I had to know what happened to that boy. It was like a sickness inside me."

I looked through the window into the café. Gail was standing behind the cash counter, ready to duck at any minute. Mark was frozen next to me. Rochester kept growling, a low sound that rose at the base of his throat and was more menacing than anything I'd ever heard from him.

Behind Hosford, I saw a Stewart's Crossing police car stop at the intersection of Main and Ferry, beneath the traffic light, directing cars away from us.

I couldn't help myself. "You didn't know about the false wall?" I asked.

"Not back then. But after a week that boy started to smell. Everyone else said it was a raccoon or possum, but I knew better. One night I broke into the Meeting House and followed my nose."

"Why didn't you tell anyone then?" I asked.

"I knew they'd blame it on me." He began to shake. "We just wanted to be left alone to smoke our dope, I tell you. But the pigs hated us and people in town used to shy away whenever they saw us. I knew no one would believe me. I broke a couple of parts off the heater so that no one else would go inside the Meeting. By the time they got it fixed the smell was gone."

He pulled the shotgun up and racked it. "I'm not going to prison. You can't lock me up. I'd rather die."

Keep waving that shotgun, I thought, and you'll get your wish. From Rick, I knew the term "suicide by cop," when somebody who doesn't have the courage to end his own life does something to convince the police to do it for him. I hoped that wasn't the way this day was going to end.

Another squad car pulled up beside the first, and two officers jumped out, guns ready, approaching quietly down the middle of Main Street. A woman with a small boy by the hand stepped out of the front door of the drugstore, saw the cops, and hurried back inside.

The sun's last rays flared against the windows of the old bank building. In the distance I heard a train's whistle. I thought for a moment about Lili. She was going to be really pissed off if I got killed, just as we were moving our relationship to the next level. I wouldn't be too happy about it, either.

"I've lived for forty-some years worrying about what happened to that boy," Hosford said. "I tell you, I've done my time."

Once again, I couldn't help myself. I had to jump in. "There's a statute of limitations for theft," I said. "If that's all you did, then the time to prosecute you has long since expired."

"Shut up, Steve," Rick said.

"It's true, though, isn't it?" I twisted my head to look at him, with my hand still on Rochester's collar. "His story matches the one you heard from Peter Bobeaux." I'd been a bit of a jailhouse lawyer when I was incarcerated, helping my fellow inmates understand the law. "There's nothing you can charge him with that would stick. You and I both know there's no way Eben could have knocked Don Lamprey dead and then gotten his body back into that narrow space without Peter Bobeaux knowing about it. Don had to get back in there himself, which means he was alive when Eben saw him last."

The two cops behind Hosford continued their slow movement toward us. A cool breeze swept down the street and shook loose a couple of dead leaves from the maple above us.

I looked back at Hosford. "That boy's family would like to

know what happened to him. You owe him that much. Help us put together a story for them."

"Is that true?" Hosford asked Rick, still holding his shotgun, though I noticed he'd taken his finger off the trigger. "You can't arrest me for anything?"

"I can arrest you, and I will, for waving a shotgun in the middle of Main Street," Rick said. "But Steve's right. The statute of limitations for theft is long since expired, and you could plead out to a misdemeanor for the gun offense and get off with a fine."

I let go of my dog and stood up. Rochester stopped growling but he looked poised to jump at any moment. "Please, Eben," I said. "Put the shotgun down, and tell your story to Rick. That's the only way you're ever going to put this behind you."

He dropped the shotgun to the ground and began to weep. I kicked the gun away from him, and Rochester lunged forward, intent on staying by my side. I grabbed his collar once again.

Rick strode up with a pair of handcuffs. "Eben Hosford, in accordance with the provisions of the Commonwealth of Pennsylvania Title 18, Chapter 61, I'm taking you into custody for displaying a firearm in a manner dangerous to public safety."

The two cops hurried up, and one of them grabbed the shotgun from the ground. "Careful with that," Hosford grumbled. "It's an antique."

The cop sniffed the barrel. "But one that's been fired recently," he said. "I can see the gunpowder residue."

Rick began to read the old man his rights as he led him down the sidewalk toward the police station. The two uniformed officers headed back toward where they'd left their squad car, beneath the traffic light.

My brain was still buzzing, though. If Hosford's gun had been fired recently, did that mean he was the one who'd shot at me the night before? And why? The only thing I'd done to attract his attention was walk my dog past his house.

Did that mean there was someone else out there who had a grudge against me?

37 – Nasty, Brutish and Short

The cops moved their car, and traffic began to pass by again on Main Street. I looked over at Mark Figueroa, who appeared shell-shocked. "You okay?" I asked.

"That guy could have killed you," he said. "Or me. Or even your dog."

I didn't want to tell Mark that I'd mourn Rochester a lot more than I'd mourn him. Though it was the truth, it wasn't the kind of thing you say to another human being.

"I took a gamble," I said. "I knew there had to be a reasonable solution to the question of how that boy died, and I guessed that Eben had it. And despite the fact that he's creepy and cranky, I didn't see him as a murderer."

"You can't tell that," Mark said. "When I was in college, I went on a summer study program in England, and a girl I was friendly with started to date this bartender at the local pub. A bunch of us used to hang out with him, play darts, drink pints, talk. When the summer was over I went back to college and she stayed in Cambridge with him. A couple of months later he got angry at her and broke her neck."

"That's awful," I said.

"And all that time my friends and I spent with him, none of us had any idea he could do something like that." He shook his head. "You're crazy, Steve. Do you have some kind of death wish?"

"No, I don't," I said. "I just get an idea and I have to see it through."

That sounded eerily like my justification for hacking, and all of a sudden the aftereffect of all the adrenaline hit me, and I sunk back in my chair. Why did I keep doing things that put me in danger? It wasn't a death wish. I wanted to live too much for that. But it was the same kind of insatiable curiosity that had gotten me into trouble in the past.

I'd escaped this situation without harm. But what about the

night before, when someone had shot at me on Ferry Road? It had to have been Eben. Why else did it seem like his Mossberg had been recently fired? Had Rick asked Peter Bobeaux if he'd shot at me? Surely he'd have mentioned it if he had, and if Bobeaux had admitted then Rick wouldn't have let him go.

I'd have to get Rick to ask Eben where he'd been the night before, and if the cartridges the crime scene team had found matched Eben's gun. If they did? Then despite what I'd said to him about prosecution from the past, I'd see that he was arrested for attempted murder. Nobody shot at me and got away with it.

The realization hit me, and I shuddered. Suppose he'd hit me, killed me? Lili would have been devastated, and I would have put Rochester through the same thing he'd gone through with Caroline.

He sat up on his haunches and rested his head against my knee. I loved that familiar pressure, that physical sense of connection with him. We were bonded. How could I have risked that for something so stupid as a cowboy challenge to Hosford?

Could I even have shot the man if it looked like he was going to shoot me, or anyone with me? I thought I could. I remembered the feel of my hand on the gun's butt, the heaviness of the metal, the sense of power that holding it gave me.

I'd met some stone cold killers when I was in prison, even got friendly with one of them, a Mexican-American named Balbino. I never asked if that was his first or last name, but I spent a lot of time with him in the prison library, researching other cases like his. He told me that every person he'd killed had taken a little something out of him, to the point where he wasn't sure what was left.

That was the case with Eben, it seemed. There were plenty of old hippies around; I'd seen them in New York, Silicon Valley, and Bucks County. Some of them had been addled by drugs, while some simply loved the lifestyle they had found way back then. But what was wrong with Eben was more than just the passage of time, or being left behind by a culture that hadn't survived. The death of Don Lamprey, whether it was his fault or not, had taken something out of him.

Mark was still lost in his own thoughts as Gail came out of the café. "What was that all about?" she asked. She sat between us and set her cell phone on the table. "I couldn't hear inside the café but when I saw that shotgun come out of his bag I completely froze."

Mark explained to her, frequently stopping to complain about my actions. By the time he finished I felt even worse. Rush hour traffic on Main Street crept past, all those commuters and soccer moms having no idea what had just happened, probably complaining about traffic and how their kids wasted too much time online, and what were they going to have for dinner that night?

"He seemed like such a nice old man," Gail said. "I've bought candles and soap from him in the past but I didn't need anything today."

"You're probably the only person in town who thinks he's nice," I said. "Most people think he's a crank. Even the Quakers don't like him, and they're supposed to be nice to everybody."

"Even more reason why you should have avoided him," Mark said. "When I first moved here, I thought Stewart's Crossing was this charming little town where nothing bad happened."

I shook my head. "Everybody has secrets, whether they live in a big city or a small town. And bad things happen wherever you go."

Gail's phone buzzed, and she said, "I realized while I was watching Eben that if anything happened to me, I didn't want to die feeling like I'd missed any chances. So I called Declan and left him a message." She picked the phone up and stood, then walked a few feet away to talk in private.

"Listen, I'm sorry I put you in danger," I said to Mark. "Once he pulled out that shotgun I should have just sat down and shut up and waited for Rick. That was a stupid move on my part. I get caught up in my own head, and I forget about the effects what I'm doing will have on other people."

"I'll survive," he said. "You had no way of knowing he had that shotgun with him. And you did a good job of talking him down." He sighed. "And I agree with Gail. You know, life is short, don't let opportunities pass you by, all that crap."

"Thomas Hobbes said life is nasty, brutish and short," I said.

"Yeah, well, old Tom got it right," Mark said. "I suppose I could look for some new carpet for Friar Lake. Maybe even get Joey to help me with the samples." He smiled.

Gail came back to tell us she had plans to see Declan on Saturday night, and Mark said he'd call Joey and see if things could still be salvaged. He left, and Gail went back inside, but I stayed at the café, finishing my coffee and petting my dog. I drove Rochester back to River Bend, and we took a long walk around the community.

A little girl with training wheels on her pink bike rode past, wearing a matching pink helmet with a silver tiara glued to the top. I remembered riding my bike into Stewart's Crossing, baseball cards flapping on the spokes, blue plastic tassels hanging from the handlebars. The sense of freedom I felt, able to go wherever I wanted. I might have only had change in my pocket, but the world was mine.

Our parents had never thought of bicycle helmets then, car seats or not smoking or drinking during pregnancy. And we'd survived. I knew a lot of kids who died, but it was the kind of thing you couldn't prevent – leukemia, head-on collisions, house fires and plane crashes.

Did I still think I was bullet-proof, the way my Eastern students did? That because I'd survived childhood, I could make it through anything? But mine had been a simple, protected life back then. My parents loved me, gave me shelter and food and books and the sense that I could do anything I wanted if I only tried hard enough.

I had fulfilled those dreams they had for me – a very good small college (Eastern); an Ivy League graduate school (Columbia); a decent career and marriage to a nice Jewish girl. Then, like a house of cards I was tired of playing with, I had knocked it all over. Goodbye career, wife, freedom.

I thought I'd learned a few lessons in prison, but here I was, forty-plus years old and still doing dumb stuff. Would Lili break up with me over my actions? My head said that I'd acted rashly and put myself and others in danger. But my heart said I'd do it all again. Would I ever be able to marry those two so that I'd act like a real grown-up all the time?

I pulled my cell out of my messenger bag, eager to speak to Lili and tell her everything that had happened. I'd missed having someone in my life like that for too long, and I knew I was lucky to have found her. But then I put the phone away. This had to be handled face to face, as I'd done when I told her about hacking into the reunion database.

Rochester hopped into the front seat of the Beemer and we headed upriver. It was going to be sweet when Lili and I lived together, I thought. No more long phone calls, no more drives between our homes. As long as she would still have me when she knew what I'd done.

38 – Barbecue

There was no answer at Lili's apartment, and her phone went right to voice mail. Could she still be at work? I dialed her office, but it was after five and neither she nor Matilda answered.

That's when I noticed the text message icon on my phone. *Developing more pix @Adam's. TTY 2morrow.*

Crap. I didn't want to have to wait that long to tell Lili what had happened, and I didn't want to leave her a voice mail, or a note on her door, or send her an email. I wanted to see her, talk to her, hold onto her and make sure she was all right with what I'd done.

But I couldn't. So instead, I drove Rochester back to River Bend, poured some chow for him and boiled some pasta for myself. After we ate, I turned on one of the dog shows on TV, and I pointed out things to Rochester that I thought he could do. On screen, a German shepherd posed, an Afghan hound walked with her tail erect, Yorkies and Maltese obeyed commands, Shih-tzus flowed across the stage as if their coats were watery. The trainers had an almost mystical rapport with their dogs, an unspoken connection that led to seamless movement.

I had that with Rochester, I thought. Sure, he pulled on his leash, hid sometimes when I called him, wouldn't take pills easily. But give us a case to work together, and we were a machine.

At eleven, I took Rochester out for a solitary walk. It was chilly, and an angry wind swept the dead leaves past the darkened houses of my neighbors. A straw couple in patchwork clothes swayed together, an owl hooted, and Rochester chased after something that scurried beneath Bob Freehl's hedge. I looked up at the sky, hoping for a star to wish on, but all I saw were clouds scudding past.

I drove to work Friday morning in a dark mood. I needed to talk to Lili and make sure she was okay with the way I'd put my life, Rochester's, Mark's and even Gail's in danger the day before. She could see that as indicative of the fact that I was too much of a loose cannon to commit to.

On one hand, I had found some measure of justice for Don Lamprey – but had I ruined my own future in doing so? Even Rochester seemed aloof, as if he was mad at me, too.

It was hard to concentrate at work, and I often found myself staring into space, wondering about Lili and our future together. At lunch, Rochester and I walked down the hill to the lakefront, and the old ranch house where the mendicant friars had lived. It was chilly, with the bite of winter in the air, and I was glad I'd brought a jacket with me.

While he nosed around the corner of the house, I thought about the way those mendicants had lived, forsaking worldly attachments for a life of service. I had no interest in that—I wanted to have people around me, to go out to dinner, luxuriate in possessions, enjoy the company of my dog.

But everything I did seemed to contradict those goals. I didn't kid myself; my marriage to Mary had been on the rocks long before I hacked into the credit bureaus. But it was that act that drove the knife into our marriage. By the time I returned to Stewart's Crossing I had no money and only the few things my father had left me in his will.

Rochester had started me on the road back to life. I knew I had to get a job to provide for him. Instead of wallowing in self-pity I had to walk him, feed him, play with him. I thought that must be how Tamsen had felt after her husband died in Iraq – that she couldn't go on, but that she had to, for the sake of her son.

Rochester had gotten over his pique, and he romped over to me, a stick in his mouth. I tugged on it. "You've got to release it if you want me to throw it for you," I said. He did, and I sent it sailing across the overgrown lawn between the house and the lake.

This was my life, I thought. If I had nothing else, if Lili broke up with me, if I lost my job and the friendships I'd cultivated with Rick, Mark, Gail and others – I'd still have my dog. He rushed back to me with the stick in his mouth and an expression of doggie devotion on his glowing, golden face.

Around three o'clock, Rick showed up at Friar Lake. "What brings you all the way up here?" I asked.

"I took a full statement from Eben last night, but I need to get one from you, too. Since I appreciate the help you gave me yesterday in talking him down, I thought I'd save you the trip to my station and come up here. Thought I'd see what the place you're always talking about looks like, too."

"I've been thinking about yesterday," I said, as Rick sat down across from me. "I should have been mature enough to realize that Eben was dangerous, and that it was up to you to resolve the situation. I have been so focused on not hacking , that I lost sight of the fact that hacking is just a symptom of my not thinking through the consequences of my actions."

"Don't beat yourself up too much. I guess the saying isn't true after all," he said, smiling. "If you're actually learning from your mistakes, that means you can teach an old dog new tricks."

"Hey, you're older than I am," I said.

When he smiled and said, "By three months," I knew we friends again.

"I spoke to the DA this morning," he continued. "He agrees that the statute of limitations for the theft of the money and the drugs has passed. But Eben doesn't have a sportsman's permit or a license for the Mossberg. That's either a third-degree felony, or a first-degree misdemeanor. Basically a slap on the wrist."

"That's all?"

"There's one other option." He paused. "The crime scene guys retrieved a couple of shell casings from the entrance to River Bend, where you were shot, and they match Eben's Mossberg."

"So he's the one who shot at me?" My heart zinged for a moment. *Got you, creep*, I thought. "Why would he?"

"He's not admitting to shooting you, but my guess is that he must have been paying attention to you. He might have seen you help me out at the Harvest Festival when we found the bones, maybe he saw the two of us around town somewhere. Then you went walking past his house. That must have spooked him."

"So you can prosecute him, right? Attempted murder?"

"That's a different story," Rick said. "His gun was used, and his fingerprints are on it. But to eliminate reasonable doubt, we'd have to prove that he's the only one who had access to the weapon, and that he had a motive to shoot at you. A good attorney could tear you apart on the witness stand. Were you interfering in the investigation? Had you made any efforts to contact Eben? That kind of thing."

There was another pause. "His attorney could call me to the stand, too, and make it seem like I violated procedures by using your help."

"Which would get you in trouble," I said.

"Yeah. But I'm a big boy. If I have to take my medicine I will."

I remembered my prison conversations with Balbino. And suddenly, what happened to me didn't seem to matter so much. "You know what?" I said. "Eben's paid enough, holding his secrets for forty years. I don't see any point in dragging this out, do you?"

"He broke down yesterday," Rick said. "Sobbing. How bad he felt."

"Where is he now?"

"Had to arrest him for waving that gun around. He spent the night in the county jail, and then he appeared before a judge, who granted him bail."

"So he's out?"

"On his way out of the system as we speak. You'll never guess who's posting the bond for him."

"Edith Passis?"

"Close, but no cigar. Hannah Palmer."

"The clerk of the Meeting?"

"Yup. She says that the Friends look after their own. But if you're not going to press charges, the judge will probably let him off with a warning and a fine."

I thought about it for a moment. I could obsess about Hosford, carrying anger inside me the way I'd blamed Mary at first for motivating me to hack into those credit card databases, and all the other things that had sent me to prison. It had taken me a long time to let go of that, to accept my own responsibility and move on. It was time to do that here, too. "I'm okay with letting him go."

He pulled out a tape recorder, and we went through everything that had happened. "When I get this transcribed, I'll email it to you for review, and then ask you to print and sign it." He hesitated, then said, "On another subject. I invited Tamsen and her son over for a barbecue tomorrow evening. I was hoping you and Lili would join us with Rochester. You could bring the signed transcript with you then, and it would really help me out. It's going to be the first time Justin sees me with his mom as more than just his coach, and..."

"I'm not sure I'm still seeing Lili." I told him about my failed trip upriver, that I was waiting to talk to her in person. "But I can come with Rochester."

I remembered that Gail and Declan had a date on Saturday night and suggested that Rick invite them. "And Mark Figueroa is supposed to be getting together with Joey Capodilupo. Why don't you call Mark and invite them, too?" I asked. "Edith, and Hannah and her family? Make it a big party and nobody will feel that awkward."

"Sounds like a plan." He paused again. "Thanks for all your help on this, Steve. We can both feel good about giving some closure to the Lampreys, and seeing that Don's bones get buried out by his family."

That was cold comfort, I thought, if solving the mystery resulted in losing Lili.

Rick left, and I stared out my office window at the blustery afternoon. Eben Hosford had gotten himself in trouble, I thought, because he had held his secrets for so long. I wasn't going to do that to myself. I picked up the phone and dialed the main number for the Fine Arts department. "Hi Matilda, it's Steve Levitan," I said, when Lili's secretary answered. "I don't want to talk to Lili right now – I just want to know if she's in her office."

"Some kind of surprise?" she asked.

"Something like that."

"Yes, she's here. She usually stays until five on Fridays."

"I'm on my way," I said. "If she tries to leave, can you stall her?"

She laughed. "I can do anything if I set my mind to it."

"Words to live by," I said.

I grabbed Rochester's leash and he bounded over to me. I locked up the office, and on my way into Leighville I made a pit stop at Genuardi's grocery. I picked five bouquets of roses in red, pink and white from the bins by the front door.

"You must be in big trouble," the cashier said to me as she

rang them up.

"You could say that." I paid and carried the roses out to the car. A few minutes later I was parked near Harrow Hall, and Rochester and I were on our way to Lili's office.

"Oh, my," Matilda said when I walked in. "How beautiful! She's on the phone but you can stick your head in."

I thanked her, and unhooked Rochester's leash so he could go into Lili's office first. I'm not stupid; I know the power of the dog.

I heard Lili say, "I'll call you Monday then," and hang up the receiver. Staying hidden, I stuck the five bouquets of roses inside the door and waved them like a white flag.

"You can come in," she said, laughing.

When I walked in she had Rochester's paws up on her lap and she was receiving doggie kisses. "Five bunches!" she said. "What kind of trouble do you think you're in?"

I laid the flowers down on her desk and kissed her. I was worried that it might be the last time I'd get to, once I told her what I had to say, and I wanted to make it count.

"Wow," she said, when we finally parted. "Hello to you, too. But you've really got me curious. What's up? You didn't hack again, did you?" she asked. "I already told you that it doesn't matter to me, as long as you're careful."

"It wasn't hacking," I said. "Let's sit down."

She sat behind her desk, and I sat in the visitor's chair, like a misbehaving student come to the department chair for discipline. Rochester slumped to the floor by my side.

I told her about the confrontation with Eben Hosford, how he'd pulled his rifle. "Rick and I managed to talk him down," I said. "Rick took him back to the station. After it was over I realized the person I most wanted to be with was you. So I'm here."

Lili was quiet for a moment. Then she said, "I thought when I quit photojournalism I left behind all the hotshots and the adrenaline junkies. Obviously not." She reached out and took my hand. We'd had this conversation before, how Lili had come to rural Pennsylvania to find a quieter life. And how I had difficulty controlling my curiosity.

"Do you think we're doomed to love the same kind of person

over and over again?" she asked. "To keep on making the same mistakes?"

Was she saying that our romance had been a mistake? "I don't think so," I said. "Sure, you have a lot in common with Mary. You're both smart, beautiful, ambitious. Jewish, with all that means. But in the most important ways, you're totally different."

I took a deep breath. "I've been working hard to get Mary out of my head, and now I'm not sure that I need to. Because having her to compare you to makes you seem even more amazing. Your independence, your creativity, your heart. And no matter what you might think, I know I'm nothing like Adriano or Phillip. Neither of us is going to repeat the mistakes we've made in the past."

"Of course we are," Lili said, but she smiled. "But the important thing is that when we do, we'll be smart enough to recognize them and fix them."

"I'm really sorry, Lili. I should never have confronted Eben like I did. I wasn't thinking. I was just going on instinct. I promise if you agree to move in with me, I'll think before I act."

"Don't make any promises you can't keep," Lili said, but her mouth rose at the edges. She stood up and opened her arms to me.

We hugged and kissed and Rochester kept trying to nose his way between us. When we finally disengaged she said, "You need someone to look after you, and Rochester's just not doing a good enough job." She leaned down and wagged her finger in the dog's face. "You need to keep your daddy out of trouble."

He licked her finger and his tail swished back and forth.

"I know I don't have anything big enough to handle all these roses here in the office," Lili said, picking the first bunch up and sniffing. "Mmm."

"Guess you'll have to take them home," I said. I reached out for her hand and twined it with mine. "Wherever you're calling home."

She picked up all the roses and said, "Let's head to Stewart's Crossing."

* * *

Lili baked a pie with the last of the season's apples, and I brought two six-packs of microbrew beer. When we pulled up in front of Rick's house there were already a couple of cars along the street and I heard the sound of Springsteen, laughter and dogs barking from his back yard.

The temperature was perfect – cool enough to enjoy the back yard, but not so chilly that you'd need a sweater. I opened the gate and Rascal came running, chased by a cream-colored golden retriever puppy and two young boys. I recognized the younger as Hannah's son Nathaniel, and assumed the eight-year-old in the baseball jersey was Tamsen's son Justin. Rochester rushed forward and the three dogs romped together, the two boys jumping in the middle of them.

Mark Figueroa was sitting on a picnic bench talking to Tamsen, his long legs stretched out in front of him. Her sister Hannah stood near her, and I could see the resemblance between them clearly – both slim, blonde and pretty. At the far end of the yard, Joey Capodilupo had a rubber football in his hand, and he threw it toward the dogs, who rushed it.

I assumed that the hipster-looking guy with square black glasses was Nathaniel's father, because he picked the boy up and twirled him around.

Lili and I walked into the house, dropping off the pie and the beer. I uncapped two beers and joined Rick at the barbecue, where he had begun grilling burgers. "Looks like a pretty good party," I said.

"That's for me?" he asked, taking the beer from me. "Thanks."

Gail and Declan were the last to arrive, both of them looking shyly around. While Rick grilled, I joined Declan, Joey and Hannah's husband, Eric to play with the kids and the dogs. "What's your name, handsome?" I asked, picking up the little white golden. He was half Rochester's size but all muscle and had to weigh close to forty pounds. He licked my face and I laughed.

"That's Brody," Joey said. "My baby boy. Just turned a year old."

"He's adorable. How'd he get so white?"

"They call it English cream," Joey said. "All the golden puppies I'm seeing lately are his color. White is the new gold."

"I'll stick with the old gold," I said, as Rochester rushed toward me, jealous of my attention to any other dog. I sat on the grass with Rochester's head in my lap and looked around at all my friends, their kids and their dogs. It was a life I could only have imagined when I left prison to return home. Lili came over to join me and I said, "Whom dog hath joined, let no man put asunder."

"An excellent sentiment," she said. "And now let's eat."

Reviews for the Golden Retriever Mysteries:

Mr. Plakcy did a terrific job in this cozy mystery. He had a smooth writing style that kept the story flowing evenly. The dialogue and descriptions were right on target. -- Red Adept

Steve and Rochester become quite a team and Neil Plakcy is the kind of writer that I want to tell me this story. It's a fun read which will keep you turning pages very quickly. Amos Lassen – Amazon top 100 reviewer

We who love our dogs know that they are wiser than we are, and Plakcy captures that feeling perfectly with the relationship between Steve and Rochester. -- Christine Kling, author of Circle of Bones

In Dog We Trust is a very well-crafted mystery that kept me guessing up until Steve figured out where things were going. --E-book addict reviews

If you enjoyed this book, please check out the other books in the series:

In Dog We Trust
The Kingdom of Dog
Dog Helps Those
Dog Bless You

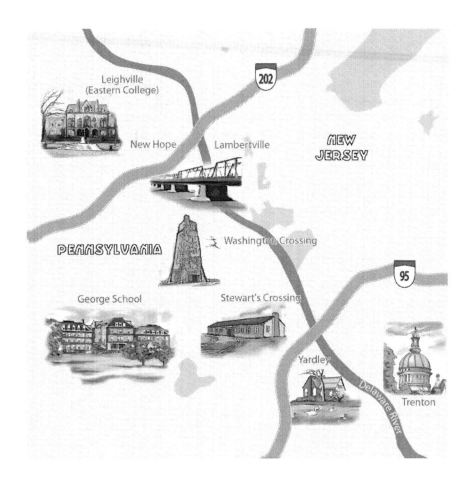

68539135R00132

Made in the USA
Lexington, KY
13 October 2017